What People Are S~~ay~~

Full Contact Performance

This book is a gift to organizations, showing their employees how to achieve win-win-win solutions by being their better selves, being better collaborators and still helping the bottom line. James is a deep thinker with a sophisticated understanding of human nature. A masterpiece!
Russell Lemle, Former Chief Psychologist, San Francisco VA Health Care System

Once in a blue moon an important book for business leaders comes along. *Full Contact Performance* is one of these rare finds. When implemented, the perspectives and practices Grayson James describes replace friction and struggles with newfound productivity and a spirit of shared purpose. I highly recommend this book for those who want to grow as leaders.
Tom Bowman, President of Bowman Change, Inc., and author of *What if Solving the Climate Crisis Is Simple?*

In *Full Contact Performance*, Grayson James draws from decades of experience helping leaders and their teams realize their potential, understand the pitfalls and possibilities of every step of the collaboration process, and see how body and mind awareness are keys to successful communication.
Charles Kremer, CEO, Access Leasing Corporation

Full Contact Performance is the field guide for the new frontier of team and leadership development. Grayson James offers a tried and trustworthy foundation for authentic human collaboration that leads to skillful action and creative interactions.

Weaving together the disciplines of language-action, the principles of Aikido, mediation, and meditation, James demonstrates not only how to do but also how to be in the 21st century workplace.

Richard Strozzi-Heckler, author of *The Leadership Dojo* and *The Art of Somatic Coaching*

Full Contact Performance details the approach and tool-set that, together, is the secret sauce to building high-performing and continuously improving teams. James has worked with me and my teams over the years, and I've seen first-hand the tremendous outcomes this approach can bring.

Mark Friedman, Chief Marketing Officer, Frontline Education, Inc.

The unique approach that James outlines in *Full Contact Performance* pays incredibly high dividends. I've had the opportunity to apply this approach in many challenging organizational transformations involving strong cultural, political and international differences, and it has consistently produced high-performing teams that deliver seemingly impossible results.

Lucy Norris, EVP, Chief Customer Success Officer, Synamedia

Listening and collaborating are staples of our everyday work lives and processes. Why does that simple process seem to break down? In this book, Grayson provides a practical approach to bridge the gap through sustained collaboration, continued behavioral learning, and team alignment. Buy the book, start practicing, and start achieving greater results.

Jeffrey Hayzlett, Primetime TV & Podcast Host, Speaker, Author and Part-Time Cowboy

Absolutely brilliant book for professionals at all levels — not once, but every year. Deep concepts from Linguistic Philosophy thoughtfully blended with practical insights with relevant case studies. I just hope, wish and pray that the book gets in the hands of at least a million professionals. Bravo!

Raj Setty, Co-founder of Audvisor and 16x Author and Teacher

Having spent most of my career in the context of collaboration and helping teams co-create solutions to challenges they face, *Full Contact Performance* reinforced many principles and practices I have learned and developed over the years, provided fresh insights into why some things work and some don't, and — most importantly — opened my eyes to new ways to think about, prepare yourself for, and conduct good, productive, and respectful interactions. Many books (and podcasts, and speakers...) can tell you what needs to be done to improve teams and how they work together, but Grayson James' book spends much more time on the how, supported with a wealth of guidance, stories, examples, and skill-building exercises. As James says (and addresses head-on), "knowing what works isn't the same as being able to do what works". If you're like me, as you start into the book you'll be taking lots of notes, jotting down pithy turns of phrase and great advice, before quickly realizing that James has already jotted down all the good stuff for you! It's there on every entertaining, informative, and easily consumed page.

David Benjamin, co-author of *Cracking Complexity*

If you lead teams, want to elevate performance, and get real results, then read this book. Grayson provides a unique and straightforward approach to getting your team to excel together. Highly recommend this read.

Shane Green, CX Consultant and Author of *Culture Hacker*

In the post-COVID world, leaders recognize that strong team collaboration is no longer a soft skill — it's a power skill. In fact, it's a major driver of organizational performance. James' book unlocks what makes real collaboration happen, moving beyond having better meetings and effective conversations to provide a more holistic understanding of the role that our bodies, our emotions and our attention also play in our interactions.

Lisa Bodell, Author of *Kill The Company* and *Why Simple Wins*

Grayson makes an important point early in the book. Your success depends on your collaborative abilities more than your title. It doesn't matter if you're the CEO or a supervisor; the way you communicate and collaborate with your team is essential to you and your organization's success.

Shep Hyken, Customer service/experience expert and *New York Times* bestselling business author

Full Contact Performance

The Internal Art of Organizational Collaboration

Full Contact Performance

The Internal Art of Organizational Collaboration

Grayson James

BUSINESS
BOOKS

Winchester, UK
Washington, USA

JOHN HUNT PUBLISHING

First published by Business Books, 2023
Business Books is an imprint of John Hunt Publishing Ltd., No. 3 East St., Alresford,
Hampshire SO24 9EE, UK
office@jhpbooks.com
www.johnhuntpublishing.com
www.johnhuntpublishing.com/business-books

For distributor details and how to order please visit the 'Ordering' section on our website.

Text copyright: Grayson James 2022

ISBN: 978 1 80341 251 1
978 1 80341 252 8 (ebook)
Library of Congress Control Number: 2022911775

A CIP catalogue record for this book is available from the British Library.

Design: Lapiz Digital Services

UK: Printed and bound by CPI Group (UK) Ltd, Croydon, CR0 4YY
Printed in North America by CPI GPS partners

We operate a distinctive and ethical publishing philosophy in
all areas of our business, from our global network of authors to
production and worldwide distribution.

Contents

Dedication

This book is dedicated to my mother, Margie, for her relentless curiosity about language and human behavior, for our countless free-range and often utterly goofy and delightful conversations, and for the support she's always shown me in the pursuit of my various idiosyncratic interests and careers.

Foreword

For most of us, our jobs make up a significant percentage of our daily life, and we spend much of this time working alongside people with different backgrounds and perspectives. Yet we often find ourselves struggling to manage these differences and get important work done together.

As I read Grayson James's Full Contact Performance, I was struck by the clarity and elegance of his insights, coupled with his down-to-earth understandings about what it really takes to collaborate well in today's organizations. And it isn't what you might think.

I've often seen brilliant people fail in groups full of other brilliant people.

What they brought to the table was individual excellence.

What they needed was collaborative excellence.

Grayson shows us that in our rush to become the best individual performer we can be, we too often neglect the skills that make great achievements possible: truly connecting with our colleagues so that we can learn together, set meaningful goals together, and then execute skillfully to realize those goals with integrity and accountability. This is what Grayson calls "Full Contact" collaboration.

Like a skilled martial arts master (which he is) who grounds his students in the overarching principles while also showing them how to apply these principles in action, Grayson takes us on a journey through the art of collaborative organizational performance. He begins the journey with five guiding principles and shows us—in unexpected and illuminating ways—how the way we speak, listen, and create stories about our colleagues (and ourselves) all shape our interactions.

But this journey isn't just theoretical. It also involves our attention, our bodies and even the way we perceive reality. Weaving together theory, examples, exercises and stories, Grayson shows us how gaining awareness of what we're doing is the starting point for transforming our collaborative performance.

In the first part of his book, Grayson helps us see collaboration with new eyes, bringing new awareness to what we're actually doing whenever we're in conversation with someone. This new awareness gives us a vastly expanded repertoire for dealing with the many types of challenges we encounter in our daily interactions with our colleagues, our bosses, our teams, or anyone else.

In the next part of the book, we're introduced to the Three Conversations of Full Contact Performance—the Learning conversation, the Design conversation, and the Fulfillment conversation—with great, real-life examples of what goes on in these conversations and how to successfully design and manage each one.

In the third and final part, Grayson brings us full circle to what really makes this book stand out from all the others in the field: The clear recognition that while collaboration certainly involves other people, the way we transform our collaborative performance is by focusing on ourselves first. This is why he says that organizational collaboration is an internal art, and he gives us a handful of simple — yet potent — practices that help empower us to do just that.

If you read Full Contact Performance and take Grayson's guidance to heart, you and your colleagues will move together further, faster, and more effortlessly than ever before.

After reading this book, I asked myself why these lessons aren't fundamental in every leader's education. Why don't we train for effective collaboration just as fervently as we train for every other subject in business courses or MBA programs?

I suppose the Tao Te Ching said it best: "When the student is ready, the teacher will appear." I'm sure you'll find Full Contact Performance as powerful and enlightening as I have.

Dr. Marshall Goldsmith is the Thinkers50 #1 Executive Coach and *New York Times* bestselling author of *The Earned Life, Triggers,* and *What Got You Here Won't Get You There*

Prologue

Most approaches to organizational collaboration recognize the importance of behaviors like *good listening, clear and constructive speaking, building trust, engaging people's full commitment, running effective meetings,* and *harnessing the diversity of thought, experience and perspectives* (to name just a few). The approach I present in this book, which I call Full Contact Performance, also values these behaviors. But in working with organizational executives and their teams over many years, I've seen that these behaviors remain distant aspirations for many people in most companies. Although most people know these behaviors are important, far fewer are actually able to *do* them in the heat of collaboration, when the pressure is on or when strong emotions are present. This is even true for those who have taken workshops or read the standard books and articles on collaboration.

Clearly, something is missing. Sustained and effective collaboration shouldn't be such a rarity in organizations. That's why I wrote this book—to share the approach to collaborative organizational performance that I've been learning over the years in facilitating challenging conversations, coaching leaders, and leading organizations. One of the things I've seen is that there is a lot more going on when we're trying to collaborate with others than we might think. I've also seen that anyone can get better at it with some self-reflection and practice. And everything you learn about collaborating with your colleagues at work applies just as readily to your interactions outside of work.

Before we get into the details, though, here's my story about how I came to Full Contact Performance...

My Journey to Full Contact Performance

In the early 1980s I was a young and inexperienced leader of a multi-campus private school system (grades 6–12) in the San Francisco Bay Area called the Independent Learning Schools. I assumed leadership of the schools just after student enrollment had dropped by more than a third during the recent recession. Over the next six years while leading the schools, there were many successes, although we also had our share of challenges and missteps—more than a few of which were of my own making, although I didn't realize it at the time.

Our leadership team of nine met monthly and on some days we would leave the meetings upbeat, focused and energized. At other times, however, the conversations seemed to go nowhere, leaving us all exhausted and demoralized. Although I knew that our collaborative performance wasn't what it could be, I had no idea how to improve it. The communication workshops we attended and the books we read as a management team sparked enthusiasm and brief improvement but yielded little lasting effect. This experience showed me that putting together a group of smart, committed and creative people together didn't necessarily lead to good collaboration. It was also clear that reading books or taking workshops on communication and teamwork doesn't always translate into new, sustained competence.

During this period, I met George Leonard, journalist, author, Aikido instructor and education reform advocate. He was researching our schools for his 1984 *Esquire* Magazine article on school reform and the next edition of his book on educational reform, *Education & Ecstasy* (in which he cited our school as a model school for the future). Our meeting eventually set me on a path that has brought me to many of the central ideas in this book.

For starters, in addition to becoming an advisor on educational reform for me and my team, Leonard introduced me to the martial art of Aikido. Sitting on the hard wooden bench by the side of the mat watching my first Aikido class, I was mesmerized by the seemingly effortless power of the practitioners in dealing with the strikes and grabs of their training partners. I took my first class the next day and was soon training every day.

Aikido is unique among martial arts in that there are no tournaments, no competitions, and no offensive techniques. Our explicit aim in Aikido is to protect ourselves while also protecting the opponent. This was a revolutionary concept to me as a beginner and it still is decades later as an instructor. The principles we practice on the Aikido mat are also remarkably relevant to our lives off the mat, in our everyday interactions. This "embodied" philosophy of mutual respect and caring for the well-being of the other has been a source of deep inspiration for me personally and in my work with teams and organizations. It is also what eventually led me to recognize that organizational collaboration is as much an "internal art" as it is an external process.

Along with Aikido, George Leonard also introduced me to the world of the "human potential movement" (a term which Leonard coined while senior editor at *Look* Magazine), to the Samurai Game® (a leadership and teambuilding simulation that he created), and to his fellow Aikido instructors, Richard Strozzi-Heckler and Wendy Palmer at Tamalpais Aikido, in Marin County, California.

Through Strozzi-Heckler, I learned about the field of *somatics*, a discipline that recognizes the deep interconnectedness of our body and mind and the value of engaging this interconnectedness through practices that enhance self-awareness and expand our cognitive, emotional and interpersonal performance. Around this time, I also began mindfulness meditation, which continues to be an important daily practice. Among its many benefits, meditation has shown me the value of using our attention in different ways—not only on the meditation cushion, but at the conference table and in the boardroom as well.

As I continued to practice and learn more about collaborative performance, I reflected back on my monthly leadership team meetings at the School and I came to realize that we had been trying to *think our way* into better conversations, which wasn't enough. What was missing was a more holistic understanding of the role that our bodies, our emotions and our attention also play in our interactions.

Towards the end of the 1980s, I left the schools to further pursue my interest in collaboration, getting trained as a mediator and facilitator, specializing in mediating complex, multi-party legal disputes within the California court system, working under a mentor, David Jenkins. These litigations typically lasted many months involving anywhere from four to 40 different parties, including lawyers, insurance representatives, expert witnesses and others.

In these disputes, each party's goal was basically to minimize their own liability and to get out of the costly and time-consuming lawsuit as quickly and inexpensively as possible. I refer to this as my "circus leader" period because that is what those proceedings often felt like to me. Each of the parties and their attorneys would pursue their various negotiation strategies and postures and it was my job to ensure that we had the disciplined conversations needed to enable them all to reach settlement. These facilitated discussions taught me further lessons, also central to this book, like...

- When nothing else is working — shut up and breathe.
- The more that people feel they're in charge of the process (but not dominating it), the more engaged they're likely to be in finding solutions.

- Although the "content" of the dispute matters, what matters as much or more is how people are thinking and interacting with each other while they're discussing the content. (If this weren't the case, there is no way that David Jenkins and I, as non-attorneys, could have successfully settled these lawsuits.)
- Coercion, cleverness and brute force aren't the only sources of power in emotionally charged and high stakes conflicts. And in organizations, they are usually the least effective and the least sustainable over the long term.

In the mid '90s I was introduced to a new approach to personal and organizational performance called *Ontological Coaching*. This was another pivotal moment for me. Leading the program were Julio Olalla and sociologist and author Rafael Echeverria, Ph.D. Central to their work was what is sometimes called the "language-action approach." Olalla and Echeverria were both former colleagues of Fernando Flores, the first to bridge the worlds of the philosophy of language with the world of business, bringing the emerging understanding of linguistic action to the challenges of business performance. (This approach was initially developed in the 1950s by Oxford professor J.L. Austin and then further developed by UC Berkeley's John Searle, and Fernando Flores, among others.)

Following my introduction to Ontological Coaching, I had the good fortune to work with and learn from Rafael Echeverria for several years, establishing this language-action approach as a central pillar in my work with organizational executives and teams—together with those already-mentioned practices from Aikido, mediation, mindfulness meditation and other mind-body disciplines I've studied over the years.

I continue to be inspired by the rich and often subtle interplay between our thinking, our attention, our bodies and our performance with others. This book shares some of what I've been learning over these decades with executives and their teams about what I now call "Full Contact Performance."

Of course, my journey continues and this book is a work in progress along the path. I hope you will find it helpful in your own collaborative performance.

About This Book

If you're a senior executive leading multiple teams or functions, you know that your company's success hinges on how well your leadership team members think and learn together and how they ensure that *their* teams are aligned around what matters most for the business.

If you're a manager or team lead, you know how critical it is for your team to solve complex problems together, to engage skillfully with folks on other teams or functions, and to execute impeccably — to do what they say they're going to do and to take responsibility for the outcomes.

Even if you're a sole contributor and have nobody reporting to you, you still need to work with others — even if it's just your boss (sometimes the most challenging person to collaborate with).

With few exceptions, if you work in an organization, you interact with other people. Some of the folks you must collaborate with may be delightful to work with, and some you might never choose to work with in a million years. Yet there they are, and here you are. That's life in organizations, even for the boss.

◯

I wrote this book for anyone working in an organization who wants to transform, or at least greatly improve, their collaborative performance at work.

Collaboration is certainly not a novel topic. There have been plenty of books and articles written about it and countless workshops and business school courses on the subject.

Many of the executives and teams I've worked with over the years have read these books, taken the workshops and could fill pages with techniques and formulas for how to listen better, handle differences, deal with conflicts, build trust, improve accountability and much more. Yet when these same people encounter difficult collaborations, all that knowledge— those techniques and formulas—is often inaccessible to them, especially in the heat of difficult collaborations when strong emotions are rampant; when conflicting perspectives are present and immovable positions taken; when folks are struggling to solve vexing and recurring problems or when they're just plain stuck in their collective tracks.

That's one reason you won't many find tips, techniques or formulas in this book. Another reason is that even when folks *are* able to apply them in challenging situations, their collaborations still often don't work and frequently get worse, not better. (We'll look at why this happens later on.)

In place of how-to's and formulas, I offer what I consider to be far more helpful, which is *a different way of thinking about and approaching collaboration,* along with *specific things to pay attention* to *and practice* on your own and when you're collaborating with others. Some of what you'll read may strike you as quite different from what you've read about or learned before about collaboration. From a conventional perspective, some of it might even seem heretical.

Work with people in all sorts of companies over the years has shown me that giving them new ways of paying attention and new ways of understanding what's really going on when they're attempting to collaborate (along with new practices) is what helps people truly transform their collaborative performance.

So, if you're looking for simple answers, or *what-to-do-when,* this book might not be for you. But if you're looking to gain greater understanding about what's happening in those difficult collaborative encounters that test your patience and your benevolence, if you're looking to collaborate more skillfully with your colleagues—regardless of the specific circumstances or personalities you're dealing with—then this book may be just what you're looking for.

How This Book Is Organized

This book is organized in three parts. Part I is about building new awareness about what is really happening when we're collaborating (or trying to). We'll look at the five principles and the basic building blocks of effective collaboration, examining the different ways we can use our attention and the specific actions we take whenever we open our mouth to speak—or our ears and brain to listen. We'll see how we use our words to construct the stories and beliefs that govern how we perceive and behave, along with the central, yet generally overlooked, role that our body plays in every collaborative situation we encounter—even those encounters that play out entirely in our own imagination. Finally, we'll explore the relationship between our words, our bodies and our emotions and why this under-appreciated relationship matters so much for collaborative performance. Following most chapters, I'll offer some simple practices for reflecting on what you've just read and cultivating greater awareness of what's happening in your collaborative encounters at work. I encourage you to take advantage of these practices.

In Part II, we'll look at the three main types of conversations in organizational collaboration. Using examples and anecdotes, we'll see why these three conversations are important and how to approach them.

In Part III, we shift our focus squarely back onto ourselves. Here, we're reminded that, regardless of the circumstances or personalities we may be facing, we, ourselves, are always the central figure in our collaborative encounters. We'll revisit a recurring theme in this book: the power of shifting our attention back to ourselves, beyond the specific content, circumstances or thinking we may be engaged in with others. I'll offer a handful of simple practices that will expand your capacity for clear thinking and skillful, respectful collaborative action, even in the toughest situations. The Epilogue offers some final thoughts on Full Contact Performance.

If you're inclined to hop around the book at random, that's fine, but keep in mind that many chapters of the book—especially those in Parts I and II—build upon previous chapters, so you'll probably get the most out of the book by reading those chapters through in order.

Part I

Gaining Awareness:
Words, Body & Attention

Chapter 1

Introduction to Full Contact Performance

Not too long ago, your ability to make things happen in your organization often hinged more on your position in the company and what you knew than on your ability to work well with people. If you were the boss, you could just tell people what to do and it would often happen. That's not so true in many organizations today.

Much of what you accomplish today is more a result of your capacity to work well and solve tough problems with your colleagues than on your formal position, or what you know. Titles, expertise, and business acumen still matter, but they won't get you very far unless you can also collaborate well with all sorts of people, many of whom you have little, if any, control over.

It can be challenging enough to collaborate with people on your own team whom you know and work with every day. But increasingly, you must do it with people from entirely different functions, backgrounds and cultures. And more and more of this collaboration—even before the Covid pandemic—is happening virtually and across multiple time zones and multiple cultures.

Your success today depends more on your collaborative capacity than on your title or what you know.

What makes collaboration so necessary today also makes it more challenging. Although people in yesterday's organization worked just as hard and were just as smart as people today, they didn't have to contend with the onslaught of new information and the demands on their attention that we deal with every moment. The tempo of our lives and the pace of change has sped up, while the traditional lines between personal-business, home-office, and even customer-competitor-partner, have gotten fuzzier. This doesn't just affect how we work. It affects how we think, how we feel, and even what happens in our bodies.

Our brains, our physiological systems and our health are reflecting this always-on, hyper-connected lifestyle. While our average attention span has shortened, our nervous system's demand for constant and novel stimulation seems to have mushroomed. Many people may feel super productive because they're getting so many things done in a day, but the quality of their reflection, their decision-making and their ability to deal with difficult challenges or conflict often tell a different story. So, while the importance of skillful collaboration has increased, it's also gotten more challenging.

Before we go further, let's take a closer look at what Full Contact Performance is and what makes it different.

What Is Full Contact Performance?

For many years when first meeting with a new team, I'd start by asking team members to tell me what good collaboration looks like. While there were some differences across companies and cultures, their answers were almost always similar. Here are just a few of the most common items they listed...

- Transparency – be honest and direct
- Be a good listener – listen to understand
- Respect people and their viewpoints, even if they're different from mine
- Build trust
- Create a safe, collaborative work environment
- Have clear and shared goals
- Accountability – know who is responsible for what

This is a good list. The bullet points could be included in most working definitions of good collaboration, and these behaviors are universally cited in books, articles and workshops on collaboration and communication.

The issue is that, although these behaviors really can work, they're not all that common in organizations. Not even by the very executives who listed them as examples of what good collaboration looks like. There is something missing between the *idea* of these effective behaviors and actually doing them. Filling this gap—helping people to *do* what works in organizational collaboration and not just *describe* what works is where Full Contact Performance comes in.

Full Contact Performance recognizes that knowing about something and being able to do it reliably in different settings and in difficult circumstances, is a challenge. But it's a challenge that can be overcome if you know what to look for and are prepared to work with yourself. I say "work with yourself" because that's where the real action is when it comes to transforming your collaborative performance, as we'll soon see.

Full Contact Performance is about cultivating specific practices that make all those good behaviors listed above not only accessible but—with practice—natural and almost effortless. It all begins with gaining new awareness of yourself and your orientation to the people and circumstances around you. This awareness encompasses...

- The words you and others use—specifically the *speech actions* you're taking whenever you open your mouths to speak, the *stories* you tell yourselves to make sense of what's going on around you, and the different types of conversations you're having or not having as you're trying to get important things done together.

- The feelings or emotional states that you and others are experiencing about the conversation, meeting, project team or organizational culture you're involved in.
- The way you're using your attention and how your attention may be revealing or limiting what you can do in your interactions with your colleagues and circumstances you encounter.
- The relationship you are having with your own body as you're trying to solve challenging problems and work collaboratively with others, which includes the sensory signals, and habitual nervous system tendencies that condition how you respond to the people and circumstances you encounter.

It's Not About *Them*

Organizational collaboration is about getting valuable things done with other people. So when our collaborations get stuck or falter, it would seem that the problem has to do with those people we're trying to collaborate with.

This is what usually happens when we hit rough patches in our interactions—we assume the problem lies with those other folks out there... and then we try to solve *that* problem of *those folks*—to fix, change or work around them, especially the ones who "don't care"; who don't listen well; the ones who dominate conversations; those who just sit back and wait for conversations to end; those who perpetually seem to operate in their little bubble; or... all the others who are just generally "uncollaborative."

Overcoming other people's collaborative shortcomings seems like it should be a good strategy if the goal is better organizational collaboration. But if this strategy really worked, then most organizations would be highly collaborative places. That's not the case.

Collaboration certainly involves other people. We can't and shouldn't ignore them. But our collaborative performance hinges much more on us, *ourselves*, than on the people we're trying to collaborate with. This is the little secret about collaboration that has always been hiding in plain sight.

This book recognizes that the path to transforming your collaborative performance starts with you, not with everyone else. It will provide you with a new understanding and new awareness about what you're doing when you're trying to collaborate with others. It will illustrate the basic principles that are at play in every interaction you have and provide examples and practices you can use to cultivate your collaborative competence, regardless of your role or position in the organization or who you're attempting to collaborate with.

Some of the things you'll be reading about in this book will strike you as familiar and perhaps even obvious. But we'll be looking at many of these familiar terms or concepts from a different perspective and perhaps with greater precision than you're used to. Other things you encounter may be quite new, perhaps even confusing at first. If this happens, I encourage you to stay with it, to try on the new concepts or practices before reaching any conclusions. This is how you'll expand your collaborative capacity.

Good Collaboration Is Sustainable

You collaborate when you want to achieve an outcome that you can't realize on your own. The outcome may be hitting your quarterly sales targets, meeting the next software release date, or improving your customer satisfaction ratings. Or it may be reducing product defects, improving your margins, or completing a cross-functional project on time. Whatever the desired outcome, there could be many ways of getting there, at least in the short term. But not all these ways are equally effective or sustainable in the long run. Some will weaken your future collaboration efforts with those people the next time around. And just as importantly, when collaboration isn't good, it won't necessarily draw out the best from you or the people you're collaborating with, even if you do hit your numbers this quarter or complete this project on time. If you're not collaborating well, you won't be learning as much as you could from one another, you probably won't make the best decisions, and at some point, your execution will suffer.

When collaboration is good—when you're making "Full Contact" with your colleagues—the good goes way beyond the immediate transaction or project you're working on. Voices, perspectives or ideas that are often left unsaid or swept under the rug find a place at the table. The energy that often lies untapped in meetings finds a path forward. The more groups learn how to make Full Contact together, the more confidence they gain, the more creative they become, and the lighter things feel—in contrast to the heavy sense of skepticism or resignation people often feel when collaboration isn't happening. Full Contact Performance is also a lot more fun. When people are making real contact with each other, they look forward to meetings instead of dreading them. We all like to be part of something when we feel that we're contributing and making a difference. All this happens effortlessly when people are truly able to do the things on their lists of "what works in collaboration" I mentioned earlier.

Surprisingly, once you get better at making Full Contact with others, the particulars of who you collaborate with become less of an issue, because you've discovered that good collaboration is not all about *them*, but more about *you* and how you choose to engage with them. Again, this doesn't mean the folks you're collaborating with don't matter—or that every one of your collaborations will magically be transformed and successful. Not every collaboration may work out as hoped, but even the most challenging ones will still have a much better chance at success. And importantly, you'll probably end up with better relationships and feeling better about yourself even when those collaborations don't go as you'd wished.

Why Is It Called Full Contact?

The term "Full Contact" is borrowed from the martial arts. It refers to a type of training in which participants literally make full contact with one another—they don't hold back with their strikes, kicks or throws. When your training partner or opponent isn't holding back, you need to stay awake because you can get hurt. But you can also learn a lot. Having to deal with someone's full, focused energy shows you where you're weak, off-balance, unfocused, or just unprepared. It reveals your habitual assumptions, both about yourself and about the other person. It can also reveal your opponent's strengths and weaknesses.

The moves in the martial art of Aikido (as with many Chinese and other martial arts) are designed to use the opponent's own force and energy to contain, pin, or throw them. This is much easier to philosophize about than to pull off as your opponent is barreling down on you, but it boils down to how you've embodied the techniques, how you're directing your attention and how *unified* you are within yourself—your intention, your movement, your energy, your focus, and your connection with the ground under your feet. What starts as an oppositional interaction (your opponent was attacking you) is transformed into an experience in which you feel that you're *working together*—joining with, absorbing and redirecting their energy, rather than fighting against it. That's what we practice on the Aikido mat, but we can practice these same principles at the office without any martial arts experience.

With human bodies, there are only so many ways to push, pull, grab, grapple, strike, kick, or throw someone, and many of the moves we practice on the Aikido mat are similar to those in many other martial arts. It's the *intention* to protect our opponent that distinguishes Aikido from those other arts. This intention is also at the heart of Full Contact Performance: To approach every collaborative challenge, every conflict or impasse, as an opportunity to respectfully connect and strengthen our relationships with our colleagues, so that we can learn, make better decisions together and execute better together. That's very different from applying communication or negotiation techniques to the person in order to get our way or protect our ideas, perspectives or positions.

On the Aikido mat, we take turns attacking each other and practicing our techniques in response to those attacks, over and over, day in and day out. The more senior students adjust the intensity of their attacks to the level of their less experienced training partners, delivering attacks with just enough force and speed to allow the other person to practice and learn, but not so much that they get overwhelmed and just keep reacting habitually.

As we progress in our training, our training partners challenge us more. The attacks come faster, harder and less predictably. Punches that were soft and slow when we were beginners now land with more impact if we don't get out of the way or properly absorb and redirect the blow. The tolerance for mistakes gets narrower.

This is how we continue to learn. Our training partners must up their game so that we can keep upping our own. If our training partners continue to hold back, giving us weak or unfocused attacks, we'll get very good at dealing with those types of attack, but we'll be unprepared to deal with a true, committed attack when we encounter one. We'll develop what organizational psychologist Chris Argyris called "skilled incompetence." Skilled, because our behaviors have been learned, practiced and mastered over time, but incompetent because they don't work—they don't achieve our intended aim.

To keep learning, we eventually need to make full contact with our training partners. At this stage in training, engaging with full contact is an expression of our respect and commitment to each other's growth and development. It would be disrespectful to do otherwise. And it wouldn't be nearly as interesting.

When our training partner brings their full, committed energy to the attack and we're able to engage skillfully without being reactive or aggressive in response, it's an extraordinary feeling, both for us and our training partner. When we join fully with their movement with no other agenda or motive, then for that brief moment we are like a single organism—just long enough to safely redirect their attack (generally into one of those joint locks, pins or throws). But again, to do this we need to be grounded, relaxed, and unified in our ourselves. This is what enables a smaller martial artist to handle a much bigger, stronger or faster opponent without getting hurt—and without hurting the opponent. And here's what's so fascinating: your training partner often gets up from the mat feeling more relaxed and more energized than he or she felt just moments earlier, before they attacked you.

Full Contact with Your Colleagues

It's similar in organizational collaboration. When we're feeling grounded, relaxed and unified in ourselves—when we have embodied the basic principles of Full Contact Performance—it's much easier to make contact with people who have very different perspectives, styles and even goals from our own. We're able to listen with curiosity and interest instead of impatience, frustration, or just waiting for our turn. Because we're more comfortable in ourselves, we're better able to tolerate and manage the strong emotions that may arise in truly candid conversations, and we're better able to stay engaged and constructive—without withdrawing, needing to protect ourselves, or dominating the conversation.

21

When we can make Full Contact, then even when an interaction hits a wall and folks feel confused and unsure how to proceed (which can happen in even the best of collaborations), this contact gives us the confidence to keep going while we figure out a good path forward together.

Another Type of Contact

There is another way in which Aikido and other martial arts point us towards Full Contact. It has to do with the *quality of connection* we are making with our training partners. On the training mat, when we're making Full Contact with our partner, we can sense their balance and movement, the force and direction of their energy, with just the lightest touch on our part. Our finely cultivated ability to sense *ourselves* enables us to sense them as well. In collaboration, when we're clearer and more aware of ourselves and what we're doing, we're also better able to pick up on our colleagues' subtle cues, to notice more about their choice of words, their body language, their energy and what they're trying to accomplish. Our body will register the non-verbal cues of others and we can notice our body's responses to further understand what's happening. It all starts with making contact with ourselves.

Full Contact Principles

There are five principles at the heart of Full Contact Performance. These principles remind us what to pay attention to and how to work with ourselves and others more skillfully. They are all interrelated—as you get more familiar with one, you'll probably start noticing how it relates to the others. Here are the five principles...

Principle #1: Awareness

It starts with Awareness—of our words, our body and our attention.

When it comes to organizational collaboration, our biggest challenge is that we're often not aware of what we're doing. We're not aware of the actions we're taking and how those actions are impacting the people around us, as well as ourselves. More precisely, we're not aware of the actions we're taking with our words, our body, or our attention. We're not aware of how our built-in connectivity with the people around us can cause even the "best" technique to go sideways and weaken trust.

When we're not aware of what we're doing, it's also difficult to change. Because it's hard to change what we can't see, gaining new awareness is the starting point for Full Contact Performance.

While we can acquire or improve some skills simply by gaining more knowledge or learning new actions, this isn't the case when we want to improve our collaborative performance. It also demands that we gain an expanded awareness of what we're doing while we're taking those actions. And by actions I'm referring to the things we do with our words, as well as what we do with our bodies and our attention.

We all know that we collaborate with our words, through our conversations. But our words aren't just mental constructs conjured up by a disembodied brain. All the words we use and the conversations we engage in, take place in our body. We think, plan, speak, listen, and lead our teams in our body. That's the same body that experiences all sorts of complicated sensations and emotions while we're interacting—all of which influence what we say next and how we say it. And the converse is just as true: Our words and conversations take up residence in our bodies. They shape our nervous system, are mirrored in our posture, our gestures, our breathing, in the hormones coursing through our veins and the neurotransmitters circulating in our brains. Our conversations are never just cerebral transactions. They are fully embodied interactions.

23

And what about our *attention*? We may pay attention to our colleagues' body language and to the words they're saying, but that's often where our attention remains—on the people *out there*—especially when they're not doing or saying what we think they should be doing or saying. But the way we use our attention determines where our energy and resources go, so it's important that we manage our attention skillfully. Although it's rarely covered in books or workshops, we can learn to use our attention in many different ways—including directing our attention to our attention itself—which has profound and unexpected implications for collaboration (and for many other areas of our lives).

Principle #2: We are already connected

Our bodies are wired for connectivity. Watching slow motion video replays of people in conversation reveals that our bodies are in constant interplay. We continually adjust posture, gestures, eye contact, tone of voice (and much more) in subtle and mostly unconscious response to each other's cues. Our nervous systems are exquisitely tuned to respond to one another in ways that are both obvious and invisible. And it doesn't matter whether we're enjoying the interaction or not— we are still viscerally and neurologically connected with the people around us.

But this hard-wired connectivity doesn't mean we are always aligned, in sync, or collaborating well together. It doesn't mean we are making Full Contact. We can't help but influence and be influenced by each other, so the question is, *Are we using this connectivity to collaborate well, or is our connection polarizing us, keeping us stuck, driving us further apart?*

Principle #3: We are where the action is

It's easy to assume that our collaborative challenges happen because *that person over there* is just uncooperative or *that team* doesn't care. As if we're just passive victims of other people's actions. But there's much more to it than that. We are *always* active participants in our collaborative challenges—we just may not recognize how our actions are influencing those other people, or in some cases, even recognize that we're taking any action at all.

Whenever we are sensing, perceiving, thinking, speaking, listening, planning, even just sitting quietly by ourselves and reflecting... we are engaged in action. Much of this action happens below the level of our awareness: Even when we believe that the things happening in the conversation around us are just happening on their own, *we are still acting*, simply by perceiving and interpreting those things in the particular ways that we each do. *We are always at the center of our interactions.* Becoming more aware of how our own action is at the core of our collaborative encounters enables us to free ourselves from stuck interactions and find new and more helpful ways to contribute to our collaborations.

Principle #4: It takes practice

As our awareness of our own actions grows, we discover new moves we can make to transform our collaborative performance. But then we need to *practice* those new moves so that they'll be available to us when we really need them. One of the major reasons good collaboration remains so elusive, is also why just reading books about flying airplanes doesn't make good pilots; why just studying about surgery doesn't make good surgeons, and why just showing up on game day doesn't make professional athletes. Skill requires practice. To get better at organizational collaboration, we need to do more than take workshops, read books and just show up to the meeting—we need to practice with focus and feedback, and ideally with support from a trusted coach or teacher, as well as from your "training partners" at the office.

Principle #5: Our intention matters

As my colleagues and I have seen with executives and their teams in diverse companies and cultures all over the world, people can do all the "right things" and still not collaborate well with their colleagues. As I said earlier, sometimes those "right" techniques actually make things worse, weakening trust and increasing polarization.

Although tools and techniques are essential in many situations, when we're trying to collaborate with other human beings, they're not enough. Nobody likes to feel "techniqued," even if the technique is executed perfectly. We don't like feeling as if someone is trying to control us like a machine or handle us like a trained animal to get their way.

When it comes to interacting with our fellow human beings, the *intention* underlying our actions matters as much or more than the specific techniques or actions we may take. For organizational collaboration, the intention to engage with curiosity, to learn together and to design a new future and make meaningful commitments to one another is the type of intention that's needed. Otherwise, all we're left with is empty techniques and negotiation strategies.

It goes beyond just getting our way on this immediate project or that short-term objective. It means treating each project and every objective as an opportunity to build trust and strengthen our contact with our colleagues. That's the intention underlying Full Contact Performance. When you're clear in this intention, then even imperfectly executed techniques can often work—because they're not aimed at working *on* the other person—they're aimed at working *with* the other person. When you're *not* clear in this intention then—no matter how many books or articles you've read—your old habits will likely take over when things get rough, and those old habits are frequently aimed at getting everything you can in the short term, often at the expense of the longer-term learning, decisions and relationships that are important for sustained collaborative performance.

Although aimed at organizational managers, anyone who lives, works or collaborates with others in any setting can also apply these principles and benefit from the practices that reflect them. My clients routinely tell me how this approach has helped them to transform their relationships outside of the office — with their spouses, kids and friends — as much as inside the office.

Reflection & Practice – Your Collaboration Case Study

In a notebook or on a device, please follow the instructions and answer the questions below:

Recall a tough collaborative challenge you've faced in the past or may be facing currently.

Write down a brief description of the collaborative challenge or problem as you see it. You may include descriptions of the individuals involved, the role(s) they played/are playing in the collaborative challenge and the actions you saw/see them making.

Hang on to this description as you read on. You can think of it as the beginning of your "Full Contact Case Study," which we'll be referring back to, so you can practice applying what you're learning.

If you're having trouble recalling a challenging collaborative encounter, here's a real example that you can use for your reflections as you continue reading...

"Care Doesn't Care" — A real life collaborative challenge

A couple of months into the Covid pandemic, I was asked to help a leading tech company resolve a troubled collaboration between Sales leaders in the Latin American region and Customer Success leaders, mostly based the U.S.

New sales in the Latin American region had been growing exponentially for the past year and this trend was expected to continue, even amidst the pandemic. But, although new sales were looking good, it was taking too long for customers to get up to speed with the products they were purchasing and they were opening far more technical support tickets than in other regions. Those support tickets were not—according to the sales team—being resolved quickly enough or fully solving customers' problems, which was frustrating to customers. What brought this issue to the CEO's attention was the recognition that many of these new customers were at risk of canceling their subscriptions early or not renewing at the end of their contract period.

A cross-functional team made up of 16 or so Latin-American based sales leaders and U.S. based technical support and customer success leaders had been convened to address the issue and the team had met several times already by the time I was asked to help out. I was told that little progress had been made in these meetings and that the conversations were getting more acrimonious with each meeting.

In my first video meeting with the team, the tension and frustration were palpable. After introducing myself, I asked that we take the time to go around and hear from each person about what problem(s), in their view, the group was here to address.

Almost to a person, people expressed their frustration and impatience with the conversations thus far. After this venting they each then launched into their proposed solutions. It became clear early on that this group was all over the map—there was no clear business problem the group was focusing on. In place of a business problem, they instead focused on people problems—the Sales folks were convinced that the problem lay with the Customer Success folks, who either didn't seem to care about the customers, or clearly lacked the competence to help the customers even if they did care (or both).

As the regional Sales team saw it, if the tech support agents would resolve customers' issues adequately then customers would be able to get up to speed quickly and would have no issues. If the customer success team were doing their job, customers would be happy and would stay with the business and renew their subscriptions. These views were captured in the phrase, "Customer Care Doesn't Care" which had become the rallying cry in the region.

No surprise that this mantra didn't go over too well with the folks on the Customer Success side, who felt unfairly and incorrectly singled out as the cause of a problem that was far more multi-faceted than the Sales folks were willing to admit. In fact, as Customer Success folks viewed things, the primary issues lay at the feet of the Sales team, which frequently, according to Customer Success, sold the wrong products to customers, creating a flood of unnecessary tech support tickets and planting unrealistic expectations in customers' minds about what the products were capable of.

This is a classic dynamic in organizations (as in so many other places): Thoughtful and committed people who have come together to solve a problem that impacts all of them find themselves locked into opposing narratives and fixating on the folks on the other side as "the problem." And folks on both sides, feeling unfairly targeted by the other, do their best to deflect and defend themselves from the other side's claims—which only hardens the others' views.

On the surface, there appeared to be little appetite amongst team members for venturing out of their respective camps to find common ground. But the intensity of their emotions and the energy they were putting into their tirades told me they were desperate to break out of this stuck place and find a way forward together. They just didn't see how. They were unable to make contact with one another, and they were all (along with the company, and even some customers) paying a price for it.

Over the next six months, the group did find a way forward together, solving many critical business problems that dramatically improved the region's performance and set the stage for robust customer renewals and sustained growth. Just as important, folks figured out how to forge stronger relationships and renewed trust—how to make contact with those on the "other side." This would allow them to continue to raise and address tough new problems together into the future, which is what good organizational collaboration is really all about.

How did they do this? That's what we'll be exploring throughout this book. Again, feel free to use this example for your "Case Study" reflections. I'll also be returning frequently to this example, and many others, to illuminate the key principles and practices of Full Contact Performance.

Chapter 2

Managing Your Attention

I remember it very clearly—the instructor in my driver's education class telling us that wherever we go with our eyes, the steering wheel will follow. When we turn our head to look at that billboard, our hands follow and soon the car is veering onto the shoulder. In other words, our body follows our attention. I still think about it when I'm driving and catch myself getting overly focused on things other than the road in front of me.

Several years later, on the Aikido mat, I heard the phrase "energy follows attention" and it occurred to me that this was what my driving instructor had been saying. Not only does our attention influence our movements, it influences our entire physiology as well as our thinking. What we pay attention to shapes our experience of the circumstances we encounter and of ourselves.

It's easy to experience the importance of attention in Aikido when a training partner is trying to push you over. Focusing your attention on your head, or on your thoughts, you'll be easy to topple. But if you move your attention down to the center of your body, or to your feet, you'll be much harder to push over. Try this with a friend and you'll see how powerful just a simple shift of attention can be.

There are practices in many healing, spiritual, and martial arts traditions that involve the use of attention to bring about changes in the body and mind. Different traditions use different words, such as "mind directs energy," "energy follows attention," or, "the energy (or power) flows where the mind goes," but they're all pointing to the same thing: the way we use our attention determines our performance, whether we're performing solo, or with our colleagues at work.

Despite the powerful role it plays in our lives, however, attention is rarely recognized as a factor in organizational collaboration. It's one of those things we take for granted. We say that some people are very focused, while others are easily distracted ("he has ADD"), but that's about the extent of our relationship to attention. Attention, however, isn't binary. It's much more than just being focused or not. There are many different ways of using our attention, and we can learn to cultivate and use our attention in ways that can improve our collaborative performance.

I *Am* Being Collaborative!

When my colleagues and I lead workshops with managers and teams, we see a common phenomenon across companies, cultures and countries: As the workshop participants begin to closely examine their own challenging conversations for the first time, they are, almost universally, *surprised.*

They're surprised to realize that they're not doing what they thought they were doing in those conversations (and were instead doing things they thought they *weren't* doing). Holding up a mirror to their own conversations reveals the sometimes-uncomfortable truth that *they aren't always aware of what they are actually doing in their conversations.* Or of how what they are doing impacts the people around them.

Now, we all do this at times — we think we're sharing our views skillfully only to discover that everybody else in the meeting thought that we were being arrogant and close-minded. Or we're respectfully questioning someone's idea but later hear that the person felt personally attacked by us. We can't be aware of everything, and when we're feeling pressure or frustration it can be even more challenging to notice what we're doing.

When workshop participants explain why some of their difficult collaborations go sideways, their explanations are typically other-focused: *"That other person (or team) wasn't ready," or "they're difficult personalities," or "they just don't get it."* Just like the folks from Sales and Customer Success in the "Care Doesn't Care" story. These are the kinds of explanations that any of us might make when our collaborative difficulties don't improve or get worse even though we've done "all the right things." This doesn't just happen in our collaborations, of course, but in many other areas in our lives.

This phenomenon partly reflects how the nervous system responds to challenges or adversity, activating the well-known "fight or flight" arousal response. In this mode, our attention narrows to focus on the perceived threat or challenge *out there* (along with a myriad of other physiological reactions that prepare our body to deal with the challenge). Although helpful for some situations, this reaction isn't so helpful for many other challenges in our modern day lives, including our collaborative challenges.

Again, although those people *out there* are certainly factors in our collaborative performance, the primary challenge is usually *in here*. And to change what's going on *in here* we first we need to *know* what's going on in here. We need to know what we're doing. As the saying goes, *"If you know what you are doing, you can do what you want."* Conversely, if you don't know what you're doing, you have little choice in the matter.

Victims of the Invisible

A 2006 paper published by a Duke University researcher states that more than 40 percent of the actions people perform each day aren't deliberate decisions, but habits. I suspect the figure may be much higher. And this isn't a new thing: In the late 1800s, William James declared that *"All our life, so far as it has definite form, is but a mass of habits."*

Our biggest challenge—and greatest opportunity—in any area of performance is *knowing what we're doing while we're doing it*. Most of the time, in collaboration as in other areas, we're flying blind. In place of awareness and deliberate action, we're operating on auto-pilot. Our habits are at the controls.

One basic function of attention is that it enables us to gain awareness, which opens the door to learning and transforming our performance.

Habits are, by definition, self-perpetuating. Operating below the radar of our consciousness, they are difficult to notice and therefore difficult to change. Also, when habits are running the show, we're not being fully present to what's happening in the here and now.

This is one reason why some meetings feel like such a waste of time: although our bodies are all in the same room or video conference together, our conversations aren't. Some people are speaking or listening from some place in the past, habitually colored by their historically conditioned experiences or memories, while others may be habitually operating in some imagined future. No wonder it can be hard to have meaningful conversations!

Just to be clear, habits aren't a problem, per se; we probably couldn't survive long without them. The ability to mentally automate certain tasks is certainly advantageous from an evolutionary standpoint. Our automated routines enable our brains to do much more, with much less neural real estate. And there are plenty of habits that we each have that are healthy and valuable.

It's those habits that aren't serving us so well that are worth examining. Such as those habitual patterns of thinking, feeling or directing our attention that keep us indulging in unhealthy lifestyle choices, or that continue to hinder our performance or relationships.

Researchers have been learning a lot recently about habits and how to change them. For some kinds of habits, we can simply change the environment, the process, or the tools we're using, and the habit may recede or disappear.

But that doesn't work for every type of habit. For many of the habits that influence our collaborative performance, awareness is a necessary ingredient. We must become aware of what we're doing when we are speaking and listening; what we're experiencing and doing in our body; what we're feeling emotionally, and how we're using our attention. Otherwise, we'll continue to be carried along on our automated trajectories, like Raul was, in the following example:

Raul's Habit

Raul was one of those team members in the "Care Doesn't Care" example I described earlier. A manager in his early 40s, Raul was a central figure in the region, and he was also a dominating presence in that first team meeting I joined. With a sharp intellect and a forceful way of expressing his views, he could barely contain himself when folks offered perspectives that differed from his own. His commitment to solving problems was evident to me, as was his habitual tendency to repeat himself, to cut people off, and to jump straight to promoting his own "solutions" without acknowledging that others might view the problem entirely differently.

I decided to call Raul after that first meeting because I thought he had been pretty out of control and it might be helpful going forward for us to have a personal connection together. Before I could even get out a "Hello," Raul immediately apologized for his behavior in the meeting, which he recognized as inappropriate and unhelpful. We discussed his behavior and I agreed that some of what he'd done was unhelpful and polarizing. Without any request on my part, he promised that he was going to really "rein it in" going forward.

In the next team call the following week, Raul was quite subdued—for the first 15 minutes. Then, he launched into the similar behaviors as before, even accusing others of cutting him off mid-sentence and of having no interest in seeing or addressing the "real" issues in front of them. As I intervened in the conversation, I could see him start to pull himself together, looking sheepish and perhaps a little discouraged with himself. He was clearly trying to "rein it in," but it was a little too late because at this point in the meeting, one of the senior leaders in the meeting just laid into Raul, letting him know that she was done with his immature and dominating behavior. This shut him down entirely for the last few minutes of the meeting.

The next day, Raul reached out to apologize to the leader who had called him out, and then he called me. He was ashamed and repentant. And also, clearly stuck in some powerful conversational habits that were becoming detrimental to his standing on this team, and possibly in the company. (Someone else in the meeting referred to his typical behavior as "outright bullying.") I shared with Raul my hypotheses that his unintended but habitual behaviors were creating the very dynamics that he was accusing everybody else of perpetuating. He quietly agreed, and then he once again "promised" to turn over a new leaf going forward.

While I appreciated his sincere intention to change (which I did), I told him that it would likely not be an overnight transformation. It would require some time and practice to gain more awareness about himself and his behaviors, and to cultivate new patterns of behavior in the heat of challenging conversations. I gave him a couple of simple grounding practices to work on, which could help him better manage his attention and his emotions when he felt himself getting amped up.

Unfortunately, Raul wouldn't have the opportunity to put those new practices into play on that particular project, as he was booted off the team before the next meeting by the senior leader who had called him out in the last conversation.

Raul's story underscores the habitual tendency for our attention to fixate outside of ourselves and onto the apparent threat "out there," when we're feeling challenged. It also highlights the impacts that some of our habitual coping routines may have on our collaborations (and our careers). For Raul, the threat appeared to be coming from the folks in the meeting who opposed his views. The real threat, however, was his own habitual behavior—including his inability to *pay attention to himself* in the meeting, while it was happening. Until Raul is able to manage his attention more skillfully, it will be difficult for him to rein in his unproductive behavior.

Our attention matters because it holds the key to new awareness about ourselves and others, which opens the door to new learning and behavior.

Using Our Attention

Here are a few of the ways we can use our attention:

1. We can zoom in on the fine details or zoom out to see the bigger picture.
2. We can focus outside of ourselves on the people or circumstances around us, or direct our focus back inward, to ourselves as the object of our attention.
3. With respect to ourselves, we can focus our attention on *what we're doing* (activity focus) or *how we are experiencing*

the activity (experiential focus). And we can get even more precise by shifting our attention (like changing the channel on your TV) between our *thoughts* (mental channel), our *physical sensations* (body channel), and our *emotional state* (feeling channel).

4. We can also change the "level" of our attention. In other words, we can be fully immersed in the interaction, task or experience we're in, or we can shift our attention to a place outside of that fully immersed experience to look back in on it.

Most of us use our attention in these ways every day although we might not be aware of it. Let's take a closer look at how our use of attention shows up in our collaborative encounters...

Zooming in & Out

We've all become experts at zooming in and out with our fingers, or double clicking on our devices. We pinch our fingers and thumbs together on our devices to zoom in for a closer look, or we pull them apart to zoom out to see the bigger picture. Zooming in calls the object out of its background, enabling us to home in on the details, the fine print. It turns our focus into a narrow spotlight.

Conversationally, we zoom in so as to examine some aspect of it more closely, to understand it better. It may be a particular problem or solution, a goal, strategy, anything.

In contrast, zooming out is more like a floodlight. It gives us a view of the bigger picture. Our peripheral vision comes into play and we can see connections that aren't apparent to us when we're narrowly focused. We zoom out to orient ourselves within the broader situation, conversation or problem we're trying to solve.

We zoom in and out all the time. It's important for everyday navigation whether we're literally driving to a new destination, or figuratively navigating the ins and outs of organizational life, the marketplace, or our relationships.

Zooming in and out also has an important physiological dimension that impacts our collaborative performance. In Aikido we refer to this process of zooming our attention in and out as using *hard eyes* or *soft eyes*, which we'll look a little later.

Activity or Experience Focus

Our attention often has a mind of its own, and that mind is influenced by all sorts of things, both outside of us and inside of us. Our attention can orient itself outwardly to the circumstances, activities or people *out there*, or inwardly to the internal environment of our experience, to our thoughts, feelings and bodily sensations. Both types of attention focus on what's happening, but from different vantage points. Raul's habitual focus, like that of so many others, was predominantly *out there* on the other people he was working with. Especially when someone out there disagreed or challenged his thinking.

Activity Focus

Outside of ourselves, activities and circumstances are constantly vying for our attention. Sights, sounds, smells and other sensations pull us towards them, invited or not.

There is the avalanche of social activities out there, including social media, that are hell-bent for a share of our mind. Plugged in as most of us are to electronic media for so many hours a day, it's easy to relinquish control of our attention to what's out there—to people we don't know, companies that know more about our preferences and lives than we do, and to computer algorithms we don't notice yet which dictate how we use our attention. In what has been called the Age of Distraction, we must work very hard, and often pay more money, to minimize the steady stream of advertisements and opinions coming at us through our devices.

Habitual *activity* focus is the default way of paying attention for many of us because the world out there can be such a captivating place. Daniel J. Levitin, cognitive psychologist, neuroscientist and author, explains it like this: "the brain's arousal system has a novelty bias, meaning that its attention can be hijacked easily by something new – the proverbial shiny objects we use to entice infants, puppies, and cats. And this novelty bias is more powerful than some of our deepest survival drives: Humans will work just as hard to obtain a novel experience as we will to get a meal or a mate. The difficulty here for those of us who are trying to focus amid competing activities is clear: The very brain region we need to rely on for staying on task is easily distracted by shiny new objects."

Experiential Focus

Of course, shiny new objects don't only show up "out there." We are fully capable of manufacturing them ourselves, even when sitting quietly with our eyes closed. This is the other world of distraction that requires no electronics, no social media. It doesn't even require other people. It's the rich and compelling world of our interior—our thoughts, feelings, images and bodily sensations.

We can cut ourselves off from all of the normal distractions that make up our lives, cut ourselves off from all human, animal or machine contact, and the mind will still generate a steady stream of "material" that can be much harder to quiet than any smart device. Studies of people in physical and social isolation show how our minds step up to fill in the blank space, to create sensation and experience in the absence of input from outside.

You don't need to do hard time in solitary or undergo sensory deprivation to experience this. If you've ever attempted to meditate, you know how hard it can be to let your attention remain quietly focused on your breath, for even a few minutes.

When we deliberately shift attention from the activities we are doing or that are happening around us, to *experiential* focus, we can attend to our thinking, to our feeling, or to how we are sensing ourselves in our body while we're doing whatever we're doing. "Changing the channel" in this way is a helpful way to change what we're aware of, and also to change how we're performing.

Our *Thinking* channel includes our mental activity — reflection, remembering, planning, evaluating, analysis — pretty much anything we do in language.

Our *Feeling* channel includes our moods and emotions.

Our *Sensing* or *Body* channel encompasses all the different types of physical sensations that occur in our bodies including everything from temperature (heat/cold), tension, relaxation, constriction, expansion, vibration, tingling, streaming, to movement, spatial orientation, balance, and even our imagination and visualization (seeing without using our eyes).

Each of these channels reflects an aspect of our relationship with the world. At different moments, in different situations, one of these channels is likely dominant. Each of these channels may have potentially valuable information about what's going on: within ourselves, in our interactions, and in our relationships with the people and circumstances we encounter. Becoming conversant with each of these channels and getting better at switching between them helps us become more aware of what we're doing.

Shifting Levels and Meta-moves

So far, we've talked about zooming in and out and switching from activity to experience focus. Now, let's look at shifting our attention from one level to another...

When we are fully immersed in an interaction, task or experience, we're operating on the first level. Let's say we're having a conversation, reading a report, playing tennis or doing any other activity, and all of our attention is focused on that activity. We're not thinking about what we're doing or how we're doing it, we're just doing it.

First level of attention

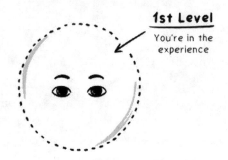

1st Level
You're in the experience

To shift to another level, we deliberately step back with our attention to a place outside of—or beyond—that fully immersed experience we were just in, so as to look back in on it. I call this deliberate shift of our attention a "meta-move." If the fully-immersed space we were in a moment before is Level One, then we've just moved to Level Two. Here's a simple illustration of a meta-move...

Second level of attention

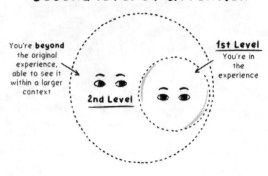

You're **beyond** the original experience, able to see it within a larger context

2nd Level

1st Level
You're in the experience

Here's a simple example of shifting levels...

At the All-Hands Meeting

You're gathered together with many of your colleagues in the large meeting room, watching a live-stream video of the CEO talking about the challenges and opportunities facing the company in the months ahead. It's the quarterly All-Hands meeting. And because the CEO is a riveting speaker (and because you're deeply invested in the success of this company), you're fully engrossed in the presentation. Your experience is direct and immediate. Your thoughts, your body and your emotions are fully engaged; you're not thinking about the fact that you are in the All-Hands meeting — you are just in it.

Let's say you committed the crime of leaving your cell phone ringer on and you suddenly receive a call, which jolts you and everyone else in the room out of the All-Hands meeting and back into this meeting room. You fumble to turn off your ringer, while some of your colleagues are chiding you about the interruption, but a moment or two later, you're all back "in" the All-Hands meeting. Immersed in the CEO's words and the implications of those words.

Your experience of being fully immersed in the All-Hands is that first small circle — First Level — the direct experience you were having. Your ringing phone thrust you momentarily into that second concentric circle, where you remember you are in a meeting room with your colleagues watching the CEO.

As the meeting ends, you and your colleagues start filtering out of the meeting room, reflecting together about what the CEO had said, how he said it and what it might mean for your teams. No longer in the All-

Hands (the first circle) you are now talking *about* the All-Hands—your conversation is taking place in that second circle. You have gone "meta" to (beyond) the All-Hands, which allows you to think critically about what you observed in the All-Hands. You might discuss how you thought the CEO looked, the quality of the live-stream, the poor attendance by some other teams, the timing of the information and much more—all from the perspective of that Second Level.

As you listen to your colleague's comments about the All-Hands you realize you hadn't noticed many of the things she had clearly noticed, even though you were both there listening to the same thing. This colleague is opening up a whole new dimension to the All-Hands for you and you mention this to her. Bingo—you've just made yet another meta-move, jumping beyond this second level, taking your friend with you! You're now talking about the conversation you are having with this colleague about your experience of the All-Hands meeting.

In this new level you are observing what you just did or experienced in a new way, and probably noticing things about that first level that you might have missed before—like how you were doing whatever you were doing—your assumptions, beliefs, objectives, strategies and perhaps the results of what you were doing. This shifting from one level to the next isn't anything foreign or esoteric—we all do it whenever we're learning a new skill and we pause to reflect on how we're doing and what to do differently (this meta-move is sometimes called "going to the balcony"). What we don't always do is make these meta-moves deliberately when we're engaged in collaborative interactions or when we're trying to solve complex problems.

We'll be returning to this concept (and practice) of shifting attention levels throughout this book and revisiting these basic levels.

Again, when you make the meta-move from the first level to the next, you'll notice things you couldn't see before. You might notice details about what has been going on in that first level—such as that the CEO seemed to be choosing his words very carefully when describing the outlook for the business over the next few quarters. And because you're no longer inside of that first circle, you may also notice patterns or relationships more clearly. You might realize, for example, that the CEO used the very same careful words in his last two All-Hands meetings. The point here is that you can learn more about what's *inside* the circle by stepping *outside* of it. And when you step outside of that first level with other people, you will all probably see and learn even more.

This process of shifting levels is sometimes referred to as *Second Order* or *Double-Loop* learning. Going forward, we'll refer to the different levels (reflected by the smaller circle within a larger circle or open space) as *First Order* and *Second Order*.

It may seem as if making a meta-move is the same as zooming out, but it's not. We can zoom out indefinitely within the same level or frame of reference, and although we'll gain a wider view of things within that level—more background, less detail—we won't be able to see what we'd see from outside that circle. A wider angle isn't the same as a different level in terms of what we can observe.

When we make a meta-move, it's like injecting "space" between ourselves and what we're doing or seeing within that first level. This new space also seems to affect our nervous system, which appears to quiet down when we deliberately shift our attention out to the next level. In fact, this may partly explain why meta-moves are so useful: they act as a reset for our body and mind, so that we can be more present to what's going on around us (and inside of us).

To Meta-Move Is Human

If you've had any experience with mindfulness practices such as meditation, this idea of meta-moves will sound familiar. Many mindfulness practices are themselves "meta-move" practices in which we bring our attention to ourselves, using bodily sensations, thoughts, feelings (or even our attention itself) as focus areas to assist us in cultivating this meta-capacity. The many benefits of this type of practice have been well researched and include improvements to cognitive and executive functioning, stress reduction, immune system resilience, and many others.

In his book *The Information* James Glieck suggests that the advent of writing was an evolutionary meta-move that jump-started a new era of human evolution. By committing words and thoughts to writing, the writer (and future readers) could now look back at that thinking and reflect on it (for at least as long as the clay tablet, palm frond, or other writing technology lasted). But we may have been making meta-moves from the very beginning of language. How else could we agree that this sound or grunt was going to mean, *"A tiger is at the watering hole just over that hill, so grab your club and let's get out of here—fast!"* Or, *"I'll lend you this spear if you share what you kill with it."*

Meta-Moving Doesn't Mean Detaching

Directing our attention beyond the specific thing we're doing or conversation we're having doesn't mean we're removing ourselves from it or checking out. It's also not just being in our heads, cut off from our experience. Injecting more space into a conversation with a deliberate meta-move can do the opposite— it can enable us to be more fully present to the conversation, be more open to the people in it—with more perspective and less reactivity.

As Jack Kornfield describes in *A Path with Heart*, "Sometimes we are in the middle of our experience. Sometimes it is as if we sit down on our shoulder and notice what is present, and sometimes we can be aware with a great spacious distance. All of these are useful aspects of our awareness. They each can help us sense and touch and see our life more clearly from moment to moment."

Conceptually this may all make sense, but it isn't always easy to do. Partly because the circle we are habitually operating within—like any well-worn habit—is so familiar to us that we don't even notice it. It doesn't appear to us as something we could even step outside of; it's just *how things are*. At times, like electrons being forced out of their orbits, circumstances may bump us out of our comfortable circles, and we feel as if we've been given new eyes. But we don't have to wait for circumstances to push us out of our habitual circle. We can learn to make these meta-moves more deliberately, and help our colleagues do it, too.

Parents and Magicians

Before we move on, let's look at one more way that we can use our attention. It's related to the earlier theme of Activity focus vs. Experiential focus, but it's a little different. When we do it well, it can be a powerful meta-move that can significantly de-escalate a charged encounter. It's basically shifting our attention from the person, behavior or situation that may be challenging, to... something else. A couple of examples will illustrate the general concept:

This first example is well known to parents or anyone who has taken care of young children. It's the time-honored trick of *distraction*—pretending to shift your own attention in order to divert or redirect an upset child's attention, as in, "Isn't that a cute puppy?" or "Let's get ice cream!" It works best with younger children. (With older kids, distracting moves like this are more likely to be met with some version of "stop trying to change the subject—I'm not a child!") Now, I'm definitely not suggesting that your colleagues are children and that you should simply try to redirect their attention whenever you hit a rough patch in your conversations. Instead, I just want you to know that there are times in many collaborations when the group's focus just gets stuck on a particular point, idea, explanation, problem or solution. In these situations, making a meta-move publicly can help. Simply pointing out that the group may be digging itself deeper into its hole and inviting folks to step back and reflect on the conversation can often allow groups to see what they're doing with new eyes. Making meta-moves with colleagues—especially when done explicitly—can create new space for gaining awareness, learning and innovating.

The second example works with both children and adults. It's what good magicians do. They must be more subtle and skillful than most parents to pull it off, and they often use their bodies, their words, their props, and their own attention to bring about the desired result—that is, to get us to shift our attention away from one thing and towards another, so that we don't notice what they do when our attention is elsewhere. (They also usually must do it surreptitiously for it to work—which is not what I'm suggesting for your colleagues.)

On the Aikido mat, when a training partner is coming at you with a punch to the face, that fist can be totally mesmerizing. Your peripheral vision narrows, and your movements, techniques and strategies all merge to "become" that fist. But if you keep your attention on that rapidly approaching threat, you'll either get hit or react in some habitual and probably ineffective way. So, you have to practice shifting some of your focus away from the incoming strike, without actually losing your connection with the opponent or checking out. You can do this in several ways:

You can zoom out to take in the bigger picture—your partner's balance and posture, other people or objects in the area, even the empty space around you.

You can shift your attention to some place on their body (generally other than their striking fist), which—if you do it effectively, can draw their attention to that place as well, weakening their strike (our attention doesn't only direct our own energy—it can also influence their energy as well).

You can focus on some real or imagined point on the ground or the space around you, turning your eyes, your head and even your entire body towards that point. Again, if you do it well and remain engaged with your opponent, it can often derail the attacker's focus, giving you an opening that wasn't there before.

Although a fist to the face is not the same as a conversational challenge, our bodies generally react similarly. In both types of circumstances, it may matter less what we shift our attention to, as long as we shift it decisively and stay present while we're doing it. The key is to not remain spellbound by the attack—or by this colleague, conversation or situation.

Here's another example:

I'm in a conversation with Sheila, a colleague I've known for quite a while. As usual, she is dominating the conversation with her forceful energy and ideas—so much so that it's hard to get a word in edgewise. Also as usual, I inwardly grumble about how annoying she is to work with. The more frustrated I get, the more focused I become on what a problem she's always been for me. Because *she* is the problem I need to solve (to succeed with my work), I naturally focus on *solving the problem of Sheila*. I may try many different strategies or techniques to get her to shut up and listen to *my* ideas, *my* needs, but they all just fuel the fire, making her even more aggressive and oblivious.

Here's how I would explain this situation: I have let my own attention become captured by Sheila's behavior, to the point where my entire focus is on her and how problematic she is. Just as our hands on the steering wheel follow our eyes on the billboard, with all my attention fixated on Sheila, all my energy, creativity and resources are now also directed towards solving *the problem of Sheila* ("energy follows attention"). I have become the victim of my own narrowed attention, which has also narrowed the possible responses I might make in my interactions with Sheila. But what if I make the meta-move of shifting my attention off Sheila and her behavior for a moment and focus on my own body, thoughts or emotions (which is, after all, where the problem is being experienced)? And what if I made another meta-move, with Sheila this time, in which I share with her what I'm feeling and that I would like her to consider some ideas I've been entertaining, so that we can discuss them along with her own ideas? If I can do this from a relaxed place without treating her as the problem to solve, she just may relax a little too, and be more receptive to a more balanced conversation.

These simple examples show how powerful our attention can be. Aside from altering our own experience, shifting our attention can significantly influence the perceptions, thoughts, emotions and focus of other people—and as some politicians understand, even entire populations. But trying to manipulate other folks isn't the primary reason for shifting our attention, and it can easily backfire if that's our motive. The primary reason to shift our attention is that it expands awareness—so that we know more about what we're doing—and therefore have more freedom to respond effectively to the people we're working with.

When we bring our deliberate attention to some part of our body, our physical energy accumulates there, often bringing sensations such as heat, vibration, tingling, contraction, releasing, etc. When we are overly focused on what a colleague is doing or not doing, our energy and actions accumulate around *that person or behavior*, which can cause them to intensify whatever they're doing. When our own energy is aimed at another person, we often inadvertently intensify the very behaviors that we are hoping would change. What's more, when our attention is fixated on the person or problem *out there*, our world narrows down to that person or problem, which inhibits our capacity to respond skillfully or creatively. Just like we "feed" the tantrum our child is throwing in the middle of the grocery store by focusing on it or fuel the dominating behavior by that colleague sitting across from us.

It's common to fixate our attention outwardly when we experience difficult circumstances or interactions. And while it might seem irresponsible to take our attention away from the problem we're experiencing, that is often exactly what we need to do to get a stuck collaboration moving again.

Hardwired for Connection and Reciprocity

Now let's apply this practice of shifting attention to the principle of connectivity....

First of all, the principle of connectivity recognizes that we are connected with one another via our nervous systems—through our sensory perceptions: what we see, hear or otherwise sense in each other's presence. But what we perceive in each other isn't just determined by happenstance. It has a lot to do with how we're using our attention.

When I'm intently focused on trying to change or fix you, because I see you as the obstacle to my successful performance, this focus—this way of using my attention—will naturally express itself in my words, my posture, my gestures and my energy—in my very way of being around you. And you'll pick up on this and will likely feel judged, rejected or otherwise at risk, and your nervous system will react in kind by fixating your attention back on me as a threat, as the obstacle keeping *you* from feeling okay and getting your needs met. Then in turn, when I sense this response from you, my beliefs about you are reinforced, which further intensifies my attention on you as the problem to fix... and on and on it goes. It's how our innate connectedness coupled with our tendency to reciprocate so often plays out. In this instance, this connectedness and reciprocity happen to be working against us.

Conversely, when we're treated with respect, understanding, and the presumption of good will, we tend to be more respectful, understanding and generous in return.

We are already wired for connection. We just need to learn to use this connection to make Full Contact.

Our connectedness can lead to virtuous or to vicious cycles. In the context of organizational collaboration, when we don't use our attention skillfully, our natural connectedness can foster weakened trust, defensiveness, inability to learn from one another, and ultimately, poor execution. When we manage our attention well, this same connectedness brings us closer together to learn and perform better. Because we are connected, when I shift my attention *away* from you as the problem it often allows you to relax your defensiveness or your attachment to a particular view or position.

We are all pre-wired for Full Contact; we just need to learn to use this wiring for good.

Reflection & Practice – Using Your Attention

Over the next week, practice noticing what you're doing with your attention at least three or four times a day during any of your conversations with others. Using a notebook or device, write down your answers to the following questions:

1. *How you were using your attention during that interaction. Where was your focus?*
   - Were you mostly *zoomed in* on the details, or *zoomed out* on the big picture?
   - Were you mostly focused on the *other people* in the interaction, or on the *content* of the conversations—the agenda topics, data, or circumstances being discussed?
   - Were you focused at all on *yourself*—your feelings, thoughts, or bodily sensations? If so, what did you notice?
2. *Now, speculate about how the use of your attention might have influenced your own and others' thinking and behaviors during the conversation.* Don't worry about getting these answers right—this is your own private speculation, for your own learning.

Chapter 3

The Five Speech Actions
(or, *Doing Things with Words*)

We all know that words *lead to* action. Marketers and ad agencies have long understood the power of words to conjure up emotions, yearnings, entire lifestyles—to drive the listener or reader to buy. Leaders use words to inspire action on the battlefield, on the factory floor, and in the voting booth.

But words do more than lead us to act. They *are* action in their own right. As Echeverria says, "to speak is to act." In your organization, "talk" is the most valuable asset. And it may also be one of the most poorly managed assets.

Casting Spells with Words

Historically in many cultures, certain phrases or word formulas were used to cast spells. These incantations were believed to have magical qualities—words could help avoid disaster or rain down Armageddon. "Spell words" could cause individuals to fall ill or die and crops to wither. Or they could protect your loved ones and bring fertility and prosperity to the land. Words could change the world.

And that is still true today. In the words of J.L. Austin,[1] "We do things with words."

Our tools and technologies, our organizations, communities and nations are all products of our words. Whenever we open our mouths to speak, we are taking action, not just preparing for the real action later on. This applies to all the different types of "speaking" we do, including typing documents, texting, emailing, posting to social media (even "liking" and "friending" is talk). Talk drives organizational alignment, performance and innovation—or organizational dysfunction and excuses. It depends on how well we're using it.

A Handful of Actions

Whether we're defining our company's strategic direction or shutting a company down; analyzing data or inventing a new business model; whenever we're fixing, building or even destroying things—we are doing it with just a handful of actions or *speech acts*. These are:

- Assertions
- Declarations
- Requests
- Offers
- Promises

These five speech acts not only act upon the world *out there*, they also shape how the world shows up for us, *in here*. They influence what we perceive and don't perceive, what we think, and how we feel about things. They strengthen our connection with one another, or they drive us apart.

We weave speech acts together to tell ourselves stories to help us make sense of things, and to predict what things will happen next.

Even our identity—our sense of who we are in the world— grows out of the speech actions we use. All this with just a handful of words.

Okay, not *just* words.

Words Incarnate and In Context

Words don't come out of nowhere. And once spoken (or thought) they don't just evaporate in the ether. Our words come from somewhere, and they go somewhere—they are listened to by someone—even if it's only us listening to our own internal chatter.

Our words are *embodied*. They arise in and are expressed through our bodies, not only our mouths (or our writing, typing or signing hands). And this isn't just metaphorical.

When we listen to what others say (or what we say to ourselves), our brains actively create meaning from the words we hear (we listen with those same five linguistic actions). We interpret for meaning and we absorb that meaning into our bodies. As we'll explore further in Chapter 9, the way we interpret words affects our entire nervous system. Some speech acts we listen to (or speak) trigger the release of hormones that amp our bodies up for action. Others invite us to relax and chill out. Still others flood us with feelings of warmth, connection or confidence—or their opposites. Our words and the actions they express shape our mood, our posture, our gestures and even our tissues—often in ways that we're not even aware of.

If you are a native English speaker, you probably consider the future to be in front of you and the past to be behind. And when you talk about the future, your body probably sways forward slightly (and backwards when talking about the past). But this isn't so for everybody.[2] If Aymara were your native language (likely because you grew up on the region of the Andes where Aymara is spoken, or were raised by Aymara speaking parents), you'd likely lean or gesture backwards slightly when talking about the future, and forward when reminiscing about the past.

Sensing the World through Our Words

Most of us in Western cultures believe in separateness. We believe that we are each discrete, separate "selves," living amidst many other separate selves, within an environment that is also separate from us. But sages, and now scientists are recognizing that this notion of separateness is a false one: No organism can be distinguished apart from the environment in which it exists. Systems biologist Humberto Maturana and others speak about the continual "coupling" with the surrounding environment that defines every organism, including humans. Although we may be inextricably coupled with our environment and everyone in it (another way of talking about that hard-wired connection we each share with one another), that's not always our felt experience. And that's partly the result of the words we use to describe ourselves and to distinguish ourselves from one another and from everything else in the animal, vegetable and mineral kingdoms. Creating distinctions is one more thing we do with our words, but then we often "believe" these distinctions, forgetting that they are purely "linguistic," and not how the world actually is.

Just as our various body parts are not independent of our whole body, neither are they isolated from our thoughts or our emotions. All of these "parts" are different expressions of the *whole* that we each are. And this *whole* is also always in relationship to, and part of, the larger unity comprised of the other people, organisms and "things" in the world around us. We are not disembodied "word machines" transmitting and receiving linguistic actions in a vacuum. We are sensate creatures living in physical bodies with exquisitely sensitive nervous systems that are constantly at play with other bodies and with the environment around us. Our words, our bodies, our emotions, our attention and our relationships with the people, places, and circumstances of our lives constitute what we experience and refer to as "me, myself and I."

And it all flows from language.

Perceiving with Words

We don't just see with our eyes, smell with our noses, or hear with our ears—we also perceive with our words, through our distinctions. Distinctions serve as a sort of perceptual organ through which we perceive and interact with much of the world.

These distinctions allow us to perceive things that we wouldn't necessarily perceive without them. We use words to call ourselves out from the larger background within which we exist, and to call everything else out as well. We cleave things apart with our words, giving each a distinct name and description, which lets us focus our attention more precisely— to study, learn and act with greater granularity.

Distinctions are part of what makes experts so expert. The distinctions they've learned enable them to differentiate between what's important and what isn't, what to pay more attention to and what to ignore in the pursuit of their objectives.

What makes a doctor a doctor is her ability to see things that the rest of us don't see. When your child complains of a sore throat and you look at his throat, you may not see much at all. But his doctor may see a lot. Like perhaps certain parts of your son's throat that are subtly swollen or discolored, or other physical signs that seem to us entirely unrelated. The doctor asks questions that we wouldn't know to ask, makes diagnoses we're clueless about, and takes other actions (like taking and interpreting a throat culture or blood test) that we couldn't take. "Your son has strep throat. Have him take these pills for 7 days and let me know how he's doing."

Just to drive home the point, if you took your son to the acupuncturist, she'll likely give an entirely different diagnosis: "Weak governing vessel," or perhaps a "running liver pulse." She may stick acupuncture needles here and there, and perhaps send you home with an herbal formula to help restore your son's vital energy.

The Western medical doctor and the Acupuncture doctor are looking at the same boy but are seeing very different things because of the different distinctions they are "looking" through.

So it is with every profession, every discipline, vocation, hobby. Whether it's the Chief Financial Officer, the Marketing Director, the software engineer or the Sales Director, every discipline is characterized by its own distinctions. Distinctions represent one of the ways that we act with language, and also one of the ways that language acts upon us.

Creating Us and Them

Distinctions created with words also form part of the social glue that lets us feel that we're part of a unique group and distinct from other groups.

Shared distinctions help to foster a sense of belonging, trust and even pride with the "us" group, while also erecting invisible barriers between us and the outsiders in those "other" groups.

Teams, companies, communities and entire cultures are defined in part by the unique distinctions shared by members. This is just one reason why people in the sales department seem to live in such a different world from those in engineering; why finance folks see the world differently from the folks in Marketing. They each use distinct terms, acronyms and phrases that represent the important things they need to pay attention to and act upon to do their work. Their distinctions let them focus and collaborate with their fellow group members quickly and efficiently. When two groups with dramatically different distinctions must work together, their distinctions can get in the way. So, paying attention and helping each other become aware of the particular distinctions being used is important for cross-functional collaboration. Which brings us back to our five speech acts:

- Assertions
- Declarations
- Requests

- Offers
- Promises

Each one of these speech acts is unique. Each can also be expressed in different ways. Some may take the form of single words, others may be expressed in lengthy sentences or even treatises, but they are still speech acts. And we make speech acts every time we speak (and also when we listen). Each speech act brings with it its own particular "social obligation" or commitment that we, the speaker, implicitly make when we speak them. This will become clearer shortly.

In the next chapters we'll be examining each of these speech acts in some detail. Some of what we'll cover may appear very basic at first glance, but I encourage you to be open to seeing things you might not have noticed or thought about before. Although they may seem obvious, these speech acts aren't very well understood — or well utilized — in most collaborations. And most collaborative problems arise from misunderstandings about how these speech acts really work and how to use them effectively. As you read on, keep in mind that the point isn't to remember every little thing about each speech action, but to begin to gain greater awareness of these speech actions in your daily interactions, in real time. Doing the Reflection & Practices at the end of each chapter will help you increase this awareness, so that soon you'll find yourself noticing the speech actions you and others are making all the time, with little or no effort.

Endnotes

1 The Oxford Philosophy professor who, in the 1950s, introduced the concept of performatives, or speech acts, in lectures he delivered at Harvard University, later published posthumously in his book *How to Do Things with Words*.

2 In 2010 Lynden Miles of the University of Aberdeen in Scotland in 2006, Raphael Núñez of U.C.S.D. and Eve Sweetser of U.C. Berkeley

Chapter 4

Assertions: Telling It Like It Is

Sales of product XYZ are up 12% year over year.

We have been rated #1 in the industry for Customer Satisfaction for the past three years.

Our revenue dropped by 3% last quarter.

The earth revolves around the sun.

All the above statements describe something that can be observed and is considered factual. They are all examples of *assertions*.

See It, Then Say It

In one of his journals from 1851, Henry David Thoreau said that "first of all a man must see, before he can say." He may have been talking about assertions.

We assert facts to describe the world as we observe it. Our descriptions include the world of physical "things" like mountains, trees, rivers, houses, chairs, buildings, and all the other things we can observe with our eyes. John Searle calls these physical things *brute facts*—which seem to exist independently of, or *before*, the person arrived on the scene to observe and describe them. When we say that *Mt. Everest is covered with snow,* or *We have offices in 30 countries,* or *Our entire vehicle fleet consists of electric vehicles,* we are asserting brute facts. Someone could go and observe the snow on Mt. Everest, the offices in other countries with our company's logo on it, or each of the vehicles in our fleet to physically verify these facts.

We also routinely describe all sorts of "non-things," like laws, norms, logical or mathematical calculations, organizational roles, etc. Searle calls these *social facts*. Even though we can't see these non-things with our eyes, they are often just as real to us; we can still "observe" them and describe them with words. We can make factual statements, for instance, that *There are laws which govern how fast people can drive on the roads*, that *Lisa is the CEO of that company*, or that *Your company's tech support department takes 1.3 days on average to resolve customers' issues*. These are assertions that could be proven or disproven, even though they don't describe concrete, tangible things.

> *The key to assertions is that they can be proven true or false. They are statements that deal with facts.*

Just the Facts, Please

Each speech act has its job to do, its purpose in life. The purpose of the assertion is to "tell it like it is." It is to describe our observations, chronicling what we perceive to be true, accurate, factual.

We make assertions to inform, educate, give us insight into how things are or how they have been. Rafael Echeverria echoes Thoreau when he says that with assertions, *the word follows the world*. First, we observe the world, then we describe it with an assertion.

Assertions are, technically, "value-neutral." They are, in the ideal, unbiased and unemotional, merely faithful descriptions of that which the observer is observing. The value or significance comes later—from our *interpretations* of those assertions. Your company's year-end Profit and Loss statement consists solely of rows and columns of words and numbers. They have no meaning or significance in themselves. Just show them to someone who has no idea what a financial statement is and that becomes clear. It's not until an executive, analyst, shareholder, or SEC examiner looks at these numbers that the significance kicks in. (*Wow, this is a great looking company to invest in.* Or, *Whoa, this company is in much worse shape than we thought.*)

Similarly, in the "Care Doesn't Care" example, the chart showing how long it took on average for the Customer Care department to resolve Latin American customers' issues was made of lines, shapes and colors—all aimed at accurately depicting the performance of the Customer Care department. But the chart didn't "tell us" about the thinking, attitude, motivation or challenges of the Customer Care team. To look at the lines, shapes and colors of the chart and conclude that "Customer Care doesn't care" involves an entirely different speech act. This was not clear to the managers involved in those conversations. They had conflated the data (assertions) with their interpretations and feelings about the data (which involve declarations, another speech act which we'll look at shortly), and assumed that their interpretations and feelings would be obvious and inescapable to everyone else. Failing to appreciate the critical distinction between assertions and declarations made it is almost impossible to have a constructive conversation with the folks on the Customer Care team, who had a very different interpretation of what the data meant (and what to do about it).

To say that the speech act of assertions consists simply of "data" might suggest that they are not as "active" as the other speech acts. But consider the scientist who "discovers" a new organism, or the explorer who comes upon a new frontier, previously unknown (or unobserved). By calling these out in language—by reporting on them, *asserting* their existence (showing them in the microscope, leading an expedition back to the newly discovered territory), these organisms or places that previously did not exist for us suddenly become part of our world of facts—part of *what is*. Assertions are active and alive: they show us and others what has happened or is happening; they show us what to look for, which can point us to new possibilities for action and interaction.

Assertions Are Community Property

The late U.S. Senator Patrick Moynihan said, *"You're entitled to your own opinions but not to your own facts."* Since assertions tell it like it is for all to see, they "belong" to everybody.

We can each look at a painting, a bouquet of flowers, or a financial statement, and while agreeing that we're looking at the same painting, flowers or numbers, we also understand that we can each have dramatically different reactions to what we're seeing. But unlike beauty, which lies in the eyes of the beholder, facts don't belong to any of us alone. They are community property.

When I make an assertion, a listener expects me to be able to back it up with objective evidence that they can see for themselves. Because assertions represent what is observable, others should be able to look at what I'm describing and see what I see. That is the *social obligation* of assertions: to be truthful and provide acceptable evidence, if asked for. When our *assertions* veer away from the truth or there's no evidence to support them, the speaker's credibility can be called into question and things can get shaky (when we suspect that speaker is doing it intentionally, we call it *lying*).

When a company announces that its revenues increased 12% over last year, the expectation is not only that this assertion is accurate, but also that there is a viable paper trail to back it up. That's what "Generally Accepted Accounting Practices" (GAAP) are for, should a shareholder, watchdog organization, government regulator or consumer seek to verify it.

This is also why news companies employ fact checkers, and why courts of law have strict rules to determine what constitutes acceptable evidence (and not just hearsay, or spurious claims). And it's why the term *fake news* raises such indignation and concern, regardless of our political affiliation: Because we believe that news is supposed to be comprised of assertions that are accurate and objectively verifiable by anyone—not just reflective of someone's subjective bias or agenda.

Which brings us to an important but nerdy point about assertions: assertions that are false (based on faulty data, or even fabricated out of thin air) are still assertions—they're just false assertions. Today, most would agree that the statement "The solar system revolves around the earth" is false. But, although false, it's still an assertion. The term *assertion* refers to the *speech act* we're making—not to the truth or falseness of that speech act, nor to the thing or concept it's referring to. Assertions are not the things they are describing any more than product brochures are the products they depict, or numbers on a balance sheet are the actual dollars they represent.

There is another way in which assertions are community property, and it has to do with the agreement that exists within any given community about what is generally accepted as true or as false. Just as an assertion carries with it the *social obligation* of being factual and true, that social obligation exists within a larger *social agreement* about how "factual" and "true" are actually defined.

Within the accounting community, there are agreed upon standards for recording financial transactions and reporting on those transactions. These are codified within the GAAP framework of standards. This framework is what enables anyone in the community (or outside of it) to examine a company's financial reports and determine the validity of the assertions made about the company's finances.

Similarly, the scientific community has its own set of standards and practices that enable people to determine the "facticity" of assertions made within that community.

Each community is defined, in part, by its particular standards and practices for determining what's true and what isn't. And those standards change over time, as the community, technology and the rest of the world changes. Some of our cold, hard facts today will certainly be displaced by newer, "truer" facts five years, or five days from now.

The history of science is partly the history of how true *assertions* evolve with the advent of new technologies, new distinctions and new theories that alter what people in the community can observe. Like the formerly true *assertion* that the planet we live on is flat, and that it occupies a coveted location at the center of the universe. For millennia at least, these were incontrovertibly true assertions for many cultures around the world, supported both by our felt sense of the world (of course we'd fall off the edge of what we call the horizon), and in some cases bolstered by the specter of torture or death for anyone brazen or ignorant enough to suggest an alternate (and heretical) assertion.

Reflection and Practice – Assertions

Reflect on your Personal Case Study (or the "Care Doesn't Care" example) and see if you can recall any assertions that were being made by you or others in the conversation(s). Please write these down.

1. *Were any of these assessments in apparent conflict with one another?* If so, how did folks handle these apparent conflicts—did people challenge the validity of the assessments that seemed to contradict their own? Did they treat the contradictory assessments as if they were personal opinions of the person(s) citing them?

2. *If the individuals were able to resolve the apparent conflicts of assertions, how did they do that, and do you think everyone felt satisfied with the outcome/decision?* Did anyone feel as if their assertions were not considered by others to be as valid or legitimate as some other assertions? If so, how would you think the person(s) whose assertions were not seen as valid felt about the conversation? How do you think this experience may have influenced them going forward in these or other conversations with the same people?

3. *Over the next few days try to notice as many assertions as possible in your conversations, paying particular attention to how you and others relate to these assertions.* As you read further about the other speech acts, this particular speech act of asserting will become even more clear.

Chapter 5

Declarations: Making It What It Is

We will be the #1 brand in the luxury car market.

Our vision is to be earth's most customer-centric company.

She's a great leader.

We will expand our product offerings into the European market.

This go-to-market strategy represents our greatest competitive advantage.

I love that idea!

These are all *declarations* — our next speech act. If assertions tell it like it is, declarations *make it what it is*. If assertions aim to describe what is true about the past or the present, declarations conjure up the future. They create new conditions or contexts that guide our thinking, expectations and actions towards a future to which we aspire.

Declarations perform their enchantments as they are spoken, which is why J.L. Austin called them "performatives."[1] When a manager says, "You're hired," the speaking of those words "does" the hiring.

We use declarations to mobilize ourselves and each other to action, to establish expectations about future behavior, to shape or reshape our own and others' experience of things. We use them to bring into being things like relationships, jobs, communities, entire countries. This is a tall order, and yet we use declarations to do things like this every day.

Before 1776, the United States of America didn't exist. Then came the *Declaration of Independence*, followed by the rest of the Constitution. What started as a blank page on Thomas Jefferson's writing desk gave birth to a new country with 13 new states that hadn't existed previously, three distinct branches of government, and a host of laws, codes and radically new relationships with the rest of the world that would continue to evolve for hundreds of years. And it all grew out of a declaration.

For declarations, we could turn Thoreau's comment around: "First a man must say, before he can see." Or, as Echeverria says, for declarations, "first comes the word, then comes the world."

Let's go back to the declaration, *You are hired*. Until the words were spoken, the job was just a future possibility. The words, *You are hired*, spoken by your newly-declared-in-the-same-moment employer is what *made* you an employee. Those words didn't *describe* the hiring process, they actually *performed* the hiring. Until those words were spoken, you didn't have the job and after the declaration, you did (assuming you accept the job — which would be another declaration). The declarations *You are hired* and *Yes, I'll take the job* change your world, your employer's world, and the worlds of many other people affected by this hiring, setting into motion all sorts of planning, investment and other commitments involved in bringing about this new reality.

Just to further distinguish assertions from declarations, once this declaration has been made, it would be a true assertion to say that you are an employee of that company. Similarly, when the magistrate says, *I now pronounce you husband and wife*, he is not *describing* a marriage between two people (which would be an assertion); his utterance (his declaration) "does" the marrying. Once the declaration has been made, it creates a new *fact* which the couple can now truthfully assert: *"We are married!"*

The most inspiring speeches are declaratory, "breathing energy" into our lives, moving us to think or behave in new ways, to overcome challenges, to make fundamental changes to our lives, as the following examples illustrate...

Nelson Mandela – "An ideal for which I'm prepared to die."

Considered to be one of the most important speeches of the twentieth century, Nelson Mandela spoke in the courtroom where he was being tried in 1964 on counts of espionage, furthering acts of communism and aiding foreign powers, and where he was later convicted and sentenced to life in prison. His three-hour speech, made from the defendant's dock, ends with the declaration, "I have cherished the ideal of a democratic and free society in which all people will live together in harmony and with equal opportunities. It is an ideal for which I hope to live for and to see realized. But, My Lord, if it needs to be, it is an ideal for which I am prepared to die."

Steve Jobs – "Keep looking. Don't settle."

Jobs was revered for many things, including his speeches that challenged the audience (and the marketplace) to transcend the mundane and conventional, and to aspire to something greater. In a 1997 speech, he told the audience how Apple products "are for people who aren't just out to get a job, but for people who want to change the world."

In his classic 2005 commencement speech at Stanford University, he drew upon pivotal moments in his own life, declaring, "You've got to find what you love. And that is as true for your work as it is for your lovers... Keep looking. Don't settle."

Although perhaps not as lofty as the above examples, when your company's management team finalizes next year's revenue targets, or the CEO announces the company will be acquiring an important rival, they are also making declarations. Goals, objectives, strategies, mission, vision, values—all declarations. Again, these statements aren't describing how things were or are—they are announcing to the listener how the world will be; or at least how the speaker intends it to be. Organizations are built and fueled by these declarations.

If we were to say that we create much of the world—what we see, do and experience—with our declarations, we wouldn't be far off the mark.

From War and Peace to Your Daily Latte

Although they can be monumental, not all declarations are. They range from announcements of geo-political scope (including war and peace) to expressions of love, faith, annoyance and even rage, to the canned value statements hanging in some corporate lobbies. Here are a few examples of common declarations we make or hear every day...

Thank you.

I want that promotion!

I don't know how to do this.

I'm not good with numbers—I don't think I should apply for that position.

Employees are our number one priority.

Just do it.

Double decaf, almond-milk latte, no foam—mobile order is ready!

Declarations are ubiquitous. As simple as *Yes* or *No*, they can change the course of our lives. They are also a featured speech act in the Design conversation—one of the three fundamental collaboration conversations which we'll cover in Part II.

We'll concern ourselves with two types of declarations, what we'll call *directional* declarations and *comparative* declarations (or *assessments*).

Directional Declarations

Directional declarations set us or others on a particular course for the future. They include vows, proclamations, edicts, policies, mandates, statements of vision, mission, goals, strategies, and so forth.

We will put a manned mission on Mars by 2020.

Our target for Gross Customer Retention next year is 96%.

I want you to lead the Sales team in this region.

I accept your offer to lead the Sales team in that region.

I'm going to lose 20 pounds in the new year.

Your call is important to us. Please remain on the line and a representative will be with you shortly.

Good directional declarations animate and move us to feel things and do things. They communicate the speaker's intent to the world. Assuming that the speaker is sincere, we expect her to behave consistently with her words.

The CEO sets a new direction for the company by declaring, "We are going to double our investment in R&D and consolidate our product lines to be more focused going forward." Hearing this, we expect the CEO and her team to behave accordingly — to double the company's investment in R&D, to trim down the product offering, and so forth. If these things don't happen, we begin to doubt either the sincerity or the competence of the CEO — or both. Cynicism and resignation show up when leaders' actions are repeatedly out of sync with their declarations (which is one reason why talk is seen as cheap in some organizations).

Although declarations are not community property, they absolutely impact our standing in the community. So, pay attention to the expectations you set in motion when you make directional declarations: The world will expect you to act accordingly — to *take you at your word*. When you don't, your words become empty and your public identity and "trusty-ness" will suffer.

Before we leave the theme of directional declarations, here are a few more examples. They are a little different from the earlier examples. Rather than explicitly stating the "direction" the speaker is taking or wants others to take, these are more personally disclosive about the "state" of the speaker. The specific actions that might follow might be less explicit, or left unstated altogether, but the declarations themselves are not necessarily any less important or meaningful...

I am hungry.

That was a great meeting.

I apologize.

I love you.

I don't know how to do this.

I am scared (or excited, or confident, or any other emotion).

I'm ready to take on that challenge!

These types of declarations are one of the ways that we connect with others on a personal level—by telling them what is going on with us. If you're familiar with "I Statements" you'll recognize that they consist primarily of declarations: *When you say or do [something], I feel [uncomfortable, frustrated, hurt, excited, happy, etc.].*

When we make these types of declarations, we are disclosing to the listener what we are feeling, thinking, or sensing in our bodies. While these declarations are informative and do describe our experience, they are still *not* community property—they are not assertions. They are subjective, private property. This is part of the power of making these types of disclosive declarations: Listeners who hear us make them tend to recognize that there is nothing to argue about—our experience is our experience and we're simply sharing that experience—not inviting an argument about right or wrong, true or false (which is why *I statements* can be so powerful).

We'll look at Comparative Declarations in the next chapter.

Reflection and Practice – Declarations

1. *Take a moment and reflect on some of the most significant declarations you've made in your life.* These may include decisions about which schools to go to, which jobs or careers

to pursue, which friends or partners to be with, and so forth. Think about how these simple declarations might have changed the entire course of your life trajectory.

2. *Next, think about declarations you've made in your life that seemed important at the time, but which your later behavior didn't express.* New Year's resolutions, declarations to stop smoking, lose weight, start exercising, etc., are common examples of declarations that frequently don't "stick." What impact do you think these declarations and subsequent behaviors may have had on your own self-confidence? On the way others perceived you?

3. *Reflect on your Personal Case Study (or the "Care Doesn't Care" example) and see if you can recall declarations that were made by you or others in the conversation.* How do you think those declarations influenced the way others perceived the person making the declarations? Which of these declarations seemed to instill greater trust and confidence in the group? Which declarations may have generated less trust or confidence?

4. *Thinking about your Personal Case Study or any other important collaborations you may be involved in, reflect on any declarations that may be "missing."* By this I mean opportunities for someone (perhaps you) to make a meaningful and committed declaration that could catalyze new thinking or new action that might move the conversations and performance forward.

5. *Finally, over the next several days, you will likely start noticing more declarations being made by you and others around you.* When you notice these declarations, reflect on the influence you think they have on you and others. Which declarations seem to make the most difference for people? Which don't seem to make any difference or might even hinder performance? For those that don't seem effective, what might make these declarations more impactful?

Endnote

1 John Searle, professor of Philosophy of Mind and Language at UC Berkeley, further developed this understanding of linguistic action, which one of his doctoral students, Fernando Flores, later introduced to the world of business. Rafael Echeverria worked with Flores, has authored many books and articles (mostly in Spanish) about this approach to language and action, and is considered a pioneer and thought leader in the field.

Chapter 6

Assessments:
Comparative Declarations

You may remember Pet Rocks. For millions, if not billions of years, rocks lived a mostly quiet, humble existence. Except for their utility in construction, arrowheads, catapults and other essentials, most rocks held little market value. At least until the 1970s, when many Americans suddenly discovered that they could not live without their own Pet Rock. And neither could their friends and loved ones, so they bought a lot of Pet Rocks as gifts. Almost overnight, rocks had become (sorry) rock stars. Pet Rocks came swaddled within their own little nest inside their own box, accompanied by a 32-page *Owner's Manual* which included instructions on teaching your Pet Rock to "sit," "lie down," "roll over," and "attack."

Pet Rocks earned their "inventor," Gary Dahl, millions of dollars within about six months of hitting the market. Then, some months later, the Pet Rock craze was over. Rocks were suddenly once again just rocks—objects to be built upon, stepped over, skipped on the lake, dug out of the garden, and occasionally hurled at an enemy ("attack!").

So where was the value of Pet Rocks? Clearly, it wasn't in the rocks. When Shakespeare's Hamlet said that "there is nothing either good or bad, but thinking makes it so," he could have been talking about rocks because their value—just like the value of your company's products, services, building, people, and everything else—lies in the how people are assessing them.

Value is never a *property* of things, circumstances or people. Value is not a thing at all—there is nothing objectively *there*, no innate property of something wherein the value resides. Value is always an assessment, which is a type of declaration made by someone comparing or evaluating one thing against another, or against some standard, expectation or preference. And we know that assessments of value change over time even though the objects of those assessments (the rocks, for instance) may not change a bit. This applies just as much to the Pet Rock's more exalted cousins—gold and silver, for instance—as it does to the rocks in your garden.

Returning to the company's P&L from earlier, although the numbers themselves are neutral assertions (community property), the executive, analyst, shareholder or SEC regulator who looks at them will interpret these neutral numbers and *assess* what those numbers mean to them or their audience. Depending upon whether you're the executive, the shareholder, the industry analyst, or an industry rival, you could react very differently to the same P&L numbers. You'd form your own subjective assessments, which remain your private property.

Some other words we use to refer to assessments include opinions, appraisals, judgments, evaluations, and critiques. Although most people know what assessments are, they're still very often confused with assertions, and this confusion leads to many of our collaborative problems. For example, the following statements are all grammatically similar:

Jose has attended every one of our project meetings.	Jose is a collaborative person.
Linda is our lead product designer.	Linda is a poor manager.
Our company makes accounting software.	Our company makes great software.

Although grammatically similar, the statements in the left column are entirely different speech acts from those on the right. The assertions on the left describe facts, while the assessments on the right express our opinions.

Both the assertions and the assessments are "about" Linda, Jose and "our company," but what they each tell us is very different. They are very different actions, with different social obligations (to be factual in the case of assertions, and to behave consistently with the assessments, in the latter case).

To further highlight the distinction between assertions and assessments, following is a brief description of Barnes & Nobles, Inc., the bookseller, taken from its website. Note that it consists mostly of assertions...

Barnes & Nobles, Inc is one of the major bookstores in the USA with over 665 branches all over 49 states. Aside from this, Barnes & Nobles also sells DVDs and videos, music CDs, magazines, etc. and has distribution rights to nearly 10,000 publications.

And here are brief excerpts from Barnes & Noble's much longer Mission Statement—consisting primarily of declarations (including assessments the company wishes to generate in the marketplace):

Our mission is to operate the best specialty retail business in America, regardless of the product we sell... As booksellers we are determined to be the very best in our business, regardless of the size, pedigree or inclinations of our competitors... Above all, we expect to be a credit to the communities we serve, a valuable resource to our customers, and a place where our dedicated booksellers can grow and prosper...

Both of the above statements tell us something about the company, but what they each tell us is very different.

Assessments Are Private Property

I am excited about the progress this team is making!
I don't like the way our margins are trending.
That was an engaging presentation, Barbara.
Cool!

As assessments these statements are subjective. They "belong" to the person making the assessment. And although assessments go by many names, one thing remains constant: Assessments are never true or false, right or wrong. They are only mine (or yours) to know and experience. Assessments are private property.

Because they don't *describe* the things they are about, assessments reflect more about the person doing the assessing and the standards he or she is using to make the assessment, than about the person, circumstance or thing being assessed.

Again, just to review...

Assertions are about facts; ideally, they are observable by anybody, which makes them "community property." Our social obligation when making an assertion is to provide acceptable evidence to prove that the assertion is true.

Assessments are a type of declaration in which we compare one thing to another, or to some standard. They are entirely subjective, which is why they're "private property." As a type of declaration, our social obligation when making an assessment is to behave consistently with the assessment.

In the Beginning, There Were Assessments

According to the Old Testament, assessments have been around for a long time: *God saw everything that he had made, and behold, it was very good.*

That assessment is attributed to God, but we humans also do a lot of assessing. Assessments are surely one of our critical survival mechanisms. Central to our relationships, our organizations, to every aspect of our lives, assessments dictate what we move towards and what we move away from, what we embrace and what we avoid. They determine what we decide to do next, where to invest our time, energy and money; whom to trust and whom to be wary of. We assess when picking our mates, the next book to read, how to spend our vacation. We assess for profit and also for sport.

In organizations, we assess our products, services, strategies, and tactics. We assess value, performance, risk, capacity, quality, opportunity, and leadership. We assess our colleagues, bosses, teams, customers, partners, and our rivals. And, of course, we also assess ourselves. All of these assessments guide our actions. You're reading this book because of some assessment you have about your own collaborative capacity or that of your colleagues.

Although we've always assessed, these days, making assessments has been exalted to a global obsession—perhaps even to the pinnacle of human achievement. For every 60 minutes of live sports coverage, there are scores of hours devoted to assessing the game, the plays, the players, their personal lives and more. We're constantly harangued to "Like" this, "Don't Like" that, give "thumbs up or thumbs down," to "fill out the survey at the end of this call to tell us how we are doing."

We are endlessly entertained and fascinated by what commentators (professional "assessors," also known as pundits) want to tell us about who did this or said that, and what it means. But we don't stop there—we also assess the assessors, not just for the quality of their assessments, but for any number of other qualities, even their sex appeal. (If you must, put "TV Guide's the 23 Sexiest Political Pundits and Anchors on Television" into a search engine and assess your heart out.)

One other reason assessments are so important to us is that they determine *who we are* as human beings. Our identity is tied to our assessments.

Tissue, Bone and Assessments

We know that our words don't simply describe the world; they also construct the world that we experience. Our social identity is built out of words.

When I say that Jose is 5'11" tall and weighs 165 pounds, or that Linda is 42 years old and has worked at the company for 6 years, I am using *assertions* to describe something about Jose's and Linda's *physical identities*. But when I say that Jose is collaborative, or that Linda is a poor manager, I'm not describing their physical properties. Instead, I am *declaring* Jose to be collaborative and Linda to be a poor manager. And as private property, my assessments disclose just as much or more about *me* and how I experience Jose and Linda, as they do about Jose or Linda. But that's not all: When I make these assessments, I'm also participating in the "construction" of their *social identities*.

We all have social identities—ways that we appear to others, based upon our behaviors and ways of being, and these social identities reflect the kinds of assessments that others make about us, good, bad or neutral.

These social identities are central to our collaboration since the way we each show up to others influences the commitments those others will want to make with us.

As I said earlier, the *social obligation* we commit ourselves to when making a declaration (including assessments), is that our behaviors will be congruent with our declarations. When we say that Jose is a collaborative person, that assessment will determine the types of requests or offers we might make to him or involving him. Because we say "he's collaborative," we might invite Jose to join an important project team, and we might not extend that same invitation to Sam (because "he's not collaborative"). And we'd be unlikely to promote Linda into that open Vice President position if we assess her as a poor manager.

Our social identity determines our standing within the community and with one another. It determines the opportunities and possibilities available to us—and it's built largely out of words, out of the assessments that others have of us and that we have of ourselves. (It is also built by our bodies and our way of

81

being—by the way we stand, move, sit, speak, listen—and the assessments this demeanor generates, but more on this later.)

Remember the "Care Doesn't Care" example from earlier? What type of speech act is the phrase "Care Doesn't Care"? Although it purports to describe a factual state about the Customer Care department (that they don't care), it's actually a declaration. There's no way of really knowing what the Care department does or doesn't care about. If you were to state this sentiment more clearly (and more skillfully), it might sound something like, "In my opinion, the individuals who work in the Customer Care department do not seem to care about the customers they're serving, because... (and then you'd provide some specific observations – assertions – to explain why you've arrived at that opinion). But we often just voice our assessments without recognizing them as assessments at all, which often creates problems.

Every assessment is based upon some behavior, action, or way of being that we or others observe. By *way of being*, I'm referring to the general experience we may have of someone— their energy, the way they move and show up in their body, their predominant moods and ways of dealing with people and circumstances. As we know, assessments can change when the person making the assessment changes, as well as when the person or thing being assessed changes. Just as assessments aren't static or fixed, the social identity created by those assessments also isn't static or fixed—it's dynamic and alive. It changes and evolves as the assessments the identity is built upon evolve.

Our social identity determines the doors that open for us and the doors that are closed to us. And the path to every one of those doors is an assessment.

One of the common challenges we encounter with respect to social identity is the tendency to forget that it's based upon dynamic, living assessments, and instead treat it as a fixed or innate property or characteristic of the person. When we do this, it's like we're turning people into stone, like Medusa, treating their social identity as something permanent and "true," like an assertion, rather than the subjective assessment it is. This can profoundly limit the person's possibilities for learning and personal development. But—to keep with the stone metaphor— that's like assuming that the value of a Pet Rock lies in the rock itself, not in someone's assessment of the rock. In this case, the human being is the rock, and this way of relating to the human being can keep our relationships and collaborations frozen in place. This is what we do when we characterize someone, which we'll examine in more detail shortly.

When I learn new behaviors and develop new competencies, my assessments about myself will change, which changes *who I am* to me. And if they're paying attention and aren't living in a fixed mindset, others' assessments of who I am will likely also change.

If we understand that the social identities we attribute to our colleagues are fluid and open to revision based upon new assessments, then we're free to question and update our assessments, and to remain current with those colleagues, "updating" their identity—at least in our eyes—as they (or we) learn, grow and are otherwise shaped by life. This is how our relationship with them can remain current and alive.

A Few Assessment Challenges

Assessments are core to everything we do in our lives and our organizations. But there are some challenges we can encounter when making or listening to assessments. Here are a few to watch for...

Incessant assessment. Assessing is so central to being human that it often occurs automatically and unconsciously. While normal, this can also get in our way. Constant assessment about what we're doing, what other people are doing, how circumstances are going, what we like and don't like, etc., can create a barrier that keeps us from being fully present with who and what is right in front of us, here and how. It can also keep us from being fully present with ourselves, bodily and emotionally. Because assessing is a mental activity, when we constantly do it, we're constantly relating to people and experiences from a conceptual place, which can keep us a step removed from the direct experience of the moment. It's impossible to truly listen to somebody when we're continually assessing what they're saying, how they're saying it or who we think they "are."

Fortunately, we can learn to diminish this incessant chatter by gaining more awareness of our habitual tendency to assess and of our assessments themselves. This lets us cultivate new ways of interacting with people and circumstances that are not solely and automatically "in our head." (This is why we're devoting so much time to assessments and all the other distinctions in this part of the book—to help you expand your awareness of what you're doing.)

On the Aikido mat, many new practitioners are so busy assessing everything they're doing, they stifle their own learning. Their assessments distract them from focusing on what the instructor is teaching, and from sensing their own bodily movements and experience. Learning how to notice their habitual assessments is sometimes the most important early lesson for them to learn—even before they learn specific Aikido techniques.

As on the Aikido mat, so at the office: Learning to notice and become more aware of our assessments as we're making them helps us to connect more fully—to make full contact—with the people we're collaborating with. *Treating all assessments equally.* Not everybody's assessments should be given equal weight. If I'm trying to learn something

new, I need to be able to discern whose assessments I can trust—
who has sufficient expertise, experience and positive intent—
who's feedback, guidance or instruction will serve my learning.
Just because someone may have strong opinions about how to
pilot an airplane, perform surgery, or run a global software
team, doesn't necessarily mean they can do any of those things
well. Same if my team and I are trying to make an important
business decision or chart a critical new path into unknown
territory. We generally want the assessments from someone
experienced and qualified to help us—or at least more qualified
than we are in this area. If we treated everybody's assessments
as equally valid, granting everybody equal authority, we'd find
ourselves in a big mess.

*Thinking that our critical assessments are our most valuable
contribution to the people or teams we work with.* There's an important
place for critical assessments, for challenging people's thinking
and behaviors, and for constructive, "negative" feedback. But
not as a steady and sole diet. It's pretty easy to be the person
who pokes holes in other people's thinking, who finds the
problems in things and points out all the ways that something
may not work. But if that's your primary and habitual way of
contributing, your contribution is probably less valuable than
you think. And when you believe that your highest and best
contribution to others' ideas, strategies, behaviors or people
is to criticize them, you can destroy the possibility of fruitful
collaboration. You're probably also not going to be much fun to
be around, either.

Some corporate cultures exalt negative assessments, equating
criticism with rigor, discipline, and "hard-nosed" business
acumen. These are places where folks are rewarded for finding
fault, poking holes, seeing the problems in things. These are
also places where people are often punished for appearing soft
by expressing openness towards new ideas, or for not shutting
down unconventional ones.

What I often see in these cultures is fear, anxiety and rigidity. Fear of not being seen as intelligent. Anxiety around not having all the answers, and rigidity in the face of change and uncertainty—which generally call for greater flexibility and agility, not the opposite. These cultures are rarely fertile grounds for learning, taking risks, or disruptive innovation. They aren't fertile places for Full Contact Performance, although many of the people working in these cultures are starving for it.

When we believe that our highest and best contribution to every new idea, strategy, policy or behavior is to criticize it, we may just be toxifying the environment for everyone around us, including ourselves.

Making Better Assessments

Because every decision we make in our organizations, and in our lives, hinges upon assessments, it would be nice to have certainty that our assessments are good ones. Unfortunately, that's not possible; assessments just don't work that way.

But there is something we can do to help us make more useful assessments and fewer misleading or unhelpful ones. And that is to "ground" our assessments, to subject them—and the factors that influence them—to examination. Grounding an assessment with our colleagues or others can reveal inconsistencies and biases in our thinking and highlight influences that could cause us to make weak or "ungrounded" assessments. While not a guarantee, the process of grounding our assessments can improve the likelihood that our assessments will lead to good decisions.

Think of a lightning rod, that metal pole sunk deep into the ground that's wired to your house's electrical system. It's there to prevent injury or damage by directing lightning that might strike (a powerful electrical charge) safely into the ground, rather than into your desktop computer, your gas pipes, or your sudsy bathtub.

Grounding your house keeps you safe by diverting dangerous electrical charges away from you and your stuff. Grounding your assessments helps to keep you and your team safer by bringing habitual assumptions, unconscious biases, or emotional reactions you might be having into the light of day where you can examine them and see how useful (or not) they might be.

There are five basic questions you can use to ground your assessments. Taking the time to ask yourself and your colleagues these questions can help to clarify your thinking and either further support your assessment or show you where the assessment may not be so well-supported. Grounding your assessments together with your colleagues can lead to more learning and better decisions, which leads to better execution downstream.

Here are the five questions for grounding an assessment

1. Towards what end are we making this assessment? (When considering this question, it often helps to also clarify the *domain of action* to which the assessment applies.)
2. What are the relevant facts (assertions) we're relying on to make this assessment?
3. What are the standards we're using to make this assessment?
4. What factors might be influencing this assessment? (including emotions, unexamined assumptions, and team, company or industry blind spots, among other potential biases)
5. How might other people whose opinions we value assess this?

We'll walk through each of these grounding questions with an example...

To Invest or Not to Invest

The leadership team was deliberating about whether to invest in a new initiative that was unlike anything they'd done before. If successful, it could drive sales for this business unit into new markets and introduce products to entirely new customer demographics. But because it was so different, this initiative would require significant investment in people and consultants with the expertise that the company didn't currently have. It would also mean a shift in priorities away from what the business unit had been doing in the past, and towards the unknown.

The opportunity was the brainchild of a team member, Phillip, known for his unorthodox, and often very creative, thinking. His forte was envisioning new possibilities and directions that didn't occur to other folks on the team. But he wasn't especially known for seeing those new possibilities and directions through to fulfillment. The team felt that going through the grounding process together would be helpful both to validate the basic concept, and to enable them to identify any issues or concerns they should factor into their planning if they moved forward with the initiative. Here is the abbreviated Grounding process we went through over the course of several conversations, to arrive at a shared assessment and decision about the concept...

1. *Towards what end (and within what domain of action) are we making this assessment?*

In this case, the answer was simple: The team wanted to increase sales for their business unit by tapping into previously untapped markets and engaging new customers.

The team agreed that the *domain of action* was *lead generation*, which would primarily be handled by the Marketing team. If successful, this investment could result in many more qualified sales leads entering the pipeline, leading to more sales, increased revenue, and a larger, more diversified customer base.

Pay Attention: Sometimes, when teams are asked to be very specific about their ultimate objectives, they discover that there are multiple answers to the question, and those answers don't always jive. Even when it seems obvious, take the time to articulate together that future vision—that answer to the question *Towards what end are we making this assessment?* If you're not aligned on the fundamental purpose of the assessment, you could have a hard time arriving at a shared and well-grounded assessment—or you'll arrive at a clear assessment, but that assessment may not actually lead you to where you want to go. Same for the *domain of action.* There could be many different domains of action that could be relevant to our assessments (there could be multiple ways of increasing the number of sales leads in the pipeline, for instance), so specifying the particular domain relevant to this future you're designing could make a big difference. When teams try to take short-cuts by assuming that all team members already agree about what they're after and why it matters—without checking their assumptions—ungrounded assessments can lead to weak decisions, which lead to poor execution.

2. *What are the relevant facts (assertions) we're relying on to make this assessment?*

The team identified several key assertions:

This approach was based upon an extraordinarily successful model in an entirely different industry. There was plenty of market and financial data about the success of that model that the team looked at before considering this approach.

The VP of Marketing was excited about this approach, and the head of Sales felt it could be a "game-changer."

Although there was strong support from other departments and Phillip was clearly in his creative wheelhouse with the project, it would be a new and very different type of project for the team. Nobody had ever worked on anything quite like this before (assertion), which could create challenges (assessment).

Pay Attention: Assessments are based at least in part upon past experience, observations, events or other factual data. Take the time to discuss the assertions you are each looking at and compare notes. If necessary, seek out additional assertions along with any supporting information behind them to minimize the potential for habitual or other biases to influence thinking. There may be just as many assertions that don't support your assessment as those that do seem to support it. Going through these data points together can help you to arrive at a more grounded assessment.

3. *What are the standards we're using to make this assessment?*

Some of the standards the team was using included:

The project needed to be scoped and executed in phases, with Phase One rolled out within 7 months (by year end). This was a tight, but necessary timeline.

It needed to produce observable impacts on the sales pipeline (specifically new sources of qualified leads) within 3 months of Phase One being rolled out.

The continued support of the Sales organization would be critical for the long-term success of the initiative, so designing in periodic checkpoints with Sales would be part of the plan.

Pay Attention: Every assessment is based on some standard. The standard may be a level of quality, attainment, timeframe or other performance metric, as in some norm or benchmark: For instance, the standard of service expected at a five-star restaurant will be different from that at a neighborhood diner. Your performance expectations of a new hire fresh out of college won't be the same as someone with years of experience in the role. The standards for governance, management controls and compliance are usually different for public companies than for privately held companies, even of similar size and in the same industry.

When we change the standards we're using, our assessment often changes as well. Ask yourselves whether the standards you are using are relevant, up-to-date and well-matched to the particular assessment you're making. It's common for different people on a team to be using different standards when evaluating a decision, policy or course of action, often without realizing it. Because standards aren't always explicit, it's good practice to take the time to draw out and discuss the various standards people are using in order to arrive at a better understanding.

4. *What factors might be influencing this assessment? (including emotions, habitual assumptions, blind spots held by individuals, the team, or the company, and other potential biases)*

Phillip, who conceived the initiative, was widely liked and respected for his creativity, but he also had a somewhat checkered history with the company. He'd come up with many brilliant ideas over the years, but his track record on seeing them through to completion was not great.

For this initiative, his boss had deliberately teamed him together with Brock, a new manager, who was a strong project manager and also had technical skills that Phillip lacked which would be needed to drive the initiative forward.

Phillip was enthusiastic and certain that the initiative could be wildly successful. He was sure that the value of the initiative would be obvious to everyone who saw it, and that once the demo was built, it would just take off. Brock, on the other hand, could see the possibilities, but shared privately with me that he was anxious about his relative lack of experience co-leading a project like this. And he had no idea how to get the support and additional organizational resources he thought they'd need just to build a solid demo. So, while Phillip kept spinning off beautiful and inspiring visions of what could be, Brock kept putting the brakes on, while growing increasingly anxious. He was certain that Phillip, the other members of the team, and their boss, Serena, were becoming disappointed in him and recognizing his "obvious" inadequacy.

At one point in a video conversation with just Phillip and Brock, I suggested we hit the Pause button and take a fresh look at this fourth grounding question to see what we might uncover. With some encouragement, Brock acknowledged that he had been assessing himself very critically recently and had convinced himself that everyone else must be seeing him in a similarly negative light. The fear and anxiety he was feeling was making it difficult to see the project clearly, much less any contribution he might be making to it.

Upon hearing this, Phillip nearly jumped out of his seat and said he really needed to clear something up. He then proceeded to share his assessments about Brock directly, which turned out to be extraordinarily positive. He told Brock how much more focused Phillip himself had become because of Brock's discipline, how for the first time in many years he felt confident that one of his creative projects was really going to succeed. And he started listing for Brock, very specifically, all the things Brock had done to support both this project and the entire team, including Phillip. (That's right, Phillip was spontaneously verbalizing his own "grounding" process for his assessments about Brock.)

Brock was stunned by Phillip's words and realized that he'd been operating in his own bubble for some time now, afraid to really talk about how things were going and how he was doing. He also acknowledged that part of his reluctance to talk openly about things was that he was so much younger and less experienced than Phillip and he had convinced himself that Phillip would have no patience for Brock's concerns or assessments. As a result, he had been feeling almost paralyzed about openly sharing his concerns and ideas about the project. The simple structure of the Grounding process was an opportunity to get all of this into the open and it turned out to be transformative for both Brock and Phillip, increasing trust in their working relationship, which also paid dividends for the rest of the project team and company.

Pay Attention: Our assessments are always shaped by many different factors. Taking the time to identify some of these factors using a set of simple, structured questions often allows people to expose their emotional predispositions, assumptions and other potential biases to the light of day, where they can be explored together. Even though we can't eliminate all of them, just getting a clearer view of how these factors may be influencing our thinking and feelings often enables us to mitigate their impacts.

5. *How might other people, whose opinions we respect, assess this?* The key point here is simple: Seek out other people with different perspectives and ask them! *What are they seeing that you may not see? Are they using different standards, looking at different data? How might their experience inform your thinking?*

Although the team clearly saw the potential benefits that this project would deliver for sales and marketing, they hadn't given as much thought to its impacts on the Customer Success department. It was the Customer Success folks' job to ensure that existing customers were fully utilizing the solutions they were paying for, and to renew their subscriptions and buy additional products or services to better realize their desired outcomes.

Phillip and Brock met with Stacey, the head of Customer Success to get her input and see what they could learn. This proved to be another turning point. Stacey's response was overwhelmingly positive. In fact, she saw an opportunity to engage some key customers in being part of the project, which would increase their engagement with the company and investment with the company's products. In Stacey's view, this was a great way to increase the up-sell and cross-sell opportunities with customers.

Phillip then suggested that several executives in their customers' companies could be filmed as part of the creative story (which would also promote their own companies). This prompted Stacey to offer to partner with Phillip and Brock to enroll the executives and to ensure the full engagement of her entire Customer Success department to make the project a success. This response brought the project into a whole new light, resulting in a redesign of the original vision in ways that nobody had anticipated. It also brought new resources to the table, putting the project onto the fast track, and greatly elevating its visibility within the company.

Pay Attention: No matter how experienced, expert, or thoughtful you and your colleagues may be, your assessments are still bound by what you don't or can't see. So, seeking out individuals who may have a very different take on things can be invaluable. Even if they end up reaching similar conclusions and validating your original assessments, the exercise of submitting your thinking to someone else's scrutiny can—at the least—affirm your ideas and increase motivation for implementing them. Sometimes it can completely transform your opportunities.

Taking the time to ground important assessments helps to compensate for our individual and collective biases and blind spots. It's a simple and structured way for individuals and teams to collaboratively reflect upon and clarify their intentions, to identify relevant data and assumptions, and expand their perspectives by seeking out people who may see things differently. You don't always have to go through all five steps to improve your assessments—sometimes you may only need to consider those that could have the greatest impact on the decision. It's usually time well spent.

Finally, remember that as helpful as the grounding process can be, and no matter how well-grounded your assessment may be, it will always remain just that—an assessment. No amount of grounding can eliminate the subjectivity inherent in an assessment. Even if your assessment doesn't change as a result of the grounding process, going through the process together with your colleagues almost always generates better alignment and stronger commitment to the assessment and decision you finally land on.

Reflection and Practice – Assessments, Part 1

Please put this book down and take a few easy breaths. Notice any tension you may sense in your body and imagine that tension dissolving away, along with all the information you've just been taking in as you've read the past few chapters. No need to remember it all right now or understand it all perfectly. When you're ready, here's another practice opportunity...

Going back to your Case Study, or other challenging interaction you're involved in:

1. *What is one key assessment you made or are making in this interaction?* Write it down so that you can see it clearly.
2. *With respect to that key assessment, how have you been expressing this assessment in your interactions with others?* As a subjective assessment? As a factual assertion? As an "obvious" conclusion?
3. *How do you think others might have been (or are) treating this assessment?* And how might these ways of treating this assessment be influenced by or be influencing the conversation?
4. *Can you notice if others may be treating their own subjective assessments as factual assertions?* If so, how does that influence your own and others' response in the conversation?

In your upcoming conversations, practice identifying the assertions and assessments people (including yourself) are making and see if folks are treating these speech acts as the very distinct speech acts that they are, or as interchangeable and similar speech acts (which they're not).

Reflection & Practice – Assessments, Part 2 (Grounding Your Assessments)

In Part One of this Reflection and Practice (above), you selected one key assessment from your "Case Study." Return to that key assessment, and go through the grounding process, asking yourself each of the five questions above and writing down your answers. If you can do this together with someone else, that's even better.

For Question #5, try to find someone whom you think might NOT share your perspective about this assessment and ask him or her how they see things. Your job in this conversation isn't to convert them to your assessment, but to be curious and willing to *let them convert you* to their assessment—or to some other assessment.

In that same Case Study conversation, can you identify any *characterizations* being made by yourself or anyone else? If so, how do you think those characterizations may influence the conversational dynamic, the decisions and/or the commitments being made? You can use the grounding process to help tease apart the characterizations people may be making from the assessment(s) those characterizations may be based upon.

Chapter 7

Stories that Free Us and Stories that Freeze Us

We know how ubiquitous the speech acts of assertions and declarations are in our lives, both at work and everywhere else. We make and hear them everywhere.

Before we look at the remaining three speech acts (requests, offers and promises), we're going to see how we weave assertions and declarations (and particularly assessments) together to create *stories*. These stories aren't just for bedtime or entertainment; our stories guide, instruct and animate us. We use stories to help predict what may happen in the future and to build our relationships, our communities, our careers, our organizations, and every collaboration we engage in.

Author Jonathan Gottschall calls us "storytelling animals." Stories permeate our waking lives, and beyond. "Even when the body goes to sleep," Gottschall reminds us, "the mind stays up all night, telling itself stories."

We are almost always telling or living out our stories. When something happens that is threatening or uncomfortable, we create a story to try to understand it. Same when something great happens. We tell ourselves stories about the past, about the present, and we tell ourselves stories about what will or will not happen in the immediate or distant future.

We create stories with the information we have available to us, and also in the complete absence of information. We even create, and often believe, stories that directly contradict other stories we tell ourselves, or that contradict facts that may be staring us in the face.

Our storytelling creativity can be as varied as our experiences. For instance, read each of the assertions that follow, and then answer the questions that follow...

The boy sitting on the sofa is typing at a keyboard.

The man in his office is sitting with his elbows on his desk with his head resting in his hands.

The executive talking with that other person is grimacing.

Questions

Is the boy doing his homework? Playing a video game? Designing a videogame? Avoiding his homework? Is he lonely and trying to connect with other people through social media? Something else?

Is the man sleeping? Is he upset or anxious? Is he just thinking? Is he thinking about work? His family? Something he just heard on the news? Is he planning his next vacation? Something else?

Is the woman reprimanding her employee? Is she upset with herself and sharing her feelings with a confidant? Does she have a headache? Did she just swallow something bitter? Something else?

If you had more context, you might be able to answer these questions more "accurately." Maybe. Because even with more context, there is still plenty of room for interpretation—plenty of room to tell a very different story based upon the very same facts. As we already know, assertions are neutral; they carry no intrinsic meaning one way or the other ... until we interpret them. Until we tell the story about what these assertions might mean and why they might matter for us.

Stories about Others

Here are a few statements (short stories) from managers who are describing people with whom they've been collaborating...

Fundamentally, they aren't willing to see beyond the existing model to new opportunities that can drive revenue.

He is a very smart person who will always try to avoid doing the work himself and instead pass it on to someone else.

She's a control freak—she's OCD and will never let anybody on this team run with anything that she doesn't personally direct.

That team only wants to do things the same old way regardless of whether it addresses our customers' issues or not.

Now take a moment and imagine how a person telling him/ herself each of the above short stories would likely approach and behave towards the people or team that are the objects of those stories. How would you likely behave towards someone you see as short-sighted, or as always trying to deflect responsibility? As a "control freak"? How would you approach a team that "doesn't want to change and doesn't care about their customers"? Probably similar to those folks from the Sales and Customer Care departments in the "Care Doesn't Care story" you've already read about...

As I mentioned earlier, in my first meeting with the "Care Doesn't Care" group I asked each person to describe what was going on, from their perspective. What emerged were two overarching stories: The Sales folks were living in the *"Care Doesn't Care"* story. The title of the Customer Care team's story might have been something like *"Sales Only Cares about Sales— not about the customer's success or our company's success."*

Now imagine that you're a member of either the Sales team or the Customer Care team, and you are telling yourself a story about the folks on the other side. You're telling yourself either the *Care Doesn't Care* story or the *Sales Only Cares about Sales* story. How would you likely interact with those other people? If you're on the Sales team, you would have already determined that those in Customer Care are self-oriented, shortsighted slackers who care only for their own success (and care little about anybody else's success). Similar if you were on the Customer Care team. How would you expect this collaboration to go?

In my first conversation with the two teams, it was clear that the folks in the Customer Care department felt disrespected and unfairly accused (by the "self-righteous" Sales team) of not caring about the very people they were there to serve. They felt resentful and defensive being depicted that way. Feeling this resentment and defensiveness from Customer Care, folks on the Sales team felt confirmed in their story that the Care team didn't care—why else would they be so hostile and defensive? Although their respective stories differed in the details, these stories were playing out in similar ways—people on each side were convinced that their *own* story was accurate and justified, and that the other side's story was B.S. And both were distrustful of the other.

Locked into these polarizing stories, everything that was said by one side was interpreted through the lens of the other side's story, driving each person further away from constructive engagement with the other. Good collaboration wasn't possible within these entrenched stories. The folks could only try to protect themselves from unjustified attack and compete with one another in a game with no winners, only losers.

To begin turning things around, one of the first things we did was to shift our attention. Instead of focusing on either of the two opposing stories, I asked folks to focus on an entirely new story—the story of how things would look if this collaboration were successful for everyone on the team, as well as for the customers and the company. We could have tried examining each of their existing stories and picking them apart, but I felt that a new, fresh story that everyone could help contribute to would work better. As we shifted focus towards a successful future and made sure that we listened carefully to each person in turn (and redirecting focus whenever someone slipped back into the old us/them story), the tension in the meeting began to subside. Although we were meeting virtually, it was clear that folks' eyes and faces were relaxing, while pent-up energy began to flow.

Over the next couple of sessions together we continued to flesh out the new *shared* story together. With our attention focused on something positive that everybody cared about, the confidence of the team members grew, allowing them to listen more openly, without needing to protect themselves from potential accusations or enmity. No longer fixated on the perceived deficiencies of the others, we could examine collectively the assertions (data) that people thought were important to look at, and why. We also used the *grounding* steps you read about in the last chapter to ensure that everybody's input was sought and the assessments formed were as well-supported as possible.

We were now fully immersed in a Learning conversation (which we'll look at more closely in Part II), with members from each team volunteering to do joint fact-finding together in between sessions, sifting through data and coming back to share with the larger team what they'd learned. Along with the new story about the future performance targets they all felt were important, other new stories were also being crafted—including what problems or obstacles stood in the way of realizing their newly-envisioned future, and how they would be able to monitor and course-correct together as they navigated this new future in the coming months.

As all stories do, these new stories brought with them new emotions, new behaviors and new relationships. At one point, one of the Customer Care folks offered that the data they were now looking at together clearly *did* show room for improvement by the Care team, possibly including more rigorous training and updating of the online resources they maintained. Moved by this acknowledgement (this was first time she'd encountered anything other than fierce opposition to her comments), a Sales leader then countered that it clearly wasn't just Customer Care that was the problem—there were definitely some product sales that simply should never have happened, and that Sales hadn't always done a good job managing customer expectations. The rigid, polarized thinking, tense jaws, knitted eyebrows and clipped language that had characterized our first meeting together had now morphed into curiosity, more receptive listening, good-natured joking, and folks volunteering to take on projects with their counterparts between sessions, to keep up the momentum they were feeling.

In working with groups of different types and in different cultures over the years, I've come to my own story about the damage that our polarizing stories create for *everyone* involved — both the people the stories are about and those telling the stories. Our disparaging stories about others may allow us a brittle sense of righteous satisfaction, but these stories punish us just as surely as they punish those we're disparaging. When we believe our negative stories, it's difficult to take genuine interest in the others' views. It's difficult to learn, to make good decisions, and to make important commitments to one another. These stories inhibit us from taking an honest and critical look at how our own actions or thinking may be contributing to our problems, and — perhaps most poignant — these disparaging stories generally make us unhappy.

As I mentioned earlier, one of the common types of stories we tell ourselves (which we may not even recognize as a story) are *characterizations*. These are short stories aimed at explaining our observations and assessments about others (or ourselves), so as to predict future behavior.

It works something like this:

Step One: We observe someone's behavior: *He hasn't returned my emails; she always criticizes my ideas; that group doesn't follow the company's stated process.*

Step Two: We assess that behavior as desirable or undesirable; good or bad; collaborative or uncollaborative, and so forth.

Step Three: We attribute that behavior to some fixed character trait of the person or group: *He doesn't return my emails because he's inherently lazy; she always criticizes my ideas because she's mean-spirited; that group doesn't adhere to the company's process because they're arrogant (perhaps because all engineers, developers, artists, you-name-it, are fundamentally arrogant).*

Step Four: We don't realize that we are creating the characterization, that we are *inventing* an explanatory story, much less that the story reflects as much or more about us as the author of the story as it may about them as the *object* of the story.

Step Five: We relate to the person or group we've characterized as if those character traits are real, objective, fixed and permanent features of them (not something that we've invented to try to make sense of our subjective experience). Naturally, we expect them to continue to behave in ways consistent with who we say they are (their character) — and we therefore continue to behave and treat them accordingly, which usually further reinforces our characterizations about them. And on it goes.

In other words, we treat our stories about them as *who they really are* (mistaking our assessments for factual assertions). We forget that there is a person (us) who is making the assessment in the first place.

It's as if we're freezing the other person (and us) in time, putting on blinders that cause us to completely miss or undervalue everything they may do that doesn't fit our story about them. Even though Sam has learned to listen much better and to be open to other people's perspectives, he'll still "be" the uncollaborative person we've characterized him to be. And poor Linda — who may now have developed solid line-level management chops, will still "be" the poor manager we assessed months or years ago.

What's probably becoming clear is that when we characterize Sam or Linda, they won't be the only ones who pay the price. We too will be doomed to always see and relate to them through our static stories about them. Our misunderstanding — our confusion about what constitutes their identity — can keep us relating in very limited and unproductive ways to the people with whom we must collaborate.

In tough and deeply entrenched collaborative situations, characterizations are almost always running rampant. And naturally, the conversational "moves" people make with each other in these tough collaborations will be based upon their characterizations of each other: "Because this person is *stubborn*, I'm going to use questions to try to get them to come around to my view..." Or, "I'll ease into the conversation with some light small talk and positive feedback before getting to the point, because Sam is a very defensive and uncollaborative person." Why would we even bother to try and understand them better, to listen with curiosity and openness, if we already "know" who they are?

We Embody Our Stories

The stories we tell ourselves about *ourselves* (which include our self-assessments and self-characterizations) also matter: *I'm a people person, so I shouldn't become an engineer. I'm a stronger leader, and I deserved that promotion, not Ellen! Raju is a much better presenter than I am—I'll ask him to lead the meeting.*

Our stories about ourselves play out in what we do or don't do, and how we do what we do. They determine how we respond to the people and circumstances, the challenges and opportunities of our lives. And of course, they also shape our bodies—literally. Because stories are action (remember, they are constructed out of speech acts), they live in the neural circuits in our brain. The more we repeat our stories, the stronger those neural circuits become, literally shaping the structure of our brains—just like physical actions that we practice over and over. And this happens even if we only "practice" telling these stories silently to ourselves. As our recurrent stories become more and more habitual and automatic, they'll naturally be reflected in our posture, gestures and movements. The way we sit, stand, speak and listen all reflect the stories that live inside of us.

Perceiving with Stories

When stories are particularly compelling, they shape entire organizations, industries or cultures. They define what's normal, acceptable and rational and provide a sense of belonging for those bound together by their shared stories.

While our stories can be a source of inspiration, progress and cohesion—they can also limit us and impede our performance when they don't align with what we want to do or who we want to become. Innovators, explorers, artists, humorists and rabble rousers of many stripes are so valuable in part because they poke, prod and puncture some of the sacrosanct but outdated stories we live by and take for granted. They offer glimpses—for those who can listen—into new possible stories.

As with any habits, our most fundamental stories are often difficult to notice and hence to change. The story about modern management and production efficiency that Frederick Taylor authored over a hundred years ago is a good example...

The Modern Story about Efficiency

Did you ever wonder why we in the Western world (along with many other cultures) have such a fierce obsession with time, order, productivity, and efficiency? While a variety of forces, over many centuries, have played a hand, what pulled it all together was the simple persuasive power of a well-told story.

Around the turn of the last century, an innovative thinker and iconoclast named Frederick Taylor authored a radical new story that put him on par with Darwin and Freud as one of the most influential contributors and shapers of modern Western culture. His story ushered in a fundamentally new way of thinking about how to get work done in organizations.

He told his story in his 1911 book, *Principles of Scientific Management*, telling his readers how to apply the rigor and precision of scientific observation, experimentation, and categorization to the problems of organizational productivity and scale.

Taylor's story met with extraordinary receptivity, as it spoke directly and confidently to a frustration that had been building amongst business leaders as the Industrial Revolution was gathering steam.

Up until the early 1900s, everything was produced by hand. Even the simplest objects had to be crafted individually by craftsmen. Taylor showed us how, by breaking any work project down into smaller components, these discrete components could be produced more quickly, efficiently, consistently, and profitably, by focusing on:

- Standardization and precision – instead of continually producing each product manually by the same person from start to finish—break the process down into discrete units of work that could each be standardized and given to different workers—none of whom needed to be artists or craftsmen any longer. They just needed to be told what to do and how to do it as quickly as possible—which led to the innovation of the assembly line.
- Separating the *planning* of work from the *doing* of the work, leading to the new "science" of management.
- Experimenting and applying rigorous discipline to observing the effects of these experiments (later taken to new heights by Toyota Motors and other Japanese production methodologies via Lean Production, the Toyota "kata," etc.).
- Focusing on efficiency and productivity to the exclusion of all else.

The new distinctions and practices Taylor introduced revolutionized not only the way organizations were structured and production was engineered (as in the assembly line that Ford and Sloane put into place in their factories, with Taylor's help), but almost every domain of social activity as well, including the management of homes, farms, churches, schools, universities, and beyond.

In Taylor's story, *knowledge* was the protagonist that could overcome the antagonists of the labor, productivity, and social problems of the time. One of the key tenets of this story was that only a special class of men could hold and use this all-important knowledge: *the manager*. The rest must be spoon fed this knowledge, being told what to do, when to do it and how to do it.

Like any good story, Taylor's story has had huge emotional, as well as practical, impact. It inspired generations of leaders but it has also, as Robert Kanigel (author of Taylor's biography, called *The One Best Way*) says, "quickened the tempo of our lives, left us more nervous, speedy, irritable." Taylor's story went viral more than a hundred years ago and it continues to be a primary lens through which many of us still view the world. As Kanigel says, Taylor "helped instill in us the fierce, unholy obsession with time, order, productivity, and efficiency that marks our age." This may be changing in some companies and industries, but it's still the dominant paradigm in which most businesses operate. It's still almost impossible for many to conceive of business through any other lens.

Stories Don't Always Need to Be True

When it comes to creating reliable technology, it helps to have stories that generally match up with how things seem to function in the real world. That's what the scientific method aims to facilitate. Most major technological leaps have been preceded by new stories about how things work. The ancient story about the relationship between the earth and the cosmos led to the earliest star-based navigation systems. As this story gradually evolved, it paved the way for new navigation tools, eventually to today's GPS systems. But stories don't always need to be accurate to be impactful.

When Our Fallacy Is All Wrong

Before the story of germs and hygiene in medicine, many state-of-the-art, widely adopted medical treatments were as likely to kill the patient as to cure them. From bloodletting to leeches to lobotomies, there are plenty of now-obsolete, disproven stories that still had extraordinary impacts on the people and practices of their day. Today, our social-media platforms spew out story after story, often with little or no regard for their accuracy— in some cases, promoting tacit falsehoods— yet some of these stories fuel mass social movements, trigger radical new consumption patterns, and drive major shifts in the political landscape.

In Woody Allen's film *Annie Hall*, Marshall McLuhan's character (played by McLuhan himself) exclaims, "You mean my entire fallacy is wrong?" Michael Shermer, in *The Believing Brain*, says that while we outgrow beliefs, we don't often outgrow *belief*. We continue to cling to the conviction that there are some things (some stories) that are fundamentally believable, regardless of whether they are true, knowable, or helpful.

One reason for this may be entirely practical: Since the brain seems to predict the future based on what has happened before, it is constantly generalizing from our experience. Which means it's constantly making necessary, but sometimes sloppy predictions (predictions are stories about the future). We don't need to think about what will likely happen each time the light turns green, because 99.9% of the time a green light means it's safe to cross the street. Except when it's not. Because it works most of the time, we can often get by. And the more absorbed we are in a story, the easier it is for us to believe it, and the less concerned and observant we can become about the story's logical inconsistencies.

The content of our stories isn't the only factor in how they may serve us. What matters more is what we believe about our stories. Good stories can encourage and help us to be our highest and best selves. Less good stories can cloud our perception, prevent us from thinking through the consequences of our actions, or bring out our worst.

> *Our stories don't have to be accurate to be impactful.*
> *They just need to be believed.*

When we believe our stories and don't realize we are believing them, we'll often have a hard time collaborating with people who hold very different stories. The key is to remember that every story is—at its core—an *action story*. Stories are comprised of actions (speech acts) taken by human beings. As you might expect by now, the starting place for changing our stories is gaining awareness of them as stories in the first place. Remembering the "storyness" of our stories reminds us that, however we got them, they are still stories, built of the raw materials of assertions and assessments. I'm not saying that its always easy to change our long-standing stories, especially when they are particularly compelling and our identities are wrapped up in them, but it is often possible.

We usually have much more capacity for creating, editing, and even completely re-writing our stories, than we may assume. And when we do create more workable, helpful stories, we can practice telling them to ourselves—*changing ourselves*—before we ever even go public with them.

Because collaboration is an internal art, the most important action always lies with us. When we change our own stories, we change the nature of our interactions and the quality of contact we make with the folks around us.

Reflection & Practice – Stories

Take a moment and reflect again on your Case Study or another challenging interaction.

1. *What is the* <u>*primary*</u> *story you are telling yourself about this situation and the other people involved?* If you're not sure, then reflect on your feelings and behaviors towards the people in this situation. What kind of a story would likely be driving feelings and behaviors such as these? Write that story out (bullet points or short phrases are fine) and see how that story seems to fit your feelings and behaviors. Feel free to keep adjusting the story until it fits. I am encouraging you to invent a story that can help you to makes sense of your thoughts, feelings and behaviors—not to try to come up with the "true" story. You don't need to justify it or share it with anyone. Just gaining a little more awareness about the story you're living in can enable you to edit or update your story— and thus the thinking, feelings and behaviors that flow from the story.

2. *Next, choose one or two of the key players in this situation and repeat for them the same process you just went through for yourself in Step 1. But now, of course, in addition to your assertions and assessments about their behaviors, you'll be imagining what their thoughts and feelings might be—based upon those behaviors (knowing you can't know that for certain).* As before, write down a story for each person that might make sense of their behaviors and your speculation about their thoughts and feelings. Again, no need to justify your explanation, just write it down.

3. *Next, return to your own story about the situation and the people in that situation. But now, you're going to enter an alternate universe (one of infinite possible universes in the multiverse).* In this alternate universe, you'll rewrite your story about the other people in your situation—a story that would have you relate to those people very differently. If you're feeling resentful, intimidated, frustrated or impatient (or anything else that may cause you to discount or lose interest in *their* perspective or contribution), this new story will dissolve or

at least lessen those feelings, and instead move you towards feelings of benevolence, interest and curiosity towards them. Note: I'm not asking you to believe this new story or to change your thoughts or feelings towards these people—only to practice inventing a possible story in which those thoughts and feelings would naturally and effortlessly change—if you *were* to believe it.

4. *Finally, imagine that you are meeting with these people, and that you were relating to them from the alternate story about them that you just invented.* Imagine how you would feel, what you might say, how you'd relate to them from this new story. And imagine how they would respond to you—you who are living in this more benevolent story.

What do you imagine their behavior would be towards you? And then how would their responses in turn affect your counter response back to them? Play this interaction out in your mind. Do you see them expressing more interest and curiosity in you and your world in this alternate story? Do you see the collaboration improving? If not, what additional edits might you make to *your* story that could lead to new and more helpful behaviors both in yourself and in them?

If, in your mind's eye, you see things shifting and improving with these other people, then you may have invented a story that's worth practicing further (eventually even road-testing with those others, when the time is right). If you still don't see things improving (remember this is still all in your mind only), then keep at it—keep tweaking your story until it seems like it could actually help you to improve the collaboration.

Chapter 8

Requests, Offers & Promises

Could you open the door?
Would you mind opening the door for me, please?
Can you get the door?
I don't think I can get the door myself.
Is that door still closed?
How 'bout the door?

I've heard that there are over 600 ways to make a request. I don't know if that's true, but there sure are plenty of them — and some ways of requesting may not resemble anything like a request, grammatically speaking.

Since language is action, we make requests (or "asks") when we want or need help. We make requests when we want to learn something or we want to get something done that we can't or don't want to do ourselves, either right now or sometime in the future. Making a request is one important way we can address challenges we are facing.

One type of request takes the form of *questions*, which may sometimes be fulfilled right then and there:

What time is it?
Can you call me a cab?
What did you like about that show?
Did you complete that analysis?
May I have the salt?
What's the matter?
Are you okay?

We expect answers to many of our everyday questions now, not later. I don't want the salt for breakfast tomorrow if I'm asking for it at dinner, tonight. Answering sometime tomorrow my question about what time it is right now, won't help me.

Other requests entail action that we want someone else to take later on, assuming they accept the request. Those requests—if accepted—lead to promises, which we'll cover shortly.

Regardless of its grammatical form, every request carries with it a choice for the listener: She can either fulfill the request or not. Even a command, a "direct order," or the boss delegating a role or project is still a request, although the listener may not always feel as if No is an acceptable answer. This isn't just a theoretical notion—recognizing the inherent choice built into every request is critical for organizational collaboration as well as for personal well-being. The way we relate to this choice—whether we're the boss making the request or the employee receiving it—can spell the difference between full commitment and personal ownership of a course of action, or lip service, passivity and a smoldering sense of impotence.

Isaac, a 42-year-old Executive Vice President of Compliance for a national healthcare company and his Senior Vice President of Analytics, Sarah, each realized how important *choice* was when Isaac asked Sarah to analyze three years' worth of compliance data for the company and present her findings at an upcoming board meeting.

When Isaac first made the request to Sarah on Thursday morning, Sarah was excited at the opportunity to gain more exposure to the board. Sarah was in her early thirties and was a rising star in the company. This could be great for her career! But when she next learned that the board meeting was the following Tuesday, she realized that to deliver properly on her boss's request, she'd have to cancel her family's long-planned trip to visit her elderly mother- and father-in-law over the upcoming weekend.

Isaac was aware that Sarah had been planning a long weekend trip, but he was feeling pressure to present the compliance data at the board meeting—which the board chair had just requested of him earlier that morning. In asking Sarah to prepare and present the data, he made it clear that the project was not optional—he expected her to do what it took to deliver—even if it meant postponing her family trip. In his mind, saying No to the board chair's request was simply not an option, and he expected Sarah to feel similarly about his request to her.

As she listened to Isaac, Sarah felt her face flush and pressure building in her shoulders and chest. She reminded him about her planned family trip. She told him that she didn't want to do a sloppy job on the analysis, and then asked to get back to him after thinking through what it would take to do a good job on the project. Isaac responded, "I understand you've been planning this trip for a while, Sarah, but this is a board priority; they really need to see that data ASAP." In other words, Sarah understood, she either needed to make it *her* priority or... what? Risk pissing Isaac off and becoming marginalized? Not being seen as a team player by the rest of the team? Gaining a reputation with the board as uncommitted? Getting fired? Sarah wasn't sure what the consequences would be, but she felt certain it wouldn't be pretty.

Sarah spent the next three hours agonizing about Isaac's request, calling her husband at work to discuss her dilemma. He wasn't thrilled about the prospect of canceling the trip, but he understood what was at stake and he assured her he'd support her, whatever her decision.

Finally, after some deep breathing exercises to help calm her nerves, Sarah went to Isaac's office to let him know her decision. She told Isaac that, although she realized how important the project was, she didn't feel right canceling her trip and letting her entire family down. (She wanted to ask him why, if it were such an important project, the board chair had just sprung it on him at the last minute, but she decided to just focus on Isaac's request to her.)

As she'd predicted, Isaac was not happy. He leaned back in his chair, steepled his hands in front of his chest, and simply nodded, lines of tension carving up his face. Now it was his turn to tell her he'd get back to her later, and he turned his gaze down to the papers on his desk, indicating that the conversation was over.

Sarah left Isaac's office somewhat shaky, but as the afternoon wore on, she noticed a calm energy taking root in her body. By the time she got home and told her husband about her decision, her sense of dignity and comfort in her decision replaced her misgivings. Together, they celebrated her decision to put the family first, even though neither had any idea what Sarah would face back at work next week.

Returning to the office the following Tuesday and for a couple of weeks thereafter, there was a noticeable chill between Isaac and her. Isaac didn't make eye contact, barely interacted with her, and when he did, it was clear he was still upset. Gradually, however, the chill thawed, and things returned to normal between them, but with a distinct difference: Sarah could swear that Isaac was treating her with more respect than she'd previously experienced from him. It felt less like the paternalistic and at times condescending dynamic that she had, until then, just accepted as how things were with Isaac. It now felt more like a relationship of equals, which gave Sarah a quiet boost in her self-confidence.

They never discussed this situation again, but it turned out that Sarah's decision to decline Isaac's request had forced Isaac into a self-reckoning of his own. While he was working through that weekend preparing the analysis and presentation himself, he had time to seriously question his own role in this situation. Although still angry at her, he realized that he was also impressed with the way she had stood up for her deeper values and commitments, knowing she could face serious consequences. Maybe, he realized, he too could have declined the board chair's unreasonable last-minute request, or at least negotiated more reasonable terms.

Although this situation had a positive ending, I'm not suggesting that declining every request will end happily ever after. We all know that our choices have consequences. The key point in this example is that requests always bring with them a choice—to accept and fulfill it, to decline, or to attempt to negotiate a different understanding. Each of these choices lead to different outcomes. To lose sight of the choice inherent in a request is to diminish our sense of autonomy and agency in our lives and relationships.

Why Making Requests Isn't Always Easy

Even if making a request represents the best way out of a bind, we still don't always do it. Our own stories or emotions can get in the way: What if they say no? They might think I'm incompetent or lazy. Who am I to ask this of them? Or, If I ask them to do this, then I'll be in their debt, and I don't want to feel indebted to them. In some cultures, asking for help of any kind is seen as weakness, to be avoided at all costs.

This was the case for my friend Nathan. In the corporate cultures he'd worked in, asking for help was seen as a tacit admission of incompetence, and akin to career suicide. He told me about a friend of his who had worked in those same corporate cultures and who later worked for Nathan at another company. When this friend found himself way over his head leading an undertrained and understaffed team in a fast-growing division, help was what he desperately needed. But he never asked for it. Nathan found out about it too late, after things had gotten out of hand. By this point, Nathan had to let his friend go. And Nathan's own reputation also took a hit. In this case, *not* asking for help cost his friend his job, and tainted Nathan's own standing in the company. It was a costly lesson for them both about the importance of making requests.

If we never make requests, we'll likely find ourselves facing the same types of problems over and over again. If we don't make requests, we may never get good promises from others, and we probably won't accomplish as much as we otherwise could. Learning to make requests, even when its uncomfortable to do so, is a critical skill for good collaborative performance.

Offers

Just as requests are powerful tools to help us get things done and solve problems, *offers* are similarly powerful for helping others get *their* work done. When we make an offer, we are committing ourselves to *doing what we're offering to do*, assuming the listener accepts. In this way, offers are more "binding" than requests. When offers take the form of a proposal, they are often also legally binding, once accepted.

To make a meaningful offer, we must *have something* or *be able to do something* that the other person finds valuable. So, our offers reflect our capacity to make things happen. In the business world, this means to create value for someone (which we now know means to create the *assessment* of value in that person). The kinds of offers we can make and have others accept help to determine the value we represent in the marketplace, the kinds of jobs we can get and what we'll get paid for doing those jobs.

Promises

In our everyday lives, we use the word *promise* in many different ways. We say things like, "I *promise* I'm telling you the truth," or "I *promise* to always be there for you." We use the word *promise* because it carries a certain weight; it conveys more personal commitment than simply "I will" or "I may, if I get around to it." In common usage we can use the word *promise* more as a unilateral declaration of our intent to do something, but I encourage folks to use the word much more specifically as we'll see in a moment.

In organizations, promises are at the heart of performance. Regardless of your title, position, or pay grade, you are paid to design, make and manage valuable promises. The way you and your colleagues handle promises determines how well the organization performs and how well it satisfies its customers.

The bigger and more valuable the promises we can make (and keep), the more value we create for our organizations, and the more we, in turn, are valued. CEOs are paid more than their administrative assistants because they can make bigger and more valuable promises to the board of directors or shareholders. Same for any professional.

Different organizations and industries may value different types of promises differently, but in every industry, every corporate culture and every organization, our compensation reflects how valuable our promises are to our customers—who may be our boss, clients, or whomever is writing the check.

Promises Live in Our Words

There are some things that we can do without words, but making a promise isn't one of them. Because it's about actions we'll take and outcomes we'll produce in the future that involve some exchange of goods, services or intangibles, a promise is a pretty abstract concept. It can only be understood in language, with words.

To get into most promises in organizations, someone needs to make one of the two linguistic actions we just reviewed—either a request or an offer—and someone else must say *Yes* (to accept) that request or offer.

As with requests and offers, declarations of acceptance also come in different forms: *Yes, Sure, Of course, Yup, I hereby accept, I do, I solemnly promise, Yes Maam!, Where do I sign?...* The occasion of entering into a promise may be accompanied by non-verbal gestures or rituals: a handshake, a formal bow, spitting in the palms and shaking, or even a blood oath, but these non-verbal gestures still express or symbolize agreed-upon linguistic conventions that both parties recognize as an exchange of commitments, a binding promise.

When your boss asks you to convene a cross-functional meeting to resolve a customer's technical problem, and you say *Yes*, you've accepted her request and you've made a promise. Alternatively, if you go to your boss and offer to set up the cross-functional meeting and your boss says *Yes*, you also have a promise.

A promise is like a closed electrical circuit. The request or offer without acceptance leaves the circuit open—there's no energy flowing and no promise. Once the request or offer is accepted, the circuit closes, energy is flowing and you have a promise.

"Yes" lets the energy-and promise-flow

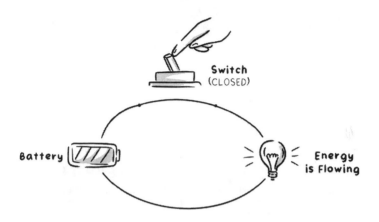

Promises well-made and well-managed are what power your organization's performance. You might associate the value you provide with your goals, strategies or projects, but promises are what bring your goals, strategies or projects to fruition.

Because promises in organizations are so important—and may at times be treated differently from some promises in everyday life—let's look more closely at what we mean by a *promise* within the context of organizations. Here's how I define it:

A promise is a voluntary exchange of commitments
made between two people (a Customer and a Promisor)
to produce a specific outcome of value at some
point in the future.

This definition applies to Customers both outside of the organization (who buy the goods or services of value from the company), and Customers inside the company (who make requests or accept offers from other people inside the company) to make those valuable things available to the external Customer.

Let's break down this definition of a promise...

- *Promises are voluntary*
- *Promises are an exchange of commitments between two people*
- *Promises are about specific outcomes of value*
- *Promises are about the future*

Promises Are Voluntary

To make a promise is to take a risk. The instant we say *Yes* to a request, we have opened ourselves to the possibility of failure—of not delivering what we promised. This could damage our reputation, our career and also our sense of confidence in ourselves, not to mention our organization's performance. No matter how committed, competent or clever we are, we can't control everything; there are likely going to be promises we're just not able to keep. So whenever we make a promise, we are putting ourselves at risk of failing to fulfill it.

In addition to the risk of failure, we also risk not being able to pursue other valuable opportunities that may arise because we've committed our time, energy, and resources to this promise. This risk applies to both parties—the Promisor as well as the Customer (who is placing her future in our hands).

For small promises, the risk may be trivial. But even small promises, when broken or poorly managed, often have large consequences. Let's say I stay home to wait for the plumber to come fix a leaky pipe at 9:00 a.m. as he'd promised. If he shows up 20 minutes late, he may think it's just an inconvenience. But this small broken promise could impact my ability to take my child to a doctor's appointment or make me late to a critical business meeting. Furthermore, I may not hire this plumber again in the future, or I might post a damning review about him on social media, which could turn an otherwise trivial broken promise into something much bigger for the plumber. We can't always anticipate exactly the consequences of breaking our promise, but we can know for sure that there will be some consequence.

Because promises entail risk, they work best when they're entered into voluntarily—through informed choice—rather than through coercion. This is why, as I said earlier, the choice—the ability to say *No*—is so important when responding to a request (or offer): it's what allows us to experience real commitment when we say *Yes*. To voluntarily enter into a promise means we acknowledge the personal stake we have in what happens; we're not just going through the motions of *Yes* to comply or get someone off our back. In organizations, I find that explicitly using the word "promise" to refer to the commitments two people are making to one another helps to remind them of this personal choice and commitment.

Strong promises are made by choice, with eyes wide open.

An Exchange of Commitments between Two People

A promise in organizations is always an exchange of commitments between two human beings—one who plays the role of *Customer* and another playing the role of *Promisor*. Without these clear roles, there might be good intentions and even strong desire, but there won't always be a good promise that delivers value.

The Customer is the person for whom the outcomes, goods, or services will be performed. It's the person who, at the end of the day, assesses whether the promise has created value and has been fulfilled to her satisfaction. The Customer is also often (but not always), the one who writes the Promisor's check. In this way, the Customer embodies the ultimate purpose and driving force behind every business, non-profit, and government organization. In business, customers may be the consumer who pays for the goods or services, your boss, your colleagues or anyone else to whom a promise may be made. In nonprofits, customers are often called *stakeholders* or *clients*; in government agencies, they're referred to by many possible names, including *citizens, taxpayers, community members, applicants, stakeholders,* and so on, depending on the context.

Regardless of what they're called, by placing the Customer at the center of every organizational promise you make, you are always aligning yourself and your team with the core purpose of the organization.

The Promisor has the expertise, resources, capacity and willingness to do something that the Customer either can't or doesn't want to do herself. The Promisor commits to fulfill the promise by doing what it takes—having the conversations or taking other actions (or ensuring that someone else takes the actions), to deliver the outcome that the Customer values. In exchange for this, the Promisor also expects to receive value in some form, which may be payment, a bonus, recognition, a promotion, and so forth.

Although they each play distinct roles in the promise, both the Customer and Promisor are bound together in mutual reliance upon each other.

One more practical point about Customers and Promisors: There can be only *one* Promisor and *one* Customer for each promise. Having more than one Customer increases the complexity of managing the promise for the Promisor. It can be difficult to fully satisfy multiple Customers for the same promise. Each Customer may have his or her own standards for assessing value and satisfaction. Forcing the Promisor to try to please multiple masters can burn time, money, productivity, and morale. Even though an entire team or company may be (and often are) the beneficiary of a Promisor's good work, always select just one Customer to represent the interests of that group for the purposes of the promise—and the well-being of all. The

Customer doesn't always need to be the most senior person, or the boss—it just needs to be someone whom the group trusts to represent the group's standards and assess satisfaction at the end of the day (the end of the promise). Similar for the Promisor—select just one person to hold accountable for the promise, even if that person may have twenty other people actively working on that promise with or for him.

Just to be clear, the terms Customer and Promisor as I'm defining them here aren't fixed, formal roles in organizations. They are only relevant within the context of specific promises. We are all Customers and Promisors at different times and for different promises, both in our organizations and elsewhere in our lives. When you hire a roofing company to put a new roof on your house, it's clear that you are the Customer because you're the one who will write the check at the end of the job (assuming it meets your satisfaction). In organizations, while this may be true for many promises, there are many other promises you might make to people whom you don't work for—or to people who may even work for you. For instance, when John in the Legal department promises to review a proposed contract revision for Cristina in Sales, Cristina is John's Customer for this promise (even though she's not John's boss and doesn't sign his paycheck each month).

But who "owns" the promise?

People often use the term "owner" in relation to promises. I avoid using this term because it can lead to confusion. The "Owner" could ostensibly refer to either the Customer or the Promisor, (or even a project manager, who is neither the Customer nor the Promisor in a promise). Is the Customer the owner because she's the one who declares when the promise is satisfactorily completed? Or is the Promisor the owner because he's fulfilling the promise? To avoid this confusion, I only use the terms Customer or Promisor with my clients, and I make sure everybody is clear about what these roles entail when they're making a promise.

Specific Outcomes of Value

Good promises specify the outcome and the value the Customer can expect as a result of the promise. So the goal of every promise is a satisfied Customer who declares that the Promisor has produced the expected value. That's it.

It sounds simple, but this way of thinking about promises actually sets a very high bar for organizational performance. This approach also, when applied rigorously, redefines organizational alignment.

Promises are cycles that begin and end with the Customer

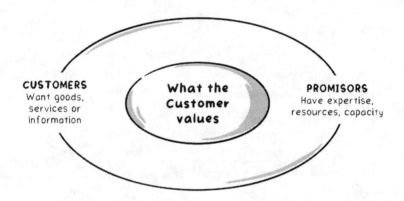

CUSTOMERS
Want goods, services or information

What the Customer values

PROMISORS
Have expertise, resources, capacity

The goal of every promise is a satisfied Customer— whomever and wherever that Customer may be within the organization or outside of it.

Very often, fulfilling a promise can involve much more than simply taking certain actions or checking off lists, although the items on the lists might all be part of what it takes to produce satisfaction for the Customer. In this approach to promises, the actions, tasks, to-do's, projects and any other *activities* you might undertake aren't *the point* of the promise, because even if executed perfectly, those activities won't necessarily satisfy the Customer.

Whether the outcome is a specific product, service, or changed condition, the promise isn't fulfilled until the Customer declares satisfaction. This shared focus on satisfying the Customer helps to keep everyone focused on the core purpose of the promise and the organization. It also fosters strong personal accountability and ownership of the results of every promise. But there are other reasons this approach to promises is helpful as well...

A Tool for Building Trust and Ensuring Alignment

Sometimes, the Customer may simply want a discrete task done, period. But even in this case, most Customers also care about the way that task is done. And they also care about how they are being treated by the Promisor while the promise is being fulfilled. You can complete a project on time and under budget, but still have an unsatisfied Customer who felt left in the dark throughout the process, was given inaccurate information, or just felt poorly treated.

The way the Promisor *manages* the promise often matters as much as what is actually fulfilled in the promise. This can include the way the Promisor communicates with the Customer and keeps her informed about challenges, risks or other relevant factors; the way the Promisor treats other people while working on the promise; the subsidiary promises the Promisor may need to make in order to keep this promise (and how well they may align with other organizational priorities, strategies or practices), and much more. Different Customers can have very different standards and expectations about how they want their promises to be managed, so it's important to talk about these expectations when hashing out the details of the promise. This is also a good time to discuss any expectations or requirements the Promisor may have of the Customer while the Promisor will be working to fulfill the promise.

There are many examples of promises that were not fulfilled, but that still increased trust and loyalty between the parties, simply by the way the Promisor and the Customer managed their ends of the promise. That is the power of making and managing your promises well.

There is another way that well-designed promises can transform organizational performance. By always placing Customers at the center of every promise and having explicit conversations about what those Customers value and expect, you help to ensure that the promises you're making will align well with the other promises your Customers and colleagues are making. (We'll go into much more detail about this in Part II.)

About the Future (and the present)

Promises entail producing some outcome of value to the Customer at some point in the future.

When we take out a mortgage to buy a house, we are entering into a promise with the lender to make monthly payments until the loan is paid off. Although this promise may not be fulfilled for 30 years, we don't wait 30 years to move in, unpack, buy new furniture, and enter into all of those other promises with utility companies, insurance agents, plumbers, roofers, and so forth. Even though the mortgage promise won't be fulfilled for many years, the promise changes our lives the instant it's made. Armed with a good promise, our lives will change right now — even before the ink on the contract is dry.

Its similar for promises made in your organization. While the completion of that financial analysis, annual sales target, new software implementation or any other promise you might make will hopefully provide value in the future, just the making of the promise — whether days, weeks, months or years before it is to be completed—may already make a huge difference for you, your team and the entire company. This promise, along with all of the other promises made by you and others you work with, are what actually constitute *the business*—the work of—the organization. This is why Fernando Flores refers to promises as the "atom of work." The company's share price is in part a reflection of the types of promises the company makes and how well those promises are likely to be managed and fulfilled.

It doesn't matter what types of promises you make, or the relative value of those promises within your organization: The more explicit you can be up front about your promises—whether as Customer or Promisor—the more likely your promises will be successful. And the more value your boss and colleagues will associate with your performance.

Six Questions for Good Promises

While we'll say much more about making and managing good promises later on, in the meantime, here are six questions to ask whenever you are contemplating or negotiating an important promise, whether you're the Customer, the Promisor, or a team member observing a promise in the making:

1. *Who is the Customer?*

As obvious as it sounds, the answer isn't always clear. Sometimes requests just seem to come from... somewhere: "Management," "HR," "the Company." Without a specific person making a clear request, it often might as well come from nobody. Disembodied requests lead the listener to treat the request in a similarly disembodied way, with little personal interest or commitment. Good promises need flesh and blood Customers (one per promise, please) to make the request and to care about the outcome.

2. Who is the Promisor?

If you don't know who the Promisor is for the promise (again, just one), you don't know whom to count on to make it happen. There's nobody to hold accountable for the outcome.

Let's say you're in your weekly staff meeting and the boss asks the team to figure out how to simplify and standardize the order fulfillment process as the business scales up. You all nod your heads and say "sure." But which of you is making the promise? Who is taking personal responsibility for simplifying and standardizing the process? Who will declare to the Customer that the project is complete, when it gets done? You all know it's important and want to contribute, but again— which *one person* can the boss (and the rest of the team) count on to get it done?

An even squishier version of this happens in many meetings where folks agree that they really "need to *do x or y*," everyone nods in agreement and the group feels as if it has addressed the issue and can move on. But there is no Customer, no Promisor, and of course, no promise. This is one of the things I often see when teams complain that their meetings are a waste of time. The team may well be talking about important issues and recognizing the need for action, but they don't actually move themselves to the action of making specific requests, offers and promises.

3. What outcomes will satisfy and be valuable to the Customer?

The outcome of a promise may seem obvious, but that doesn't always mean it's clear and helpful. When your Customer doesn't know as much about your field of expertise as you do, the best your Customer can sometimes do is guess at what's possible and speculate about how their problems might be solved. Often, it's up to you, as Promisor (who may have more expertise), to educate the Customer about what's possible and what to include in the promise.

For example, say you're the Chief Information Officer and the Vice President of Human Resources comes to your office with a request: He wants to upgrade the company's HR information system (HRIS), and asks you to put together a plan and cost proposal for migrating the current system over to the software vendor that he's selected. He'd like it before the next Leadership Team meeting next month.

You could just accept the request, put a proposal together and deliver it to your Customer as promised. Check the box.

But you know that *apparent* solutions aren't always *good* solutions. So instead of simply accepting the request at face value, you sit down with your would-be Customer to discuss it in more detail.

After asking lots of questions and learning about what is most important for him, you're better positioned to make a promise that can deliver much more value than he could have imagined — because you're the expert in this area, not him. So you ask for a week to get back to him with a revised *outcome* for the promise. Meanwhile, you have your team do some research. (You haven't yet accepted the request, so you don't yet have a promise; you've just given him a date for your next conversation about the possible promise — a date for a date.)

When you come back to him the next week, he's delighted to learn that you are prepared to deliver everything he had been looking for, but because you're proposing he go with a different vendor (whom you've also carefully vetted), you can now promise to deliver the Outcome at lower cost, with quicker implementation and more customizable features than he'd originally asked for. In other words, you've greatly increased the value of your would-be Customer's promise before you've even made the promise.

Some promises will just spell out the outcome, while others may also specify one or more of the actions that you, the Promisor, will take to achieve that outcome. Not all Customers care what the Promisor will do to deliver the outcome—just that they deliver it (without creating any new problems in the process). Other Customers (especially internal Customers— who may be the Promisor's boss, for instance), care very much about how the promise will be fulfilled, because it may impact other promises being managed within the team or organization. Or, if you are still learning the ropes, your boss may want the actions you'll take spelled out so that she can provide guidance to support your learning and to avoid costly mistakes. Whether the specific actions to be taken are specified in the promise or not, it's a good idea to raise the topic and check it out with your Customer in advance, whenever possible.

4. *How does this promise align with and support the other important promises the parties are managing or know about in the organization?*

Every promise in an organization —no matter how small or trivial it may appear to be, is part of a larger "web" of promises. Each promise in this web must align with every other promise, or there will be competing commitments and friction, which lead to broken promises and weakened performance. On a more personal level, when you enter into a new promise, it's important to evaluate how this promise might impact all the other promises you may be managing. Every promise requires some time, energy, resources and attention, so carefully assessing your capacity to fulfill and manage each new promise is an important practice for managing your sustained performance and your well-being.

5. *Due Dates—When will the promise be fulfilled?*

This is pretty straightforward. Sometimes "Whenever you can get to it" or "As soon as possible" is good enough, but unless there is already a lot of trust and familiarity between the Customer and Promisor, specify a date by which the promise will be complete. And then, if you're the Promisor, be sure that you're keeping your Customer informed if, for any reason, that date may not be met. Which leads directly to the next and final question...

6. *How do the Customer and Promisor want to keep each other current throughout the promise?*

Because entering into a promise entails a risk and a commitment for both the Customer and Promisor, it's important that they both remain informed about any changes, or potential changes, that could impact the promise. And changes could arise for either party.

In the example for Question 3, above, the VP of Human Resources is banking on the new system to be live and operational by the end of this fiscal year (which was also *his* promise to the CEO). As the Promisor, if you discover that the vendor you're planning to use may have delays in implementing the new system, then you've got to decide how to handle this information and how to take care of your Customer. It helps to talk this through during your negotiations about the promise so that you each know the other party's preferences. Some Customers don't want to be informed of potential risks to the promise unless the Promisor is certain there is a problem; others want to be told at the very first hint of trouble. Still others only want to hear about problems once the Promisor has a concrete solution lined up to deal with the problem.

The Promisor, in turn, would want to know of any changes in due dates, requirements or specifications, priorities or payment delays, among many other potentially impactful changes.

The point is that both parties have an obligation to keep the other informed so that they both know what to expect and are able to address challenges that may arise during the fulfillment of the promise. Talking about this at the start of the promise, before any challenges arise, allows both parties to manage the promise—and the relationship—more effectively.

The more fully Customer and Promisor can address each of the above questions, the more likely the promise will go well. And these questions can also be helpful when performance on your team or organization may be suffering, when accountability is weak, or when the same problems keep resurfacing. Working through these questions together with your colleagues can help you to pinpoint unclear or poorly managed promises and enable you to have the conversations needed to renegotiate or reprioritize promises that aren't going well.

Reflection & Practice – Requests, Offers & Promises

This is a good time to put the book down and take a few easy breaths. Feel free to stand up, stretch, walk around, and let go of all these distinctions we've been covering, along with any tension you notice in your body.

Now, return to your Case Study or any other challenging interaction, and reflect...

1. *Think of a promise at work in which you are the <u>Customer</u> and someone else has promised to deliver an outcome that is important to you.*

   In your view, how well are these promises being managed? What's the likelihood that they'll be fulfilled in the way (and by the date) you are expecting?

   If you aren't 100% confident of success for these promises, review the Six Questions for Good Promises and see where things might not be clear with your Promisors. This is an opportunity to have a conversation with Promisors to realign together on why the promise matters and what needs to be clarified or renegotiated to strengthen the promise and deliver the value you seek.

2. *Now think of one or more promises for which you are* <u>*Promisor,*</u> *and assess how these promises are going, both from your perspective* <u>*and*</u> *the perspective of your Customer.*

   ○ For any promises where your customer may not have 100% confidence that the promise is going well and will be fulfilled as expected, use the Six Questions for Good Promises to see where you might clarify things. Consider having a conversation with your Customer(s) about these promises so that you are both on the same page. You might need to clarify outcomes, actions, how the Customer will assess satisfaction, or dates.

3. *Finally, reflect on any area of your work in which you assess that much more progress could be made, or new possibilities could be pursued.* There may be places where you are feeling overwhelmed with things to do that you can't or don't want to do yourself. What requests might you make, and to whom, to help you achieve more of the things you'd like to achieve? Or, what offers might you make that could create new value for other people in the organization?

Chapter 9

The Body of Collaborative Performance

He's a rigid guy.
You seem a little uptight.
That project really went sideways.
I can't get over it.
How do we get out ahead of this situation?
We're over the hump.
Hey, lighten up.

What's interesting about these metaphors is that they all refer to our felt, bodily experience. That's what makes metaphors so useful—and sometimes moving—because we can relate to them directly, kinesthetically.

The words "He's a rigid guy" make sense because we've all had the sensation of seeing, touching or encountering something that feels rigid and unyielding. We say something has gone sideways because we've all experienced kinesthetically the differences in trying to manage or relate to something directly in front of us, versus something off to the side. We've seen and felt humps of all types, from humps on an animal or person's body to humps on the road (speed humps), to larger humps of terrain that we know require more effort to traverse than level ground. It's hard to think of a metaphor that doesn't refer in some way to human, bodily experience (which also includes our spatial orientation and our visualizations and imagination, which are part of our visual sense).

Metaphors reflect the intimate connection—the inseparability—of our words and our body.

The body is our tangible point of reference in relating with the world around us and the other people who share that world with us. In leading an organization, making a speech, negotiating a contract, even writing code or analyzing spreadsheet data—the body of the person leading, speaking, negotiating, coding or analyzing is the same body as the person who may be confident or anxious, excited or uncertain, focused or distracted while doing it.

Consider that...

- Holding a cold drink or sitting in a hard chair can make us a tougher negotiator.
- Assuming a grounded, centered stance enhances our own sense of self-confidence (and influences others' experience of us as well).
- Changing our breathing alters what and how we perceive and influences our cognitive performance by altering our nervous system (along with many other bodily functions).
- Doing simple movement sequences for just a couple of minutes can increase (or mellow out) our energy, strengthen our ability to pay attention, even enhance our capacity to see things from another person's perspective, and much more.
- Sitting in quiet meditation for just 20 minutes a day bolsters our immune system, improves memory and executive functioning, and enhances our ability to think clearly and perform under pressure, along with many other well-documented effects (it actually changes our brain structure).

"The most remarkable discovery of modern neuroscience is that the body controls the brain as much as the brain controls the body," observes Lawrence Gonzales, author of *Deep Survival*.

Research validates what body-mind practitioners have long known: the importance of body-mind integration for health, well-being, mental clarity, emotional regulation, and improved performance.

You often hear about the "body-mind connection," but this is misleading; it suggests two separate systems with some connection between them. Although our words (including our thoughts—the internal images we see and the words we think) may sometimes seem to emerge out of some abstract intellect or disembodied "mind," they always have a physical home—they arise within a body. And they're listened to—absorbed by—a body. Our words *reflect* our body's internal state (even if we aren't fully aware of what's going on inside our body) and also *affect* our internal state.

Just as our body is not separate from our words and thoughts, it is also inseparable from what we usually consider to be our external environment—that which seems to lie outside of the body—including our interactions with the words and bodies of other people. In our everyday experience, we might believe that the line separating us from others is bright and clear. Biologists, sociologists, physicists and spiritual teachers through the ages, however, have understood that those apparently bright clear lines reflect a crude misconception. What goes on "outside" the body isn't really outside of us any more than what goes on inside of us is just inside.

Although the brain itself seems locked inside of our skull with no direct access to light or sound, our nervous system extends through the entire body, including our organs, muscles, skin and all the finely tuned sensory apparatus that orients us within the larger environment. Our "mirror neuron" system helps to explain why our own bodies, thoughts and feelings are so strongly influenced by watching or being around other people's movements, gestures and emotions even if we're not interacting with them directly.

Bodies Connect with Bodies

Before words or speech acts, before stories or metaphors, is our body. And even before "our" body, there is that undifferentiated body with no boundaries. Our own body was not separate from our mother's body; that only came later, although hopefully the warm, connected, physical contact continued well beyond those early years.

With its exquisitely sensitive nervous system, our body is constantly at play with other bodies—even across the room, or electronically, across the globe, via phone or video calls. We are always engaged with each other in a dynamic, spontaneous (and largely invisible-to-us) interplay of sensation, movement, gesture, energy and words. Even when we're just "doing business" together, this dance of connection is still in play.

Every conversation is an embodied conversation. Every meeting is a meeting of bodies. Slow motion video replays of people in conversation reveal that we are constantly shifting our posture, gestures and eye contact in subtle, unconscious response to each other. Even when we feel antagonistic, at polar opposites from one another, our nervous systems are still connected. It's why we say it takes two to fight and two to tango.

The technical term for this synchronization is *entrainment*. Like the seventeenth-century Dutch inventor Huygens' famous clocks whose pendulums reliably (and mysteriously) came into synchrony with one another when placed in close proximity, entrainment may be inevitable for us humans, too.

Talk to seasoned law enforcement folks or soldiers who have been in combat, and many will tell you that they can *smell* when a person or situation is about to turn violent. For some others, the hair on the back of the neck or the skin tingling registers potential danger well before their conscious thoughts raise the red flag. This capacity of ours to register and respond to threats and other important environmental cues in the sub-conscious part of our nervous system, well before those signals reach our conscious awareness, is well established.

Some martial arts focus almost religiously on developing "silent talk"—the ability to sense through touch the intention of an opponent before that opponent actually makes his or her next move. At more advanced levels practitioners can sense and respond to the opponent's attack without physical contact. This type of awareness operates much more quickly than thinking — it's a direct and immediate responsiveness that can only happen because of that invisible thread that connects us to each other. This thread allows the trained martial artist to respond skillfully and instantaneously to the opponent's attack — and the rest of us to respond instantaneously (even if not always skillfully) to our conversational partners (or dance partners) without consciously reflecting or directing our body to respond.

Our body is always with us. The way we sit, stand, move and breathe; the sensations we experience in our body all influence how we feel and think about things. And how we respond to the other people around us.

Words and Bodies in Sync
Please do the following with a friend or colleague (or just do it in the mirror with yourself):

- *Raise your shoulders to your ears and keep them there. Now turn to your friend/colleague (or do it with an imaginary friend or colleague) and tell them how confident you are about the high-profile new job you've just taken (it's okay to pretend). What do you notice in your thoughts, feelings or bodily sensations as you did this? Okay, relax your shoulders.*
- *Next, tighten your jaw. Turn to your friend/colleague and tell him/her why joining the team you are leading is going to be such a great experience. What do you notice? Okay, let your jaw relax.*
- *Take a breath and hold it in. With your breath held, tell them that as their sales leader, you look forward to helping them to build their confidence and increase sales with their prospects. Again, what did you notice doing this? Okay, let your breath out.*

Did you notice the incongruence between your body and your words (*declarations* in this case) while doing the above exercises? This incongruence is clearly contrived in this exercise. But you have no doubt experienced similar, if more subtle, incongruities in your colleagues or yourself at times, perhaps feeling disingenuous or insincere when the words coming out of your mouth aren't aligned with what you're thinking or feeling. When this happens, your communications will generally lack conviction and impact. At worst, you'll generate distrust or resistance in the listeners.

The above exercise was contrived to make a point, but it's quite common for people to habitually suspend their shoulders up away from their ribcage, to keep their jaws quietly clenched throughout the day, or to never fully let their breath out—as in perpetual anticipation of some imminent threat. It's probably not so exaggerated as in this exercise, but it's there. And it communicates, often unconsciously, to the people around, and to the person in that body.

In a meeting to discuss an important project that's not going well, when I attempt to bolster the team's spirits by behaving as if things are going well, or I avoid sharing my actual assessments about things, people's bodies will usually pick up on this incongruity, even if they're not fully aware of it. If I say upbeat things but my jaw is clenched or my breathing is shallow and quick, the message my body is sending will likely drown out all those upbeat words I'm uttering. The listeners in the room will pick up on these mixed messages if they're paying attention to themselves. They'll sense something is "off" about the communication.

Every interaction we have, we have in a body and with other bodies. And much of it is habitual—automatic. But it is possible to gain much more awareness about what's going on in our bodies.

Every conversation is a conversation between bodies.

Harnessing the Power of Reciprocity

We have all probably tried, at one time or another, to change somebody else to make them more like we want them to be. Perhaps a colleague, an employee, a boss or a customer. Or a partner, lover, friend or child.

When someone is giving us a hard time, or just not acting the way we think they should, our first reaction is often to try to change them. After all, *they* are the problem—they're the one who is making us feel this way, keeping us stuck. So, we try to instruct them, direct them, finesse them, or gently guide them. But it doesn't always work as planned, and it often generates its own problems, because few of us want to be *the problem* that another is trying to solve.

Focusing on changing others *can* influence those others because of that connectivity we all share, but not always in ways that we intend. Frequently, when we attempt to change, fix, improve or transform people, it just creates defensiveness or shuts them down, making them *less* receptive to our "help," not more.

This is one reason why, even when we're doing all the "right" things that we've learned in communication workshops—active listening, open-ended questions, making eye contact, and so forth—things can still go badly. People sense our efforts to change them. But if we can shift our attention back to ourselves— to noticing what we're feeling, thinking, sensing in our bodies, this alone can create a positive shift in the dynamic.

Skillful cops, prison guards, and psychiatric technicians in crisis clinics know this well. By focusing on themselves and calming their own bodies and mind, they are better able to constructively harness their connection to the other person, calming down individuals who are agitated, anxious, or on the verge of losing physical control. They do it with their own bodies—by modulating their voice, breathing, movements, energy. Simply telling someone who is teetering on the brink to calm down often isn't enough—that person often needs to experience "calming down" in the other person. This communicates much more directly than even the most skillful words (especially when uttered by someone who is himself worked up). When we change our own nervous system, we're going to be much more effective in helping the other person's nervous system.

We don't need to be cops or psychiatric techs to tap into this connection. We can all learn to recognize and work with this connectivity in our everyday lives, because we are each already hard-wired for connection and reciprocity. We start by becoming more attuned to our own physical experience (the practices in Part III can help with this). Gaining more fluency with our bodily experience is what enables us to make Full Contact with others.

The place to start is usually to shift our attention back onto ourselves so that we can sense what we're experiencing more clearly. Strozzi-Heckler, again, reflecting on a business executive he had worked with:

Because he couldn't feel himself, he couldn't feel others. If he could separate himself from his body, then he could also separate himself from other people. Without the information from his body, he related to people as facts, figures, and abstractions. He had a powerful mind but was without compassion and feelings. I realized how dangerous it is to remove principles from feelings, especially for a man in his position.

On the Aikido mat, when someone grabs or strikes us, a movement as simple as bending our knees, relaxing and dropping our center of gravity can sometimes be enough to soften our opponent's grip on us. It's not magic—it's simply bringing our focus to *ourselves* and our way of being, which often allows them to do the same. Put simply, when we gather out attention back into ourselves, we stop "feeding the beast" that is the opponent's strong fixation on us. In contrast, when we focus all our attention on the other person and their attack, it often has the exact opposite effect, strengthening their resolve and their force.

As with our words, we start by using our attention to gain awareness—to notice what is going on and what we are doing in our bodies. In some conversations, simply focusing on what we ourselves are feeling and doing in our bodies will change us enough internally that it changes the interpersonal dynamic. Our in-born reciprocity can invite others to meet us in that new, less reactive state we've been practicing ourselves. This could explain how a truly curious and interested listener may sometimes influence the speaker so profoundly that the speaker begins listening to and understanding himself in new ways.

Learning Together in Our Bodies

Engaging the body also enhances group performance and collaboration. As we cultivate greater internal security and stability in ourselves, it becomes easier to build trust and make greater contact with others. Self-awareness is the foundation of empathy. And supporting our nervous system to become calmer and less reactive increases our capacity to remain present and effective in challenging circumstances, such as when strong emotions, conflict, uncertainty or ambiguity are present.

When teams learn and take on simple bodily practices together, the benefits are multiplied. Engaging teams in simple bodily practices can help them quickly bond, soften barriers, move beyond troubled historical patterns and connect with greater engagement, curiosity and openness. This may sound touchy-feely, but from a performance perspective it can be more practical and hard-nosed (another bodily metaphor) than many other "team-building" practices. Explicitly involving the body in the learning process is an overlooked key to rapidly improving performance, whether on the athletic field, in the operating room, or in the boardroom.

The Body Is Always Present

If any of this has sounded esoteric or woo-woo, it's really not. The body is always here in the present moment, and we can relearn how to tap into the power of our embodied experience with just a little practice.

As a kid, you probably played the game of rubbing your belly with one hand while patting the top of your head with the other. *Do that right now.* You've probably just generated some new sensations. Whatever those sensations may be, let yourself linger with them for a moment, as if they are the most important thing to be paying attention to right now.

Sensation simply refers to those bodily experiences we have via our primary *senses* — vision, smell, hearing, taste and touch, and through our internal senses, which include proprioception and enteroception. (When you have a stomachache or feel jittery, its enteroception. When you feel your legs running or your arms swinging that tennis racket, that's proprioception.)

The sensation we may be experiencing at any moment may not always be pleasurable or desired, but it's still sensation — it's still an important aspect of our experience, and it's worth acknowledging and remaining present to, when you can. Sensations provide vital information about our well-being or lack thereof, about the impacts that circumstances may be having on our bodies, and about our predispositions to react to those circumstances. If our body didn't provide us with pain signals, we would have no way to know that something may be harming us or we may be ill. People who have no pain sensors typically don't survive long.

Sensations help us to know how we are, where we are and even who we are. Sometimes, I only realize how I'm actually feeling by turning my attention to the sensations in my body.

See if you can pay attention to your posture, movement, gestures and internal sensations over the next few days as you engage with other people in your meetings, phone calls and casual interactions. Don't try to "do it better" or turn this exercise into hard work. Just practice noticing what you're doing and sensing with a light sense of curiosity.

Even when our thoughts are miles (or years) away, our body is always still present, right here and right now. Actively paying attention and engaging with our body can help us to become more present, in a direct and immediate way, with whatever we're doing and whomever we're doing it with. Engaging with the body as I'm discussing it here isn't about getting stronger, fitter, or more attractive. It's about gaining more awareness of ourselves and of what is moving inside of us. The more aware we become, the more choice we gain about what we're doing, and how we're doing it.

Reflection & Practice – The Body of Collaborative Performance – Part 1

Take a moment now to do a simple body scan, following the steps below. This is helpful for cultivating greater bodily awareness. It also helps to relax your body and mind. The aim of this exercise is simply to sense your body with a gentle attention, without trying to change or adjust your body. *You might want to read these steps into a recorder and play them back so you can listen without needing to read each step. Or, you can go to fullcontactinstitute.com and click on Performance Practices for an audio version of this exercise.*

1. Sit in a chair with your back upright, but not rigid or held. It's helpful to use a stool or chair with a firm seat and, if possible, to sit forward on the seat so that your back isn't resting against the backrest. This can help you maintain an upright, alert posture for several minutes or longer without getting fatigued or collapsing down into your lower back.
2. Start by simply sensing your whole body sitting here.

3. Now bring your attention to the soles of your feet resting on the floor, or the contact of your feet with your socks, shoes or floor. Just let your attention scan each foot without needing to change anything about the experience.

4. Next, move your attention up to your ankles and lower legs, letting your attention gently scan each area, noticing any sensations. It's fine if there is no sensation in some areas — just notice that.

5. Taking your time, continue scanning your knees and upper legs, continuing to notice any sensations that are present, without judging them or trying to change or fix anything.

6. Next bring your attention to the places where your body is making contact with the chair. Sense your bottom, and your pelvic area, noticing any sensations.

7. Continuing to simply notice without changing anything, let your attention take in your belly, lower back and the front, sides and back of your ribcage. Simply stay open and curious about whatever sensations you may notice.

   If at any point during this practice you notice distracting thoughts entering your awareness, you can treat them just as you've been treating your body sensations — with curiosity and interest, and without trying to change them or make them go away. Simply note the thoughts, and when you're ready, return attention to the body.

8. Next direct your attention to your shoulders, and then upper arms, elbows and forearms, and then your hands. See if you can sense each finger, noticing any sensations that may be there.

9. Now bring your attention to your neck, throat and head, sensing your mouth, jaw, eyes and forehead, and finally your scalp or crown of the head.

10. Finally, zoom out again with your attention to sense your whole body sitting here. You may notice that you're feeling more relaxed than you were before doing this simple practice. There may be new sensations "speaking" to you

now, because directing your attention to different parts of your body also tends to "wake" up those areas (energy follows our attention).

This is a simple form of body scanning. There are countless variations of this practice you'll find in many approaches to stress reduction, yoga and meditation. Some begin with attention at the top of the body and move downward, while others (like this one) start at the bottom and move upward through the body. Feel free to experiment and see what differences you may notice.

Once you're familiar with this practice, you can do it anywhere, at any time. Within just a minute or less, this exercise can help you reduce tension and bring you back into a more balanced and settled state.

Although there is a world of bodily sensations available to each of us at any time, we often don't attend to them, and even when we do, we may not know what to make of them. The world of sensations—the language of the body—is everybody's first language, but many of us have lost our fluency with it, relating to it like a foreign language that we just tune out. With just a little practice, however, we can refamiliarize ourselves with our body, which can have profound implications for our collaborative performance, as well as our personal sense of well-being and contact with others.

Reflection and Practice – The Body of Collaborative Performance – Part 2

This next practice is a little different...

1. Take some time to think about your relationship with your own body, reflecting upon what you've just read. Now, make a list of potential ongoing practices you might take on to expand your sense of bodily awareness and to strengthen your body/mind connection (you don't need to make any

commitments, here). Here are some possible examples, but there are certainly many more:

Yoga

Tai Chi

Chi Gong

Massage or other types of bodywork such as Rolfing, the Feldenkrais Method, the Alexander Technique, Aikido, Pilates, breath work, to name just a few (again, these are just examples).

2. Next, put aside some time in your calendar to research any of these types of practices to see which ones seem the most interesting to you.

3. Now, for the practice(s) that interest you the most, see if you can find a qualified instructor or center that you could imagine yourself attending, either in person or virtually. (If it's not convenient and you don't feel good about the instructor, it's unlikely you'll sustain a consistent practice.)

4. Finally, make just one appointment or class date in your calendar for the practice you're most interested in. (This is a personal declaration.) Don't commit to too much at first. Start with one session to see if it seems like a good fit, and go from there. If it is a good fit it will *feel good*—you'll feel better leaving the class/session than when you started. You'll also feel safe and well-cared for by the instructor—very important!

You can certainly check out more than one type of practice and multiple instructors to find the best fit, just don't set yourself too lofty a goal at first. Start small with a new practice and the likelihood of sustaining it will be much greater.

Chapter 10

Happy World, Sad World

In the last several chapters we looked at the roles and interplay of our words and our bodies in collaboration. In this chapter we'll continue this exploration by looking at one of the most common ways we communicate about this interplay—through the lens of emotions.

Although experts debate about precisely what emotions are and how they function, there is little argument that, as Ludwig Wittgenstein once said, "The world of the happy is quite different from the world of the unhappy." Depending on how we're feeling, the world may be a joyful and nurturing place, a scary or a sad place, or any other kind of place. It depends on the emotion we're experiencing. This has enormous implications for our collaboration as well as for our personal lives.

Researchers have mapped different emotional states to activity in various parts of the nervous system, and to various physiological states. Some assert that the specific physical manifestations of each basic emotion (the physiological pattern, gestures, posture, movement, etc.) are universal in all human beings, independent of cultural, social or ethnic differences. Others, including researcher and author Lisa Feldman-Barrett, see the physical expression of emotions as much more personal and individual. However, whether expressed in universal or personal ways, there's general agreement that what we call emotions have a "home" in our bodies.

When we say that we are angry, happy, sad, or anxious, we're providing a label (we're making a distinction in language) that corresponds to a particular assessment and a "storyline" that constitutes the emotion. In addition to the assessment or storyline, there's a particular bodily pattern of breathing, nervous system arousal, muscle tension or tone, hormonal activity and other physiological processes. Every emotion expresses itself through our words and through our body.

Imagine you're digging through the stuff in your basement when suddenly you encounter a big spider. You'll probably reactively pull back and hold your breath. (Similar to when a ball or a fist unexpectedly approaches your face and you throw up your hands to protect yourself.) This is reflexive, it happens without thinking—your sensory perception is mainlined directly into certain older parts of your brain, bypassing your rational, sense-making frontal cortex. It's only later—perhaps fractions of a second later, that your frontal cortex snaps to attention and you think "Wow that's a big spider. Should I kill it? Should I take it outside? No, maybe catch it and show it to the kids!" (Or, in the case of the ball or fist, "You tried to hit me!" or "What did I do?" or "What are you so mad about?") Making sense of the experience, including perhaps determining a rational response to it, happens after the body's reaction.

While some emotions are triggered instantly through the body's sensory apparatus (like the spider, ball or fist), others are clearly borne by words—assessments and interpretations (the storylines) we hold or tell ourselves to make sense of what happens to us.

Let's say you get a call from your boss—whom you know and have worked well with for years—telling you she has just taken a job at another company and the person to replace her hasn't yet been announced. This sets off a flurry of thoughts: *I'm going to miss her! Who will my new boss be? Maybe I won't get along so well with the new person? How might this affect my standing in the company, and even my career?* These thoughts and more may be going through your head, perhaps along with images of various future scenarios you might imagine. These particular thoughts—comprised of assessments, stories and images—will kick off a variety of physiological reactions, including perhaps a twisting feeling in your gut, a tightening in your chest, or heat flushing your face. Although we might each have our own specific bodily reactions to each storyline, most of us could probably agree that they fall in the general vicinity of an emotion we call *anxiety*. No spider, ball or fist in your face here—just a phone call from your boss or perhaps an email. But the emotions are just as real in the body. In this case, the words lead and the body follows; the emotion you feel originated entirely in your thinking, as do most of the stressful emotions we experience at work and in life.

Regardless of where the emotional reaction started, the storyline and the physiological changes associated with the emotion we feel will be congruent. They'll match up. This is convenient, because it means we may be able to intervene and "manage" our emotions either by changing our storyline, or by changing our bodily experience.

Just for clarity, let's distinguish between moods and emotions: Both moods and emotions express our bodily states and our linguistic storylines. Generally speaking, emotions are transitory, they have an immediate logic to them. They are *about* something; they are triggered by events, circumstances or thoughts (spiders, fists, calls from the boss). When circumstances change, so do the emotions. In contrast, moods are broader, background patterns that tend to persist over time. Moods hold on to us, keeping us in their thrall, sometimes long after the initial emotion was first triggered. They keep returning, over and over, in between the more specific emotions that may get triggered in the course of our daily lives.

We each have our habitual, go-to emotions, as well as our dominant moods. Our teams, organizations, industries, communities and nations also have their own habitual emotions and moods. You can probably walk around your office and notice distinct moods in each area, each department or each team. And visiting different regional offices of your company you'll likely also notice different dominant moods in each region.

Both moods and emotions can be highly infectious. Which is why we have pep rallies, and also why we have angry mobs.

The Story of This Emotion

Let's explore this interplay of words and body right now, wherever you may be reading this.

Take a moment and recall a time when you were sad, or if you can't think of one, imagine a scenario in which you might be sad. Now, let yourself assume the "body" of sadness. Let your breathing, facial expression and posture take on the feeling of that sadness you are recalling or imagining. Do it for a minute or so and see what you notice.

Now let that go, take a few easy breaths and do the same thing for anger. Now, how about gratitude? Acceptance?

If you were to take the time to really let your body shape itself into each of these emotions for several minutes, you'd find that your genuine emotional experience would start to reflect this bodily state, even though each emotional state was clearly contrived with your recall or imagination. If you stayed with it, you'd probably also start to notice that thought patterns (perhaps assessments or storylines) arise that correspond to the emotional state. This isn't a cheap parlor trick—it's just the way we seem to be wired: our thoughts and words occur in and affect our body.

Now let's look at some emotions from the perspective of our words. We'll start with anger...

Anger is one of the most basic human emotions and also one of the most uncomfortable for many people. Which is probably why many people seek to avoid it, tamp it down or escape from it as quickly as possible. This can be easier said than done, as anger also tends to be one of the toughest emotions to wrangle to the ground.

As you just "reconstructed" the emotion of anger in your body a moment ago, you may have noticed that, while perhaps uncomfortable, it also tends to be energizing, perhaps even exhilarating. It may involve sensations of trembling, sweating, muscular contraction and tightening. The face may lock into a scowl. (This doesn't mean that everybody experiences anger physiologically this way, or that every time you tremble, sweat, feel energized or scowl, that you are angry. As Barrett-Feldman says, emotions don't manifest the same in everybody, even though we all feel similar emotions.)

Just as you "reconstructed" anger in your body, you can also do it with your words. Jan Bowman, a clinical psychologist who specializes in experiential, somatic, and psychodynamic psychotherapy (and also my sister), describes the storyline of anger as follows: *You have done something that has hurt or violated me in some way, and I must take action to defend myself against this violation [and possibly rectify the situation].* Now, take a moment and either recall or imagine a situation that matches this storyline. Take a minute or two to do this. If you really let yourself get into the storyline, you'll probably start to notice bodily sensations arising that match the storyline.

How about the storyline for **sadness**? It goes something like... *I have lost something that was important to me. This will limit what may happen to me in the future and there is nothing I can do to bring it back or to change what's happened.*

Obviously, there could be many variations on the basic storylines you can imagine for anger, sadness, and most other emotions, but these are common scenarios and they help illustrate the linguistic dimension of particular emotions.

You probably noticed that a key ingredient in the storyline of both anger and sadness, and every other emotion or mood, is *assessment*. Assessments give each emotion its unique linguistic signature, its physiological "kick." Again, our words and our bodies are never isolated—they are different dimensions of our experience.

Here are a few more emotions, along with their storylines...

Fear, considered by many to be one of the most powerful and basic of all human emotions, has a storyline that goes something like: *This situation is dangerous for me. Bad things could happen to me which might hurt me, limit my future or even kill me. I should get out of here.*

As a social emotion, **shame** is one of the most painful emotions we may experience. Which may point to its importance for our standing—or survival—within our community. The storyline of shame would be: *I shouldn't have done what I've done. I've failed to live up to the standards of the community, and this has damaged my reputation and possibly my future possibilities within the community. I don't want anybody to know about this.* When we lower our head in shame (posture/gesture) it's as if we are trying to become invisible, as if we deserve to be alone.

Shame reflects a more serious transgression than embarrassment, but the two are often confused. **Embarrassment's** storyline is something like: *I know I've screwed up and took things too far. Most folks around here—including me—consider it inappropriate. That's awkward.*

Resignation is a common and powerful emotion in many teams and organizations. It's expressed in terms like: *This situation isn't good and there's nothing I or anybody else can do about it, so I won't do anything.*

When people feel resigned (usually as a result of feeling helpless to change things that are important to them), they become passive. They don't make many requests or offers, and when they do, these speech acts are often delivered without much energy or conviction. *After all,* says resignation, *any action is futile.* Resignation can sometimes also reflect a passive form of control, or a defensive posture taken to avoid the possibility of taking action—and failing.

Resentment is another common emotion in organizations. It simmers on the anger continuum, somewhere between annoyance on the mild end, and rage on the other extreme. The storyline is: *You've done something that is unfair and has limited my future. Although you are responsible for it, I can't complain to you directly without creating more problems for myself. Either way, somehow, some day, you need to pay for this.*

On a brighter note, the linguistic reconstruction (storyline) for **optimism** looks something like this: *Life holds both good and bad experiences. Most of the things that have happened to me and that will continue to happen to me are good. I'm pretty fortunate.*

We'll end our review of emotional storylines with **gratitude**: *You treated me well. What you've done has helped me and has likely improved what may happen for me in the future. You didn't have to, but you did it anyway, and I'm inclined to return the favor to you someday. Thank you.*

Emotions Catch Us Coming and Going

Earlier in the book, we saw how emotions can influence our perceptions—what feels *real* to us. This is important for collaboration for a couple of reasons. First, emotions serve to filter or bias what we pay attention to and perceive of the things going on around us. When we're in the grip of certain emotions, our attention can become narrowed to just those signals that conform with, or confirm, that emotion—and the stronger the emotion, the more narrowed our attention and biased our perception. Which means we may miss a whole range of other signals from the people around us—their words, tone of voice, gestures, posture, and so forth. This is one reason it's difficult to distinguish our emotions from what *may actually be going on out there.*

When we're angry, for instance, we're much more likely to interpret someone's behavior uncharitably, or as a personal affront, than when we are in a more relaxed or neutral emotion. "The function of anxiety and anger is," as psychologist Russell Lemle says, "to viscerally warn of a danger so that we take self-protective measures. To succeed at this task, we're designed to over-estimate threat. The only surefire guarantee that actual risks are never missed is giving ambiguous threats the same credence as definite ones. Better to be safe than sorry. This evolutionary adaptation was vital for survival on the savannah, but it's another story entirely with our relationships." Lemle is pointing to how our emotions influence both our perception and our attention.

Now, think about what happens in a meeting when the dominant mood is anger or hostility. It's easy to see how quickly those conversations can shut down; how the only things we notice will be things that affirm the anger or justify the hostility. The parts of the interaction that don't conform to these moods will go unseen and unheard. This is how our emotions catch us "coming" — by altering our perception and interpretations.

Our emotions also catch us "going," by predisposing and shaping what we do next — our *behaviors* — the words and bodily actions we take in response to our experience. Each emotion predisposes us for a specific type of action. When scared or angry, we are primed for very different actions than when we're feeling happy (associated with the neurochemicals dopamine, endorphins, oxytocin and serotonin, among others physiological responses). We'll be friendlier, because that's how the world seems to us.

Because we act in ways that reflect our internal experience (emotions and associated bodily state) — even if those actions aren't particularly helpful for our collaboration — it's important that we learn to recognize our emotions. And when possible, to examine those emotions so that we can minimize their potentially destructive influence and optimize the positive. Being able to look at them both in terms of their storylines as well as bodily dimensions can help us do that. Again, here's where meta-moves come in handy...

Meta-moves with Emotions

I recently received a mass email from my health care provider with a subject line that read: *Feeling bad about feeling sad?* The email ended with the words and a link: *Help fight depression with "Find Your Words. Start a conversation and help lower the stigma around mental health."*

That email illustrates a common challenge when dealing with our emotions—the tendency for emotions to pile on, one on top of another. Feeling sad may be the primary emotion we're feeling, but then we may "feel bad" about feeling sad, perhaps believing that we shouldn't be feeling it. Feeling sadness is one thing—but then assessing that sadness as inappropriate, weak, or somehow unacceptable, compounds our suffering. It can also make it harder to understand what's going on.

The email also highlights the fundamental interrelatedness of our emotions and our words. It points to the power of *going meta* to the emotions (by observing and talking about them) in order to work with them. This meta-move—of labeling the bodily sensations and/or recognizing the storyline of the emotion—especially if done without judgment—helps us move through the emotions more easily. It also helps us work more skillfully with strong emotions that surface in our collaborative encounters. (Developing this "meta-cognitive" capacity is one of the benefits that comes with consistent mindfulness meditation practice.)

When a group seems bogged down in confusion or resignation, for instance, it can be helpful to call those emotions out—to give names to the emotion—so that folks can shift their attention to themselves and the emotions they may be feeling. This can help to defuse the power of the emotions, giving people the opportunity to do a "reset" and approach the conversation from a more neutral or constructive state. By the way, when we give the emotion we're observing a name, it can be helpful even if the name isn't perfect; just the move of acknowledging the presence of a strong emotion may help to defuse it, bringing relief and enabling folks to be less captivated by the feelings.

Because emotions live in our assessments and stories as well our bodies, another thing we can do to get out from under strong emotions is to practice grounding those assessments or examining the stories we're telling ourselves, together with our colleagues. Doing this may reveal that some of the storylines underlying our feelings aren't necessarily "accurate" or even relevant. They may simply be old habits, based on outdated beliefs, trauma or blind spots. (We'll look more closely at this in the next chapter.)

Reflection & Practice – Happy World, Sad World

Go back to your Case Study—or any other challenging interaction that's on your mind.

1. *How would you describe the general mood of the other person or group you have in mind when you are interacting with them?* If you were to take a guess at the "storyline" of that mood, what might it be?

2. *How might the others in this interaction be predisposed to perceiving and interpreting what goes on—including things that you may be doing or saying?*

3. *How would you describe your own mood in the interaction you are reflecting on?* What are the common storylines that you may notice in your own thinking? What physical sensations do you notice as you reflect on this interaction (or may remember experiencing during the interaction)?

4. *How do you think you may be predisposed to interpret and respond to the things those other people say and do in your interactions?* And how might your predispositions be limiting you or keeping you (and perhaps others) locked into fixed patterns or ways of interrelating?

Chapter 11

Listening to Reality

Mark Twain once said, "I'm an old man now. I've lived a long and difficult life filled with so many misfortunes, most of which never happened." Lots of the things that we think have happened in the past or are happening now, may not actually be quite so.

Most of us appreciate that our perceptions and actions are influenced by many factors, including culture, race, ethnicity, gender, sexual orientation, family upbringing, education, life experience, professional training, and much more. Many organizations have seriously taken on the work of expanding employee awareness and appreciation for many of these differences in the workplace. While this movement is still in its infancy with much more work to be done, the importance of respecting and supporting differences is at least on the radar screen for many people and companies, even if they don't always embody this recognition consistently.

In this chapter, we'll be looking at some different differences. All of the above-mentioned factors absolutely influence how we each experience the world and interact with one another, but there are some additional factors that can have an equally large impact on our collaborative performance. And these don't always appear on our radar screen. In the next pages, we'll be looking at color blindness, disoriented pilots, blind spots, deceptive doctors, ducks, bunnies and more, to see more clearly just how ambiguous and subjective our "objective" reality can sometimes be. This chapter is the first of two chapters devoted to *listening,* and our focus here is to better understand some of the limitations we all share when it comes to perceiving how things *really are.* Recognizing and accounting for these limitations is essential for good listening.

My intention with this chapter and the next is to help you transform your listening skills. In getting there, however, you may notice that your confidence in your own capacity for knowing how things "really" are—in an objective sense—may be diminished by what you read. That's not necessarily a bad thing. My hope is that, after reading these chapters, you'll feel a little less confident and a lot more inquisitive about what you consider to be the black-and-white, factual world around you— what we call reality. This inquisitiveness will help you listen with deeper interest and curiosity to others who may see things very differently than you.

When we describe our experience with assertions, the presumption is that the objective reality we are observing— the thing, concept, or circumstance—is actually *out there* in the first place. That's our premise when we say that the purpose of an assertion is to point to something "real" in the world which we can all see or experience together. For very many assertions, this premise will serve us well. However, there are also circumstances in which the "reality" that you or I might point to is not nearly so cut and dried as we assume or wish they were—and this can lead to difficulties in our collaboration.

There are fundamental constraints that govern what we humans perceive, even if we're not aware of them in the course of our everyday interactions. We normally assume that what appears to *us* as real and factual will appear equally self-evident to the folks sitting around the table with us. So when we encounter resistance or disagreement from others about our assertions, we get impatient, indignant, incredulous, or worse. It's one thing to recognize that *opinions* are subjective, but it's another matter altogether when "obvious" facts are not seen as such by others. To temper our reactivity in these situations and to listen more effectively, it helps to remember that nobody has the market cornered on reality...

We're Never Playing with a Full Deck

Our perceptual experience feels so direct and solid to us, that we automatically assume it's an accurate reflection of what's happening *out there*. But there's skimpy evidence to support this assumption.

What we perceive is shaped and limited by many factors, including our built-in biological capabilities, our life experience, our emotions, the environmental and contextual cues around us, how we're using our attention, and a whole slew of other biases. The saying *"Just because it's obvious, doesn't mean it's true"* is more than just an empty cliché.

I have a friend with dyschromatopsia—the fancy word for color blindness—and he reminds me that even such apparently basic "facts" like Red or Green can be perceived quite differently by different observers. Greens aren't green, reds aren't red. A palette of vivid colors to one person can be shades of gray to another. What determines which assertion is true in this case is actually "majority rules." My friend happens to be among the minority of people who share those biological predispositions. So when he makes "true" assertions about red and green, they are false to everyone else. But if everyone else suddenly acquired dyschromatopsia, seeing things as my friend does, then our *reality* about those colors would change and the assertions made about those colors would be viewed quite differently.

While we're talking about vision, let's look at our blind spot. Oh wait—we can't! We all have these blind spots, and they're not just metaphorical. A certain part of our visual field is physically blocked as a result of where the eye's optic nerve, consisting of specialized light-sensitive cells in the retina (and over a million nerve fibers), exits the eye. These blind spots in our vision are biologically based, and they're just one example of our built-in perceptual limitations. We each have many more biological and non-biological blind spots that limit our ability to perceive things "as they are," and these blind spots have much more impact on our collaboration and our lives than this optical blind spot. We are blind to much more than we can see.

"In the normal course of events," says author, psychologist and researcher Robert Ornstein, "an average human being doesn't need to notice that he or she is ignorant of much of outside reality, that we see only a trillionth of what is out there, that we feel even less, just as we are ignorant of the blind spot of our eyes... In essence, we never operate with a 'full deck'..."

We know that there's a whole world of sights, sounds and scents all around us that can be measured by instruments and perceived by other animals, yet which are entirely inaccessible to us. Even though we share about 999 out of 1000 bits of our DNA in common with our pet dogs and cats (and most other species), we still understand that the worlds in which those other species live must be fundamentally different from our own. So, it's tempting to assume that because we humans are so biologically similar to one another, that we all must live in the same, *human* world. But that one bit of shared DNA that makes us uniquely human still packs a lot of diversity.

Each one of us human beings also lives in different worlds from one another. And no one of us is even operating with the same *partial* deck. My nervous system is mostly similar to yours, but it's still different enough that we can experience the same song, work of art, conversation amongst colleagues, or our team's new boss, in dramatically different ways.

Which of us gets it right? Which of us is endowed with a more "accurate" nervous system? The following examples may suggest just how partial a deck we're each playing with. Not only are we all mostly blind; we are also, as Ornstein tells us, also mostly blind to our blind spots.

Seeing What's Not There

Optical illusions occur when what our eyes are clearly telling us is just flat out wrong. The same colors or shapes may appear to be entirely different when seen in different background conditions or within different contexts.

If we were to put on glasses that make everything look upside down, within a matter of hours, our brains would adjust so that the upside-down world becomes normal (even though the glasses haven't changed).

Even our sense of time and season can change our perception: When shown the picture below on Easter Sunday, 82% percent of people identified it as a bunny. When shown the same picture on a Sunday in October, 90% said it was a duck or some similar bird. (This oft-cited picture was originally created by psychologist Joseph Jastrow around 1900. Various versions of it have been used many times since by psychologies, philosophers and others—most notably perhaps by Ludwig Wittgenstein.)

Is it a duck? Or a bunny?

Trusting Our Gut

Our own gut can often be the most reliable thing to trust. Our instincts can steer us through many challenges and situations that our intellect alone might not handle so well. But not always. In order to stand, walk or run upright, we bipeds rely heavily on the visual cues from our eyes. Our eyes take in the ground under our feet, the sky above us, and the horizon where they meet. We cross-reference these visual cues with the signals we receive from our vestibular system, which gives us our sense of balance, our relationship to gravity, and our spatial orientation. The vestibular system tells us, for instance, when we're leaning too far backward and are about to fall over.

When our visual cues disappear, say when it's very dark or we're in dense fog, we're left only with the signals from our vestibular system. The problem is that our vestibular system isn't failsafe; it can give us bum signals, which are called *vestibular* or *somatogravic illusions*. This is especially true when we don't have the earth under our feet or the normal sense of our body in relation to gravity.

Experienced airplane pilots appreciate the importance of trusting their gut—but they also know how deadly that can sometimes be. On clear days, pilots can generally trust their gut and literally fly by the seat of their pants: the perceptual signals they receive from their vestibular system are easily and accurately reconciled with their visual cues.

But without clear signals from either their visual or vestibular systems (or both), it can be difficult for the pilot to really *know* what the airplane is doing. On very dark nights with lots of stars or when flying in clouds, the perceptual cues the pilot receives from his body may be very clear, but very wrong: Is the nose pointing up, or is it in a steep dive? Is it in a pitched banking turn, or flying straight and level? It seems like it should be obvious, but it may actually be impossible to know, simply based on the pilot's gut feeling. Partly this is a result of how readily our bodies adapt to changes in our environment: When an airplane makes a gradual turn or change in pitch, it takes just a matter of seconds for our vestibular system to adjust, making this new change seem "normal," and therefore not requiring any further attention or response on our part.

Spatial disorientation can affect even the most seasoned pilots, which could lead to exactly the wrong action in response to a given situation. And the tendency to incorrectly sense the plane's relationship in space is even more pronounced when the pilot is tired, anxious or distracted. But before you get too worked up, you should understand that spatial disorientation is a well-understood phenomenon, which is one reason there are so many instruments in the cockpit (many of which are redundant, for safety's sake). Its why commercial pilots undergo constant simulation training, and why airlines regularly monitor their pilots' health, stress levels and overall fitness to fly. Commercial pilots understand the limitations of their perception and know how to compensate for those limitations, which is why flying is a lot safer than driving. (Many driving accidents occur because we drivers don't factor in our own perceptual limitations, generally assuming that we're safer than we actually are.)

Our gut feelings—however strong they may be—aren't always reliable indicators of how things really are.

Blinded by Attention

Remember the magicians I mentioned in Chapter 2? They work their magic by diverting and manipulating the audience's attention, exploiting both our instinctual and learned habits of attention. We notice more about what we pay attention to, and less (or nothing at all) about what we're not paying attention to. And paying very, very close attention to one thing can blind us to everything else around us that might otherwise be plain as day. Hence, the phrase *"the closer you look, the less you'll see."* When we're down in the weeds, even the shrubs disappear. As we saw in Chapter 2, what's *real* is partly a function of what we're paying attention to.

Healed and Sickened by Words

Well-intending doctors have been using the power of words to deceive—and heal—their patients for centuries. Placebos, those fake pills and medical "treatments" which have no actual medicinal value (and are, by definition, deceptions), can act just like actual pharmaceuticals, triggering neurochemicals such as endorphins and dopamine that activate parts of the brain associated with pain reduction and symptomatic relief. And, as Functional MRI and other technologies now demonstrate, these effects are not just imaginary. Our perceptions, along with our physiology, are apparently quite open to suggestion. Put another way, our bodies and our health may prove to be influenced as much by our intention and beliefs (and our attention) as by the substances we ingest or treatments we receive.

Until recently it was believed that placebos could only work when the patient wasn't in on the deception. But we're learning that placebos can work well even when a patient knows that the pills or treatments they're receiving have no medical value. There are now even *open label* placebos, which are explicitly prescribed as such. Several factors can influence the "efficacy" of the placebo effect for the knowing patient, such as the way the placebo pills are prescribed, packaged and consumed; the price; and even our trust that the prescribing doctor cares about us and wants us to get better. It appears that our immune system is influenced not only by the actions of others, but even by *their* intentions—or at least by our beliefs about their intentions.

Another example was described by Ellen Langer and Alia Crum in the February 2007 issue of *Psychological Science*, reporting on their study of 84 hotel workers. They told one subject group in the study that "the work they do (cleaning hotel rooms) is good exercise and satisfies the Surgeon General's recommendations for an active lifestyle," providing examples of how their work improves health. Langer and Crum told the control group nothing.

Four weeks later, when measured on a variety of factors, the control group hadn't changed physically at all, but the group that had been told they were getting good exercise had measurably improved in terms of weight, blood pressure, body fat, waist-to-hip ratio, and body mass index.

As cellular biologist Bruce Lipton says, "Your beliefs act like filters on a camera, changing how you see the world. And your biology adapts to those beliefs." Just as believing that what you are doing is improving your health, or the pill you're taking will reduce pain, the opposite can also happen: Experiments with postoperative patients showed that actual prescription pain medications were only half as effective when the patient was not aware that he or she was taking a painkiller.

Our greatest weakness is always rooted in how we're seeing things. And there is much more that we can't or don't see than we usually assume.

Seeing with Our Emotions

As we saw in the last chapter, another powerful factor in what and how we perceive is our emotions. The more secure and at ease with ourselves we're feeling, the easier it will likely be for us to remain attentive and present in a conversation involving conflict, disagreement or uncertainty. It will also be easier to notice kindness, generosity and other positive intentions that may be on display, even in the midst of otherwise uncomfortable interactions. Conversely, the more vulnerable, anxious or angry we're feeling (often referred to as "threat emotions"), the more likely we are to perceive opposition or danger where it may not exist. In the grip of threat emotions, our perceptual accuracy goes way down, and depending upon the intensity of our feelings, our colleagues can easily be seen as adversaries that our nervous system must prepare to defend against.

190 or so Biases

The common saying, "*Give a boy a hammer, and everything he encounters will need pounding,*" is about perceptual and cognitive biases—our tendency to perceive, think and behave in certain predictable, yet often "irrational" ways. At present, close to 200 distinct biases have been documented, and more will likely be added to the list.

One of my favorite biases on the list is the "Blind Spot Bias." It reflects the tendency we all share to see ourselves as less biased than the people around us. It's what lets us easily recognize biases and blind spots in *other people*, but not so readily in ourselves. This bias neatly sums up the point of this chapter, and reflects the trap we can fall into when we're trying to collaborate: When my perceptions are influenced by one or more of these biases (which feel so natural and real to me that I don't even notice it) and others aren't seeing what I'm seeing, it could be easy for me to try to "correct" those others by informing them about what *they're* blind to, perhaps even attributing their "blindness" to intellectual laziness, irrationality or other obvious-to-us factors. And we know how well those efforts usually go. When collaboration is at a standstill and people have become polarized and set in their beliefs about the other folks in the conversation, this bias is almost always at play. And if folks are also feeling anxious, fearful or angry, everyone's attention can easily become fixated on the alleged blindness, laziness or irrationality of the others, further reinforcing the polarization.

All the examples in this section reflect some type of perceptual limitation or filter, whether biological, emotional or cognitive. These, and many other factors we know about (plus many more we surely don't yet know about), affect the way the world shows up for us at the most basic level of perception — before we even get to interpreting or assessing those raw perceptions. So naturally, they'll also shape the assertions we make to describe what we experience (and our expectation that others will naturally see things similarly).

Getting Real about Reality, Together

In the "Care doesn't Care" situation, part of what was going on was that the people in Sales had no idea about what went on in the Customer Care department, and vice versa. And this led each group to view the data they'd each already collected in very limited ways. They each lacked a sense of the daily life of the other folks, including the types of challenges, pressures and commitments the others had to manage on a daily basis. So it didn't even occur to the Sales people that there might be other useful data they might collect, and other ways of interpreting the data that could be equally legitimate.

There are three things going on here: First, the types of data we collect are often limited by our habitual perspectives. Second, our habitual perspectives lead us to interpret the data we do collect in specific—and possibly limited—ways. And third, we get frustrated by the others' "obvious" blindness, and feel offended at their lack of interest in seeing what's right there in front of them. In other words, we fall into the trap of believing that our world and our worldview is the only valid one. Contrary to the cliché, the data doesn't always "speak for itself." But our assumption that it does can easily lead us to polarize and even vilify others who don't see the data as we do and therefore reach different conclusions about it.

While "true" assertions can be critically important for collaboration, it's also clear that they may at times be more subjective and less universally "true" than we think. The point here isn't to get rid of all the biases that influence our perception—that's not possible. The point is to become more aware of the unavoidable biases in our interactions so that we can approach our collaborations with a little less certainty and a lot more curiosity, humility and interest in how other people may see things. It's not always enough to simply make an assertion, provide obvious-to-us evidence, and then assume that's the end of the story. We need to remember that our own senses can be skewed, or at least differently oriented, than others. What may be irrefutable evidence to me might not be at all valid to someone else. This recognition can transform the way we speak, the way we listen and the way we try to solve problems together (which we'll look at more closely in Chapter 14 - Designing Conversations).

When I presume that my perception reflects how things *really are* (when I forget that I am as blind to what goes on around me as everyone else), I lock myself into a solitary, zero-sum universe of my own making. In that zero-sum universe there is only one "right" assertion and the rest must be wrong or somehow inferior. The challenge is that this sense of certainty can feel comforting to us, even as it renders good collaboration almost impossible. In the zero-sum universe, my job is to get others to accept my reality, or—if they won't do that—to at least get out of my way. Either way, I remain alone in my universe. Which can lead me to say things like…

It's a no-brainer.

Let's be realistic.

Get real!

What are you smoking?

Oh, you must have drunk the Kool-Aid.

Let's have an intelligent *conversation…*

In the real world…

Duh!

If you've been at the receiving end of statements like these (and we all have), you know that they probably don't make you want to snuggle up and collaborate with the person uttering them. Probably the opposite.

To break out of my zero-sum universe, I must remember that sometimes my own perceptions are simply *my own* perceptions. And others' perceptions may be equally or even more valid, even if they're very, very different. I need to leave my zero-sum universe and shift into what philosophers and scientists now dub the "Multiverse."

In the Multiverse, my way of looking at things is only *my way* of looking at them, and there are many other legitimate ways of looking, each with its strengths and weaknesses. In the left-hand column below are things I might say in the zero-sum Universe, while the right-hand column reflects what I might say when I'm living in a Multiverse...

In the Zero-Sum Universe	In the Multiverse
Who's got it right? (and Who's got it wrong?)	*Let's explore how things are showing up for each of us...*
Look, facts are facts, and the facts speak for themselves...	*What are other potential data that we may not be looking at, or different ways of organizing or interpreting this data?*
What's really going on?	*What are the possibilities we can consider or invent to solve this problem or design a workable approach?*
What's the right thing to do?	*Which direction makes most sense to us, given what we currently think we know and assume to be true?*
Here's how things are...	*Here's how I see things. How do you see things?*
In what universe do you think that could actually work?!?	*Wow, that isn't the way I see things at all—let me try to understand what you're seeing, that I may be missing...*
Let's get real!	*Which interpretation do we want to guide us in making this decision?*
Duh!	*Hmmm...*

In the Multiverse, some assertions may be accepted as fact by everyone around us, while others may not be, no matter how obvious they appear to us. Although we still might not always enjoy having our basic perceptions challenged, when we're living in the Multiverse, we'll at least find it more tolerable. And we'll certainly be better poised to learn, be influenced, and collaborate with folks who come from very different places in the Multiverse.

Recognizing that our own perceptions may be part fact and part *possibility* changes the tenor of our conversations. It allows us to shift our attention away from a relentless focus on *what's real and what's right*, towards *how might we choose to relate to things, given the fundamental uncertainty and lack of complete information to which we are all subject*? It gives priority to the question "what might work," over "who's got it right."

Now, if all of this leaves you with the disquieting feeling that there is nothing solid under our feet, that we can't even be certain about those things we call facts, that we can't know for sure what's real and what isn't—you won't be alone. I won't try to minimize or sugar-coat this feeling. But I will say that when people begin engaging with others from the Multiverse (that is, more curious, open-minded and respectful of differences), this discomfort quickly dissipates and gives way to new energy, creativity, and a more light-hearted way of working together.

Another observation is that, while certainty and solidity may feel more familiar and comfortable, it can also make us feel more anxious and defensive, because at any moment that certainty could be challenged, that solidity questioned. So, perhaps it's a trade-off: Give up our sense of certainty and the need to defend it, in exchange for more learning and stronger collaboration.

And just to clarify: Assertions are still critical for us human beings—whether we're collaborating in an organization or anywhere else. There are still plenty of areas in which our individual perceptual faculties and communal consensus allow us to agree. So, we should still hold ourselves to the standard of providing evidence that other observers could observe and accept as valid when we make assertions. And when that's not possible we might do well to treat those less solid assertions more as hypotheses—as *possibly true* statements that may need more time and examination to evaluate. Or, simply as opportunities to decide together what we'll agree and act upon.

Before we leave this theme, I want to point out that acknowledging the inherent uncertainty of things is itself a meta-move which brings us into a larger perspective. When we make this meta-move with our colleagues, it can allow everybody to lighten up a little and not feel quite so compelled to identify with or defend their positions. It can open up the doors to curiosity and inquiry, which is a lot more productive and also a lot more fun to be part of.

Reflection and Practice – Listening to Reality, Part 1

1. *Over the next few days, see if you can notice when people (including yourself) make comments that imply—directly or indirectly—that their (or your) way of seeing things is obvious, which suggests that any other ways of seeing things are inferior or otherwise questionable. Listen for comments like those shown earlier in this chapter, like "Duh,", or "Let's get real," and so forth.* You don't need to do anything when you hear these comments, just notice it, and see how you think the comments influence the conversation and/or relationship.

2. *When you find yourself making comments like this yourself, reflect on your intention when doing so.* Are you feeling impatient with the conversation and trying to speed things up? Are you frustrated with the perspective(s) being voiced by others and trying to "correct" those perspectives? Are you trying to get the others to come around to your way of seeing things? Are you feeling as if your success, well-being or reputations are somehow threatened?

3. *What might be an alternative way of challenging differing perspectives (instead of those zero-sum kinds of comments) that could foster more open and reflective conversations?* For instance, if your intent is to refocus or end the conversation, what's another way of doing that which is more direct and respectful of differences, and more likely to build trust (and less likely to feel manipulative or condescending to others)?

Chapter 12

Listening: The Art of Connecting and Inventing

Whenever organizational performance is suffering, weak listening is usually a factor, whether it's chronic under-achievement, acute operational inefficiencies or major business failures. In organizations, few things are as pervasive as weak listening, and few things can feel so refreshing and profound as encountering a really good listener.

Most business meetings are designed around speaking: disseminating information, "reporting out," presenting, advocating, updating, informing. We plan the topics, determine who the speakers will be, and then often run meetings as mostly one-way streams of information. Although presenters routinely tell us that "this will be a conversation, not a presentation," it hardly ever is. And then, when folks sitting around the table start checking their devices, looking out the window, or just not "getting it," presenters get frustrated. Why aren't people engaged? Why aren't they more open-minded? Why so closed to what I have to say? Why aren't they more collaborative?

It doesn't help that we worship eloquence and good speaking. We read books about the presentation secrets of Steve Jobs, attend Toastmasters, and study TED Talk pointers to improve our speaking skills. It's as if the secret key to leadership performance is speaking, telling, presenting, informing: As if, were we to speak clearly enough, eloquently enough, cleverly enough, or passionately enough, people will surely *get it* and good performance will ensue. This is probably not a new thing: In the first century, A.D., the Greek philosopher Epictetus was likely observing something similar when he said, "We have two ears and one mouth so that we can listen twice as much as we speak."

Mesmerized by the act of speaking, we often forget about the action at the other end. We forget that listening is what gives meaning to speaking and opens the door to Full Contact.

In the last chapter, we examined some of the ways that our perceptual faculties and assumptions may be limited (or even flat-out wrong). Now, we're ready to look at the all-important act of *listening* with new eyes. But before we do this, please do the following:

Read the five statements below, and on a sheet of paper or your device, write down what you think the speaker is communicating in each statement (as if you were reading "between the lines"). What do you think is going on with the speaker that would have them say these things? Keep your notes for later.

That department is only concerned with maintaining its own power.

This company doesn't have a clear vision.

It's easier to just do it myself. Besides, if I don't do it, it won't get done right.

Corporate doesn't understand what folks in the field really need.

Great idea, but we'll never pull it off.

Although we do all sorts of things with words, the words themselves are inherently inert, meaningless. Like inert chemicals, words must be activated—catalyzed—to create a reaction, to exert their influence. Listening is what activates the words that we and others speak. But unlike chemical reactions, listening doesn't activate words in the same way for everyone. We each listen differently, so even when we listen to the very same words spoken by the same person at the same time, those words can be understood very differently by each of us. You've probably left more than one meeting thinking that everyone was on the same page, only to learn later that each person took a different understanding away—as if you had each been in an entirely different meeting. (The Multiverse in full display!)

Receiving Isn't Listening

In his book *The Information*, author James Gleick recounts how in 1948, Claude Shannon, an engineer at Bell Laboratories said that "The fundamental problem of communication is that of reproducing at one point either exactly or approximately a message selected at another point..."

Shannon was defining the "Transmission View" of communication, which is the standard for mechanical or electromagnetic communication: the complete and accurate reception of information at one location that was transmitted from another location. If the information received doesn't match what was transmitted, you'll get incoherent messages, static, or "poor communication."

This standard works well for TV, radio, WiFi and other mechanical signals, but when we apply it to interpersonal human communications we run into trouble. First, this standard would assume that biologically we are all *equally capable* of receiving the original message exactly as it was transmitted—that the intent and meaning of the speaker could and should be understood the same by any listener. Even first graders recognize that this isn't the case—which is why the game of "telephone" is so fun. (The game wouldn't be terribly interesting if the person at the end of the telephone "line" always repeated verbatim what the person at the beginning of the line said.)

Secondly, this "transmission view" presumes that the only standard for effective human communication is accuracy. As if accurately receiving what the speaker "transmits" were all that mattered. But this presumption leaves out what are probably the most salient features of human communication, such as emotional connection and impact, conveying subtlety and ambiguity, and the acts of creation and invention. This presumption, as the last chapter suggested, is also at the heart or many collaboration breakdowns.

> *If good listening was about exactly reproducing*
> *the information transmitted by the speaker, life*
> *might be simpler—but it may not be particularly*
> *interesting or fulfilling.*

The transmission metaphor for human communication obscures what really happens when we speak and listen to one another. We humans are much more than transmitting and receiving devices, and listening is more than simply a passive or technical activity. Listening is a lot more than simply hearing.

Hearing and Listening

Hearing is largely biomechanical; it just happens to us. It happens when sound vibrations—fluctuating waves of pressure passing through the atmosphere—lap up against our eardrums. These vibrations set up oscillations in the eardrum, or *tympanic membrane*, which are then amplified by tiny bones in the inner ear, called *ossicles*. The amplified sound then travels through the fluid of the inner ear, to eventually be converted to electrical impulses bound for the brain.

Although we hear sounds all the time, we only register a very small percentage of them (part of Ornstein's "sliver" of reality). Our auditory system has a built-in filter that helps keep most of the random sounds reaching our ears from intruding on our awareness, unless the sounds are particularly novel or they conform to patterns that we associate with danger, alarm, delight or opportunity.

The sudden loud noise that startles us out of a daydream or stands out from the rest of the noises in a busy restaurant, sets off a chain of physiological reactions. Researchers call it a "bottom-up" response: In just fractions of a second, that noise travels through neurons from our ears to our brain stem and suddenly our heart speeds up, our breathing quickens, our shoulders may tense up and we instinctively glance around to identity the threat that may be heading our way. Or our body may habitually thrill to the delightful sound of our close friend walking in the door.

Up to this point, our human hearing process is similar to that of most other vertebrates (with the possible exception of those vertebrates that don't delight in *any* human being approaching them). And it mostly happens in the background, before we're even aware of it. If our biomechanics are functioning normally, the sound waves a speaker produces when speaking will be more or less "accurately" received by us. This biomechanical process is what allows us to know that we are all hearing the same piece of music, the same commands from the airline flight attendant, or the same speech by the CEO. So far, the process is pretty routine. Beyond this point things get more interesting — and much less predictable. This is where we move from the biomechanics of *hearing* to the much more variable process of *listening*.

Listening is what we do when we make sense of what we hear. It involves a different, "top-down" biological response that involves the meaning-making part of our brain, the cortex. It's how we convert the sounds we hear into personal meaning and significance. *Listening is the act of interpreting what we hear.*

We all know that in conversation, listening goes well beyond the words we hear. We also "listen" to tone of voice, to what is often referred to as *body language,* and to what we believe the speaker may be saying *between the lines, as you did in the exercise above.* We are constantly interpreting, creating meaning of it all. We do this whether we're listening to spoken words, to written words (as in reading), or to no words at all, as when we listen to silence, or when static obscures the speaker's words. We listen to what is said as well as to what is unsaid — to what may be unspoken but implied.

Listening takes place in the darkness and silence within our skull. And, although sounds are heard in the present moment, listening doesn't confine itself to this moment in time: We may still be "listening" to conversations we had hours, months or years ago, replaying them, retelling the story from interactions and experiences long since passed. In fact, we don't really need anyone else to speak a word to us— we can and do listen to ourselves, being our own audience, listening to our own words, thoughts and feelings, along with our bodily sensations.

The Action in Listening

To paraphrase Gottshall, speakers (similar to writers) do the easy part—tricking listeners into doing the heavy lifting, the imaginative work. As listeners, we are never passive recipients of information. Although we hear and listen to the speaker's words, our own minds supply most of the information in the scene—most of the color, shading, and texture. The speaker may provide the basic scaffolding of the story, but the rest is up to us, as listener.

Whenever we're listening, whether to someone else or to ourselves, we are taking action—our bodies and our minds are hard at work filtering, decoding, associating, embellishing, orienting ourselves within the stream of input coming our way, making sense of it all. Listening is at least as active as speaking— and possibly much more so.

You may have taken a workshop or read about "active listening." Active listening often includes practices like paying full attention to the speaker and the meaning she's trying to convey, making good eye contact, paraphrasing and reflecting back what the speaker is saying, using words and gestures to convey interest in the speaker, and so forth. These practices can definitely help us listen better since, as the saying goes, *message sent isn't necessarily message received.*

But even with active listening, it's still often assumed that the speaker's meaning and intent is fully and clearly embedded within the speaker's message and the listener just needs to *receive* it correctly. We can "actively listen" and still be operating within the "transmission" view of human communication. But when we do that, we are missing a huge opportunity. Instead of simply actively listening to someone, what if we asked ourselves what we could actively be listening *for*?

We can start by actively listening for some of the speech acts we've already covered, and build from there. We can listen for...

<u>The action the speaker is taking</u>. Are they making an *assertion*? A *declaration*, a *request, or an offer*? Or might they be attempting to renegotiate a *promise* we made earlier? It's going to be one or a combination of these speech acts.

<u>The stories the speaker may be telling himself</u>. This includes the assessments and interpretations they have about themselves, their circumstances, their possibilities or limitations. It also can include stories the speaker may have about us as listeners, and why they are even having this conversation with us in the first place. Paying attention to and checking out our interpretations about their stories (*our stories about their stories*) can help us better understand the next item...

<u>The context in which the communication is taking place</u>. How do the circumstances and background assumptions we might share (or not share) be shaping the meaning and action the speaker is conveying? The context of the conversation is what we use to listen to what's <u>not</u> said as well as to what is said; the context "fills in" the space around the words so that we can make sense of the whole communication, not just the discrete parts. Without context, many communications would be far messier or even entirely nonsensical (more on context in Part II).

<u>The mood of the conversation</u>. What is the speaker's *emotional state*, and what is mine as listener? If I think the speaker is speaking from a strong emotion, how might that influence the way his world appears to him? And how might my own emotions be shaping how I'm listening (which could, in turn, influence him)?

<u>The speaker's concerns</u>. What are the concerns, interests, or needs that are leading the speaker to say what she's saying in the way she's saying it? What is it that she cares about—what outcome or future might she be envisioning or seeking to create through her speaking?

<u>What their body may be telling us.</u> Some believe that a skilled observer can discern "what's really going on" with anybody just by interpreting their body language. I don't think it's as clear cut as that. I think that we each express our thoughts and feelings in different ways, and with differently conditioned bodily patterns. What's most important is that we pay attention to *how we are listening* to what they're doing with their body, and remembering that again, this is always *our interpretation*, and is not necessarily an accurate reflection of what's going on with the speaker or what they may be trying to communicate.

<u>What *our* body may be telling us</u>. I may experience sensations in my body during a conversation, and those sensations could easily influence how I'm listening. As we've already seen, our body is always present—even when our thoughts are a million miles away. There is a lot we can learn by tuning in to the sensations of our own body, which may help us to be better listeners. But as we've also seen, our sensations can also lead us astray (like those pilots who are confident they're flying straight and level but might actually be in a nose dive). Unless I recognize them for what they are—sensations in my own

body—I might be tempted to treat them as accurate reflections of the speaker, which could seriously hamper my listening and limit our communication.

Possible actions I might take. When someone speaks to us, they are often doing so in order to generate some action on our part. This action could prompt positive or negative assessments about what they're saying to us (as in validating, empathizing or challenging what they say). Or their speaking could stimulate a specific emotion that spurs us to take new action. It could lead us to make or accept a request or offer... or other possible actions. What is the *action* they may be seeking from me? What actions am I inclined to take as a result of what they're saying? It depends upon how I am listening to what they're saying.

Possibilities for the future. What am I listening to that may open up some new idea or possibility for their future, for my future or for our shared future? Sometimes, these possibilities may seem to flow directly from the speaker's words, but not always. As listeners, we can also invent entirely new possibilities through our listening. We don't always have to limit our listening to what the speaker may be saying or trying to say—sometimes, our imaginations are just sparked and our creativity engaged in ways that are only marginally related to what they're saying. Sometimes, new possibilities can be an invaluable thing to listen for, both for ourselves and the speaker.

That's a lot of things to listen for! But don't worry, you don't need to strain to listen for all these things in every conversation— that would be distracting. Just knowing what you *can* listen for and practicing some of them will already expand your listening repertoire and listening skills. If you just choose *one or two things* from the above list to practice listening for in your next conversation (or perhaps for the next week or so), you'll find that you'll be noticing more about those conversations, and probably more about yourself than you might otherwise notice.

And remember: our answer to "what am I listening for" in any conversation is always an interpretation—which we can usually check out with the speaker (which is actually one of the best ways to instantly become a better listener).

Managing the Gap

The Transmission model doesn't apply well to human listening because we don't have the biological "equipment" to faithfully and consistently receive—without distortion, bias or interpretation—what another human being is telling us. Our listening is always and inevitably an interpretation. There is always a *gap* between what a speaker says and what a listener understands.

Much of the time this gap between speaking and listening doesn't matter much. For most everyday interactions, our interpretations of each other's speaking are close enough for jazz, close enough to coordinate and get things done together pretty well. You don't necessarily need to share the exact same interpretation as your boss to know how to complete the project she's asking you to work on.

Problems arise when what we are interpreting is very different from what the speaker intends to convey—and we don't know it and don't think to check it out. This can happen when we've been working with someone for many years, but it happens more frequently when we're collaborating with folks we don't know very well, when the things we're talking about are complex, abstract or nuanced, or when we're feeling pressure to get things done *now*. These are the times when we need to slow things down and *check our listening*—either by sharing our interpretations of what the other is saying and asking for validation, or simply by asking them to restate or clarify what they're saying so that we might adjust our interpretation.

Muffling My Own Listening

When we listen to some people, the rapport we feel with them effortlessly invokes our best listening. But we don't always get to choose the people we must listen to, and sometimes listening well can be hard work.

Here are some of the things we might find ourselves doing that can hinder our listening...

- Listening only to our own words—our own stories, assessments, ideas, instead of the speaker. It's important to notice our own listening, but that can't be our sole focus, or we won't actually be listening to anybody else.
- Assuming that we've heard or already know everything the speaker may have to say.
- Getting stuck in *past* assessments about the speaker, so that we aren't available to what they may be saying right now. People and their views can change.
- Listening to solve, fix or remove discomfort. Solving problems, fixing things that may be broken and helping people deal with their discomfort are expressions of our care and compassion. But even when our intentions are good, listening in these ways can keep us from listening to what they may be trying to communicate to us. And it may not always be what the speaker is looking for or desires in the conversation.
- Listening from impatience ("I really don't have time for this."). As Fran Lebowitz quipped, "For many, the opposite of talking isn't listening. It's waiting." As in waiting until it's my turn to speak. Or waiting until we can get on to the next topic or the next meeting.
- Doing all the right things. Even if you are doing all the things you learned in the last book you read or workshop you attended, this isn't necessarily good listening—it could be just applying techniques, which is often experienced

by others as mechanical, insincere or manipulative. (This is one way that the "right moves" can produce the wrong outcomes.) That's not the same as being present, curious and receptive, even if you aren't doing all those right things.

- Getting ensnared in *the way they're making the point* (judging their choice of words, examples, or style of speaking), rather than listening for *the point itself*.
- Being so absorbed in your stories, feelings or bodily sensations that you're just not fully present with the other person(s). Important note: This is NOT the same as paying attention to your stories, feelings or bodily sensations as you are listening while still being present. When we're *totally* absorbed in our own experience, we can't really make meaningful contact with anyone else because we're just not fully there with them. We do need to be present to our own experience, but not blinded or fixated on it.

This is just the short list of things that can get in the way of our listening, but hopefully you get my point (even if you don't like the way I just made it).

When Listening Is Good

Few people would dispute that good listening is worthwhile, even if they don't always know how to do it.

Good listening can transform interactions and relationships. It creates space for the speaker to say things they might not have said or even thought to themselves. In the hands (and cerebral cortex) of a good listener, the speaker may move through challenges, resolve internal conflicts, think freshly about problems, and see new possibilities. Good listening can change the speaker as much as good speaking can change the listener.

In addition to the things we can actively listen *for*, there are two basic practices that I find core to good listening: *Quieting ourselves down* and *extending legitimacy.*

Quieting down

First—if you want to listen better you may need to quiet yourself down—attentionally, physically and mentally.

How am I using my attention in this conversation or meeting? Am I splitting my attention between the conversation, my email, my twitter feed? Am I so engrossed in what the speaker is saying or doing that I've lost touch with how I'm actually listening to her—how I'm interpreting her communication, how I'm feeling or what's going on in my body? Am I so focused on how the speaker is saying what they're saying that I may be missing what they want me to understand? Noticing how I'm using my attention right here in the present moment gives me the ability to use my attention more skillfully. Hitting the internal Pause button gives us an opportunity to check in with ourselves and get more present.

Physically, quieting the body means calming the nervous system so it isn't overly wound up or reactive. Especially when the topic of conversation, the setting, or the speaker is challenging for us, it helps to tune in (with our attention) to the sensations in the body and release whatever tension or constriction we notice. Grounding and centering ourselves (which is covered in Part III), allows us to feel our connection to ourselves and to the ground under our seats or under our feet—which also lets us feel more secure and stable—less prone to losing our cool and getting distracted. This translates into a more open and receptive presence that can better handle whatever the speaker may be saying. Because our body and mind are interconnected, when we calm our body, our mind also begins to quiet down.

Shifting our attention to our thought processes—to our assumptions, assessments, stories or images helps us to be less swayed or carried away by them (which could easily separate us from the speaker and weaken our contact with them).

Again, to quiet ourselves down, we use our attention— directing it to our bodies, to our mental activity, or to our attention itself. We may have to do this many times during a single conversation, alternating our attention between the speaker and ourselves. As we'll discuss more in later chapters, this practice of attending to our own experience doesn't cut ourselves off from the speaker but can instead do just the opposite—it can allow us to engage with them in a more receptive and less habitual way, without all the automatic reactivity that can cloud our listening. We're talking about bringing ourselves into greater contact with ourselves, so that we are able to make contact with the other person or people we're listening to.

Just focusing on quieting yourself down will probably greatly enhance your listening. It can also pave the way for the next listening practice that can be even more transformative.

Extending Legitimacy
Extending legitimacy is engaging with another person from the understanding that he is a legitimate and well-intended human being, regardless of his views, feelings or concerns—even if we strongly disagree with them or find them upsetting. It's about treating him as a worthy person.

This notion really troubles some people. How can you extend legitimacy to someone whose views or values may be completely counter to your own, or who might have little interest in your own views or values, your success or well-being? And why would you even *want* to do that?

I'll address the *Why* question, but before that I want to say that *you absolutely don't have to extend legitimacy towards anyone;*

it's entirely up to you. In my experience, there are real life consequences either way, both for others and for ourselves. The consequences have to do with: a) our built-in connectedness with others, b) our collaborative capacity; and c) our own well-being. Because we're connected, our assessments and feelings towards them will influence our interactions with them, even if we never voice those assessments and feelings out loud. If the other person is not worthy of understanding in our eyes, it will shape the way we speak to them, the things about them we pay attention to, and the way we listen to them.

If I'm convinced that Michael is a superficial jerk with nothing valuable to say (a characterization), it will be very hard for him to overcome this "jerk-ness" in my eyes. In fact, because of my bias towards him, he'll probably be even more of a jerk by the end of the conversation than when we started regardless of what he may actually say or do. Because his "jerk-ness" *lives in me* (in my assessment), not in him, I'll be filtering everything he says or does through my assessment and belief about him. And I'll design my conversational strategies accordingly, which will probably involve trying to either avoid him, shut him down, or try to get him to say or do things that I want. I may try to come on softly so as not to raise his alarm bells; I may ask leading questions to get him to where I want him; or I may take a confrontational approach and use intellectual or even physical intimidation, making veiled or explicit threats to get him to cooperate... or a thousand other variations on these themes. But, even if I get him to say *Yes*, it will likely be a short-term win. We won't have strengthened our contact—we'll have weakened it.

Few things will shut down conversation and collaboration quicker than withholding legitimacy—even if we never come out and admit that we don't see the other as legitimate. We can smile and pretend that we're supportive, but internally, we'll be shut down, which will likely shut them down. Withholding legitimacy won't position us to make better decisions, and it won't build trust or stronger commitment. Just the opposite.

Those are the transactional reasons why we might want to extend legitimacy, but there are other reasons why extending legitimacy may be a good thing, and they transcend any potential business benefit: *It's a good thing because it shapes the world we live in.*

Extending legitimacy—holding the other as valid and worthy regardless of their views, values, likes or dislikes—is something *we do*. It's an action we take; an assessment, a declaration we are making about the other person. As we know, our assessments are always more "about" us than they are about that or whom we're assessing. What this means on a personal level is that the more we negatively assess others, the more negative becomes our own world.

The story we tell ourselves about our world and the people in it are also the words that define us and our own lives. Our assessments live in us and are embodied in our neurons. They form the lens through which we see and experience the world, and they express themselves through our actions. When I'm delegitimizing people around me because I see things differently, don't agree with them or feel annoyed or threatened by them (the latter being the usual driver for delegitimizing others), those assessments aren't only defining who *they* are to me— those assessments are also defining who *I* am to me. Personally, I know that when I delegitimize someone else—even if doing so validates my righteous indignation in the moment, it doesn't make me a happier, healthier, more open, or more collaborative person.

We each live in the world of our own actions; we sleep in the linguistic bed that we make.

When I delegitimize someone else, that act of delegitimizing is taking place inside of me, too.

The dividing line between what happens *out there* and our experience of it *in here* could well be illusory. We can't really separate ourselves from our environment or the people around us. We can't identify ourselves as separate and distinct individuals without reference to the reactions and assessments we experience towards and from others. We are inextricably bound together, connected to the people in our lives.

Living in a world populated by "illegitimate others" is not working for us as individuals or as a society. Perhaps it never has, but these days, the consequences of relating to each other this way are threatening our very co-existence, in addition to our personal happiness and well-being.

When we delegitimize those with different views, values or morals, we're just a short step away from dehumanizing them, which enables us to justify almost any behavior we might inflict upon them in the defense of our own views. At the very least, it makes real collaboration impossible.

Extending legitimacy is a necessary condition for Full Contact Performance. Apart from the larger ethical implications, extending legitimacy allows us to listen to, learn and collaborate with people who may be very different from us.

If you still don't see a good reason to extend legitimacy, no problem. Instead of trying to force it, I encourage you to pay close attention to yourself the next time you find yourself in a challenging collaboration, sitting across from "that jerk" in the meeting. See if you can notice how your negative assessments may be "acting" not only upon them, but also upon you. What do you notice about your mood? Your body? Your sense of possibility and curiosity? Just this simple act of noticing may give you more choice in how you are engaging with this person.

Because it's so central to effective collaboration, we'll be looking more closely at how to extend legitimacy in Part III.

Imagining and Inventing

There is no right way to listen. Different ways of listening generate different relationships, different possibilities, different actions and different futures.

Good listeners are like artisans: They approach the speaker the way a sculptor approaches a raw piece of wood or a marble slab—with openness and curiosity. This lets them be fully present and open to what may happen next. Extending legitimacy towards their subject, they know how to be quiet and let things unfold. With their imagination, good listeners simultaneously invent what the speaker may be trying to convey, while also being shaped by it. They are continually constructing new possibilities out of the raw material of the speaker's words, body, emotions, actions and more. While they've likely practiced specific skills to become good listeners, they also know that ultimately, listening is an act of *imagination* and *invention* (and an act of checking their listening with the speaker).

Reflection & Practice – Listening, Part 2

In a moment I'll ask you to return to those five statements you reflected on at the beginning of this chapter. As before, you'll write down what you think the speaker may be saying, but now I'd like you to use some of the listening distinctions we've just covered, including...

- Actions
- Meaning
- The story the speaker may be speaking from or speaking to
- Context

- Mood or Emotion
- Their concerns
- Their body and your body
- Possible actions you might take
- Possibilities for the future

1. *As you read each of the statements below, choose two or three of the above bullet points to "listen for" in each statement.* Don't write a thesis on each one—just a sentence or two to help you practice using these distinctions in your listening. The point here isn't to "get it right," but to practice stretching your conception of what listening can be, which includes imagining and inventing...
   1. *That department is only concerned with maintaining its own power.*
   2. *This company doesn't have a clear vision.*
   3. *It's easier to just do it myself. Besides, if I don't do it, it won't get done right.*
   4. *Corporate doesn't understand what folks in the field really need.*
   5. *Great idea, but we'll never pull it off.*

You may have noticed that your "listening" to the same statements this time around has expanded. With practice and attention to how you're listening and what you're listening *for*, you'll start to notice your listening improving, along with your conversations.

Part II

The Three Conversations

In the previous section we looked at our attention, our words and our bodies—the three domains of action and experience we're engaged in whenever we're in conversation with others.

In this section, we'll look at the main types of conversations we use to collaborate in organizations. Coincidentally, there are also three: Learning Conversations, Design Conversations and Fulfillment Conversations. Each of these types of conversation has a different focus, and often a different mood as well.

Occasionally these three types of conversations proceed in a linear order: first we learn together, then we design our goals, strategy, plans, metrics, problems (or whatever it is we're designing)—then we fulfill the promises to bring to life what we've designed. But much of the time, these three types of conversation don't flow in a neat and tidy order. We may circle through and between these types of conversations many times and in different order throughout any collaboration.

Also, the lines that separate these three types of conversation can often be blurry. We might be having a Design conversation, and then realize that we're not actually clear about the facts (assertions) upon which we're basing a particular decision, or we might each have very different interpretations about those facts, which is making it difficult to arrive at (design) a shared decision or course of action. Realizing this, we could seamlessly shift gears into a Learning conversation, returning later to the Design conversation once we're all ready.

Or, we could be deep in a Fulfillment conversation, negotiating an important promise, when we realize that we're not actually clear about how fulfilling this promise might inadvertently jeopardize some other promises already underway. When this happens, we might need to shift back into a Design conversation — or even a Learning conversation — to gain more clarity.

The next three chapters will focus on each of these types of conversation. As with everything else we've looked at to this point, the more familiar you become with each of them, the better equipped you'll be to *know what you are doing* — to notice which type of conversation you might be having in the moment and to make course corrections when needed.

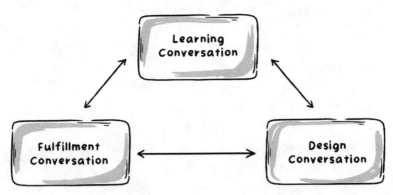

The three conversations of collaboration

Chapter 13

The Learning Conversation

The Learning conversation is where we help each other to perceive and think together in new ways by sharing and listening to how the world is appearing to each of us. This conversation paves the way to better decisions and commitments (via Design and Fulfillment conversations).

When teams or executives ask me to help them improve their collaborative performance, the two most common concerns they mention are *decision-making* and *accountability*. It may take too long for teams to arrive at firm decisions (due to analysis-paralysis, because they strive to achieve consensus at all costs, or the conversations just aren't very constructive, so they never get onto the same page together), or people don't deliver on what they said they would deliver (and nobody holds each other accountable). Or all the above.

Sometimes important decisions really do require more time. And not every promise can always be kept, even with the best intentions. But much of the time, what I find is that both ongoing decision-making and accountability challenges are symptomatic of something else: Learning conversations that were either incomplete, poorly managed or missing entirely.

Making decisions and then acting on those decisions appears to be what business is about, so that's where most people focus their attention. What isn't so evident, though, is what it takes to arrive at well-informed decisions and to commit to meaningful promises. What it takes is good Learning conversations. And they are a rarity in many organizations.

This was also true in "Care Doesn't Care" example: Folks on both sides—the regional sales team and the customer success folks, each were confident that their view was the only valid way of seeing things, and that the other folks were simply blind to "how things really are." This belief—this confidence in their own views kept them from asking questions (except for rhetorical questions, the kind that are actually thinly-veiled accusations or traps) and earnestly seeking out the others' perspectives. Until we hit Pause and set a new conversational context for the group to begin working in together, no learning was taking place, only greater and greater polarization.

When you believe you already know everything there is to know about this person, group or situation—or that the other folks on the team already know how you see things, then taking the time to have a good Learning conversation feels like a waste of precious time. But short-circuiting the learning process ends up being much more wasteful.

This is a lesson that Martin, longtime CEO of a regional healthcare company, learned the hard way.

The company had been struggling for several years to adapt to changes in the healthcare industry, and things had finally started to turn around. New member enrollments were going up, member satisfaction rates were rising, and relationships with the company's medical providers were starting to improve after years of mutual frustration and distrust. All signs were pointing to a solid turnaround. Even Martin's relationship with his board was better than ever—or so he thought. He'd known many of the board members for years, and they'd seemed supportive while he'd been focused on turning the company around.

As Martin later realized, while he was focused on "running the business," he'd put his relationship with the board on autopilot. Whereas he used to take the time to reach out to every board member frequently and ensure time in board meeting agendas to reflect together on high-level strategic issues, over the past year or so he'd just assumed that he and the board were still in lockstep, so he focused his attention elsewhere. He continued to handle his required board functions—preparing monthly reports, agendas and so forth, but that was about it. Reflecting later, he realized that board members had been raising concerns about the longer-term viability of the company for a while, but he hadn't really taken it in. They'd expressed concern that the company would be unable to compete in coming years as larger players continued to consolidate their dominance in the market and smaller companies were being acquired or just folding. Martin could have been more involved in these conversations (and should have taken a leadership role in them), but his attention remained on the immediate business problems in front of him—and setting more ambitious goals and driving executive action.

By the time Martin learned just how concerned the board was, it was too late. Two days after reporting to the board on the recent successes his leadership team had realized over the past quarter, the board called a special meeting in which they voiced their appreciation for all the great work he'd done to turn the business around... and that they sincerely hoped that he would be willing to help oversee the wind-down of the business. Martin was shocked not only by the decision itself (he felt strongly that there were other viable options available to the organization), but even more by the fact that he hadn't seen it coming—that he had missed the opportunity to learn from the board and also to educate the board about the possibilities he saw, until it was too late.

Now, you might have valid assessments about the behavior of the board, or you might say that Martin had been blind to the larger trends shaping the healthcare industry, but my point with this true story is that Learning conversations didn't happen with Martin and his board. A well-managed Learning conversation could have certainly eliminated the surprise factor for Martin, and might even have changed the direction of the organization.

We know we can't pay equal attention to everything; we can't eliminate all our blind spots, and we all get lost at times. But when we're able to learn with the people around us, we can help each other to see things we'd otherwise miss and respond more quickly and skillfully to shifting circumstances.

Learning conversations are where we compare our assertions and assessments, where we listen to understand and to invent meaning, and where we design new stories and possibilities for the future together. This isn't just some feel-good, new-age idea. We simply can't navigate the complexities and challenges of organizational performance alone, no matter how smart, perceptive or experienced we each may be. If we want to perform well together, we must get good at learning together.

Good Learning conversations don't require that everyone agrees about everything or see things the same way. They involve something of the opposite: they involve drawing out and highlighting your differences, trying on and exploring alternative perspectives to see what they might reveal and how they might expand your possibilities. (Later on, in the Design conversation, you can decide what you do need to agree on and what you don't, and what decisions you need to make together to move forward.)

For Learning conversations to be fruitful, folks need to feel safe challenging each other's thinking; inviting and exploring dissenting views and doing so in ways that continually build trust and make it easy for folks to differ and debate without feeling the need to defend their views or to always be right.

Tolerating Differences

It's common for people to feel uncomfortable or threatened when differences arise in the course of important conversations. Different perspectives and opinions, different values — especially when they're strongly held or strongly expressed — often generate strong emotions and similarly strong habitual reactions. This is the biggest challenge in Learning conversations.

Most folks know intellectually that diversity is a good thing — but the actual experience of voicing and listening to differences and tolerating the emotions and bodily sensations triggered by those differences can be difficult and, at times, even intolerable.

Because we tend to identify our thoughts and feelings with *who we are,* when someone challenges those thoughts and feelings, it can feel like a personal threat — like they're literally challenging our very being.

If we're not able to manage those powerful feelings and sensations, we'll probably act in ways that seek to minimize them or suppress them. Conversationally this may look like changing the topic abruptly, rushing to presumed agreement, cheerleading and happy talk, tossing out thinly veiled barbs at others, going silent and withdrawing, or many other reactions. Whatever form it takes, when we don't deal with our physical and emotional discomfort directly, it will usually have a chilling effect on the conversation. Because your capacity to tolerate differences and strong emotions directly impacts the quality of your Learning conversations, I provide some suggestions for doing this below. (More in-depth practices are also described in Part III.)

Managing the Conversation

Along with attending to the emotions and the body, you'll want to think about the flow of the Learning conversation. This entails designing the agenda, and then managing the agenda with flexibility as the conversation unfolds. Here are three things in particular to think about:

Give it enough time. This the hardest thing for most people in any organization, especially when they're used to just *getting on with it* — on with the next item on the agenda, the next meeting, the next decision, conclusion or takeaway. Giving it time is also hard when folks feel uncomfortable with the collaborative learning process itself, particularly the uncertainty and ambiguity that goes along with it, or the conflict and disagreement that may (and hopefully will) surface.

Many people believe that the goal of every conversation is a "takeaway." The takeaway may be a specific strategy, project or tactic, or a perhaps a definitive answer, agreement or decision, or a neatly wrapped morsel of information. Those may each be valuable at times, but they're not valuable all the time, and not in every conversation. Sometimes rushing to the takeaway short-circuits critical learning, making it impossible for the group to coalesce around a shared story or assessment that may be important. Driving every conversation to a takeaway can slow down and weaken a Learning conversation — all in the guise of "efficiency."

If you want to have a productive Learning conversation, you'll need to give it the time it needs, and you can't always predict how long that will take. Everybody has their own styles and pace of learning and even if some people seem to "get it" before others, if you rush those others, your collaboration and performance will pay a price.

Frequently remind folks that some discomfort is common in these conversations. Discomfort is not necessarily an indicator that things are going poorly; sometimes it can mean that things are going *very* well—that people are examining their blind spots, challenging their thinking, questioning their habitual assumptions. Unless it's intolerable or folks are clamming up or treating each other poorly, encourage them to stay with it and keep the learning going.

Identify the different themes that folks are talking about and see if you can tackle each one separately before attempting to package it all back together and move on. This may allow you to give each theme the time, reflection and research it may need— without which the learning may remain superficial and incomplete. This is often where you may enter into one or more Fulfillment conversations in which specific individuals promise to do additional research or analysis or have other critical conversations that can be brought back to the larger group to deepen the learning.

Learning conversations can inspire and enliven folks. But they can also be demanding. You don't always have to drive every Learning conversation to completion right then and there. Along with giving yourselves the time and additional research you may need, pay attention to when the conversation (and the group) may have reached its natural completion point for the time being. Take breaks, agree to switch topics when needed, allot time for folks to further reflect on their own or in smaller groups, or just come back to the conversation another day when things are fresh.

More Question Marks, Fewer Periods

Our conversations are often heavily weighted towards informing, reporting, advocating, influencing, storytelling, assessing. You've no doubt been in conversations dominated by *telling*. People telling each other what they think, how they feel and what's important to them — probably also telling others what *they* should be thinking, feeling, and what should be important to *them*. I call these *Tell-fests*, and you may have joined in the festivities on occasion. I know I have. And it's rarely helpful.

As the iconoclastic Tibetan lama Chogyam Trungpa Rinpoche said, "When the room is filled with you and your trip, no sensible person wants to go there. Yuck."

Telling is an important part of many conversations, but when we're always filling the conversational space with our own stuff, there's no room for anyone else. There's no room for questions or for learning. Constant telling dams up the conversational flow.

It's easy to get stuck in Tell-fests, but there is a way out and that is to make a meta-move to collaborative inquiry, which helps to clear the logjams and get the energy flowing again.

We usually have too much knowing and telling. What we need is less certainty and more questions.

Collaborative Inquiry

Collaborative Inquiry involves asking more and telling less. And then listening more. This is where Full Contact happens. Without inquiry, our conversations preclude learning and remain only about us and our own trip and, well... *yuck*.

Collaborative Inquiry isn't just a cool concept. It's a mindset and a continual practice.

We make the move to Collaborative Inquiry by asking the people we're collaborating with to share what's on their minds and perhaps in their hearts. But it's not just going through the motions of requesting that they speak honestly; that's easy to do. We must make the move with a curious mind and heart ourselves. We must actually *be* inquisitive if we want to practice inquiry. When our curiosity is genuine, then inquiry is easy and effortless; it flows naturally.

But genuine curiosity is not always so easy to embody. Which is why many people who have taken workshops on active listening or communication often find themselves wondering why their new active listening techniques or communication tactics don't work. It's because it's not about the technique or the "move" itself—it's about *how we are being as we are making the move.*

Again, if we're not feeling truly curious about how our colleagues are thinking or seeing things—or if we're not speaking truthfully ourselves—there's little chance that others will feel encouraged to do so either.

If we try to feign interest, our lack of curiosity will leak out through our posture, gestures, or tone of voice; or through the way we frame our questions, our listening, or our responses to their answers. Instead of encouraging candid disclosure and reflection, our lack of curiosity and interest impedes the learning. We might as well just return to the Tell-fest.

Getting Curious

So, what can you do if you're just not that curious about what others have to say? You can start by getting curious about *you.* Here are a few questions to ask yourself:

Do I really need to collaborate with this person or group to accomplish what I'm trying to accomplish? *If your answer is No, then consider canceling this meeting and make other plans.* I mean it—there may well be times when you just don't want or need to collaborate in order to accomplish your goals, and the best thing you can do is to just call it for what it is. If your answer is *Yes — I think I really do need to collaborate with them to get this done* — then ask yourself the next question...

Do I think there's something that I or others need to learn from each other in order to design and execute well in this collaboration? Do I think there's something else that might be important to know? If you answer *No*, then perhaps you skip the Learning conversation for now and move right into a Design or Fulfillment conversation (you can always return to a Learning conversation later) and see how it goes. If you want to dig a little deeper, ask yourself...

What may be getting in the way of my curiosity? Do I have an assessment or story about this person or team that shuts down my curiosity? Is my mood or are the sensations in my body getting in the way of my open curiosity? Would it help to postpone this conversation until another time? If so, do it. Trying to force a conversation that you can't fully engage in probably won't go well, anyway. (In Part III, we'll explore Extending Legitimacy more closely, to see how to regain a sense of curiosity and interest, when we're just not feeling it.)

These questions are about getting clearer with yourself, which is a prerequisite for being clear with others. Sometimes, just the simple act of checking in with yourself — your own mindset, mood or body — can be enough to let you reconnect with your curiosity.

As a practice, Collaborative Inquiry involves asking questions that encourage reflection, help focus our collective attention, and clarify what we care about and what we're doing together. The questions can help to reveal our unexamined assumptions, expand our collective thinking, and build alignment.

Because the point of Collaborative Inquiry is to learn, we may need to let go of what we think we already know, and even where we think the conversation needs to go. It may mean relinquishing some control over the direction of the conversation. This can feel strange if we're very used to directing and controlling our conversations and it might make you feel vulnerable because the conversation could go... anywhere.

In some organizational settings, particularly those cultures where having answers and being right is treated as your most important contribution, making yourself vulnerable by publicly seeking someone else's answers could feel like the last thing you'd want to do. Especially if you're the boss and people are accustomed to you controlling the conversation. But if your goal is to truly learn about how others are seeing things, then "humbling" yourself and asking open ended questions is what you need to do.

Going through the motions of inquiry doesn't invite real learning or contact. It just drives people further apart by signaling that we're not really so interested in what they have to say.

When the boss or other influential leaders are willing to *not* have all the answers, but instead to humble themselves and be truly curious, it can be extraordinarily energizing and empowering for others. Conversely, if the boss *doesn't* take the lead in open-ended inquiry, it probably won't happen. Instead, folks will take the boss's lead and assume its unsafe or inappropriate to humble themselves as well (the Connection-Reciprocity principle at play). Curiosity will seem too risky — and many people don't want to risk contradicting, offending or making the boss look wrong — or of looking uninformed or clueless in the boss's eyes.

Earlier, I mentioned the practice of "checking the listening." It's worth revisiting it here in a little more detail...

Checking the Listening

Checking the listening entails two questions. The first question is about my own listening: *Let me check my listening… here is what I think you are saying/doing/declaring/concerned about — am I in the ballpark?* (The specific words matter less than the spirit of the question.)

It's a great question to ask whenever you want to be sure that you are "getting" what the other person wants you to get from their speaking. I also sometimes ask this question just to insert a little more space into the conversation, to give us an opportunity to reflect a little more on what we're doing together in this conversation and how it's going.

This question is deeply respectful of the other folks in the room. It gives them a chance to restate what they've said in a different way, to clarify or emphasize a certain point, to ensure that we're going down the same path together. It also reminds us that we are each always limited to our own way of listening, which helps keep us all a little more humble, a little more curious.

The second question is: *How are you listening to what I (or others) are saying?*

Remember that whenever we speak, we are generating listening in others. But we can't always know just how they are listening unless we ask them. In meetings, I like to pause periodically to check in with others' listening, asking how they're making sense of what I'm saying, where things may not seem clear, what my own or others' speaking may be stimulating in them. I need this information if I want to narrow that gap between us — that gap between my speaking and their listening — to ensure that we're learning together.

You may have noticed that both questions about listening are meta-moves. They pull us up out of the content of the conversation, so that we can reflect on how the conversation is going and where it may be taking us.

When Inquiry Isn't Inquisitive

Not all inquiry is truly inquisitive. Sometimes, inquiry may be an expression of some concern or discomfort that the speaker may have that is being indirectly expressed in the form of a question. When this happens, there are rarely satisfactory answers to the question, and the question may simply get repeated frequently, perhaps in different ways. Here is an example from a meeting of mid-level managers who were being briefed by their leaders about an upcoming organizational change initiative...

In the first meeting of a new transformation initiative for the engineering department, Colin, a burly man with a full beard speckled with gray and a warm twinkle in his eye, started right in with his rapid-fire questions. The purpose of the meeting was to inform this team about the need and rationale for the transformation and how they would engage in the process. Colin's questions reflected astute observation and insightful reflections about the proposed change effort. But the questions were also non-stop, and none of the responses his leaders offered seemed to satisfy him.

Thinking that his questions may be reflecting his anxiety more than a need for concrete answers, I decided to test the hypothesis. I reminded everyone in the room that all their questions were welcome and valued, and I created a "Questions" space on the whiteboard wall. I wrote down a couple of the questions Colin and others had already asked, and I then requested that going forward, folks come up to the white board to write each of their questions down. This way, we could be sure to address any questions later that we didn't have time to answer in this meeting.

I commented that feeling anxiety at the prospect of a major change initiative was common, and that not all of their questions had answers at this time; some degree of uncertainty is just built-in to the change process.

Colin enthusiastically endorsed these comments and from that point on, his questions slowed to a trickle. He even began offering supportive comments to others' questions, reminding his colleagues how normal it was to experience anxiety in these kinds of situations! This was a good reminder that not every question requires an immediate answer, and the "answer" to some questions isn't the information the person seems to be asking for, but rather acknowledgement and validation for the concerns and emotions *behind* the question.

Inquiry or Inquisition?

Sometimes our questions are not aimed at learning at all. Some of these can be more like an inquisition than inquiry. I call this *confrontational inquiry*, which is the opposite of Collaborative Inquiry. It's inquiry in form only, because the questions don't seek new information or learning, but confirmation of what the speaker already believes or suspects. Confrontational inquiry can include leading questions, rhetorical questions, questions aimed at informing, embarrassing or trapping, or just demonstrating that the speaker already knows the answers he is purporting to ask for, like an attorney interrogating the opposing witness. The speaker is taking charge of both the content and the process of the conversation. It's a version of a Tell-fest, in the costume of inquiry.

Cultivating Dissent

In many teams and organizations, dissent is verbally encouraged but not actually welcomed when it occurs. Even when it's invited, dissenting views are often treated as negative, uncollaborative, an obstacle to progress, or even disloyal. Some leaders fear that if one person expresses dissent, it will spread like a virus and things will spin out of control.

I find it helpful to remember that the divergent or dissenting views are not the problem—it's the group's (and/or the leader's) response to those views that creates difficulty. If the group or even just the leader responds to dissenting views with genuine interest and curiosity, then the group can take advantage of all its members' thinking and assessments. When divergent views are shut down—even through very subtle body language or indirect comments—then the message to the group is clear: your views are only welcome if they conform to what the rest of the group (or the leaders) think or see. This always has a chilling effect on collaborative learning and performance.

Rather than a problem to eliminate, dissent can be an asset. There are countless examples in which it's been a competitive survival factor (even a human survival factor). Netflix's famous serial pricing and branding gaffes in 2011 cost the company roughly 80% of its stock price within about four months of these decisions. Post-mortems of the decisions, including by Netflix CEO Reed Hastings, concluded that the absence of dissenting views within the company was a big factor in these disastrous decisions. As a result, the Netflix leadership team kicked off a major cultural initiative aimed at ensuring dissenting opinions were sought after and considered before any significant strategic decisions were made.

Inviting and actually working with dissenting views strengthens collective learning and performance. It builds ownership of the conversation and the decisions and strengthens the execution that follows.

Lack of dissent contributed to the dramatic fall of the Swiss watch making industry when Swiss watchmakers failed to accept the dissenting view that the newest digital watch technologies (which they themselves had invented) represented the future of the marketplace. The Japanese watchmakers jumped on the new technologies and quickly rose to dominate the global market, leaving the Swiss watchmakers—who had been the undisputed leaders until then—in the dust. The 1986 NASA Challenger disaster is widely cited as one of the most public—and fatal—examples of decisions and actions that could have been avoided by the active encouragement and exploration of dissenting views. But those are just a couple of huge and very public examples.

The active encouragement and cultivation of dissent as a critical *collaborative practice* is something of a rarity in many organizations. It sounds good on paper (and in corporate value statements), but in real day-to-day conversations dissent is often avoided like the plague.

It's not just that dissent might slow things down or put a kink in someone's best-laid plans. Sometimes, it's that the dissenting views or information don't even register. They fall outside of the normal context in which people are operating (their First Order thinking), so it's difficult to even imagine how such ideas or views could be relevant.

I observed this happen with a group of highly committed leaders of a social nonprofit...

The group had been discussing how to invest their resources in the various programs they'd been running successfully for many years. The conversation had been going on for a few hours and it appeared that consensus might be near. Peter, one of the newer leaders with the organization suddenly raised the question, "I'm not sure we should really be assuming that all these programs actually need to continue, just because we've been running them for years..." There was a moment of silence, a couple of "hmmms," and a "Wow" or two. And then magically, the conversation resumed right where it had left off before Peter had voiced his thought. As if he'd never said a word. This was a group of people deeply committed to consensus and to respecting diversity of all types. It was part of their leadership ethos. Even so, I watched as Peter's expression quickly turned from excitement in sharing his comments, to confusion, and then, over the course of just a minute or so, to resignation. As he was physically starting to disengage from the conversation, I hit Pause and asked the group to share what they noticed about their response to Peter's comments. After an awkward silence, someone mentioned that his comments seemed to have just disappeared, like writing on water. This was followed by embarrassed apologies to Peter, and acknowledgements that, because his views seemed so far out there—and the group had seemed so close to consensus—they just didn't know what to do with his comments. After a few minutes of this "meta-conversation," the group resumed their discussion, incorporating Peter's views into the mix. In the end, they did reach consensus and it included the decision to discontinue two of their eight programs and refocus resources to better support the remaining six programs.

As is so often the case, this group intellectually understood the value of dissent but still had trouble dealing with dissenting comments when they arose. It takes practice to not only value differences, but welcome and engage with them.

Rather than an expression of resistance, contrariness or disloyalty, dissent can often be an expression of caring, concern and commitment. As the above examples (and many more like them) illustrate, dissenting views can often be much more valuable than unexamined agreement and consent. Even if it's coming from a disgruntled place, or not expressed perfectly, dissent can expand our thinking and our learning if we treat it with respect. Without dissenting views, our Learning conversations may be tepid at best.

Another reason dissent is so important has little to do with the *content* of a group's conversation. If team members like Peter have the opportunity to openly question, challenge and disagree with the "common sense" of the team, then free and informed choice is much more likely. Stronger commitment and ownership of the outcome—good or bad—usually follows.

On the other hand, if folks don't feel free that their well-intended dissenting views are welcome or considered, they can easily distance themselves from subsequent decisions and outcomes, as if they belonged to someone else.

Here's a challenge: When you hear a dissenting view, instead of reflexively tightening up, ignoring it, or trying to change the speaker's mind, try shifting into inquiry and ask about it. Get curious about the differences and *mine* those differences like gold for the valuable learning they may bring. (This is what Step 5 of the *Grounding Assessments* process is all about.)

Here are some sample questions that can help to elicit dissenting views (but remember—the questions are meaningless if you aren't asking them with sincere curiosity and a willingness to respect any answer, no matter how different it may be from what you want or expect to hear):

- *What doubts and reservations do you have about the direction or decision we're discussing?*
- *What are we talking about that doesn't make sense to you?*
- *What do you see as potential weaknesses or inconsistencies in our thinking?*
- *If you were in charge, what would you do?*
- *What would be in the way of you fully and enthusiastically committing yourself to what we're talking about?*
- *What are you inclined to say No to in this conversation?*
- *What do you think we may be missing?*

Our difficulty in dealing with dissenting views is much more about us and our own habit patterns, than it is about the person dissenting or their views.

A friend of mine, Peter Kindfield (an educator and former Director of Education for Steve Jobs at Next Computer), uses the term *antagonistic cooperation.* "As participants in living systems," Kindfield say, "it's our role to maintain the delicate balance of life by expressing our antagonistic contributions. It makes no sense for me, the cheerleader, to get angry with you, the naysayer. Imagine the antagonistic muscles that push against each other to keep us each from falling over when we're standing and getting angry with each other. The goal is not to stop bumping up against each other, it's to bump into each other with style and grace." Peter is describing dissent, skillfully managed. He is also describing what Aikidoists practice and aspire to on the mat every day: Moving *towards* the challenge (physical strike, grab or kick) and *joining with it* so that we can safely work with its direction, force, and energy—rather than resisting, blocking or trying to overpower it.

Cultivating Possibilities

The future consists exclusively of possibilities. There's nothing else *there*, except for possibilities that haven't yet been realized. Imagining and exploring what's possible is what we do whenever we assess a gap between where we, our team or organization are today and where we want to be. When we assess a gap between today and where we think the market (or technology, society, etc.) is heading, when we face challenges that we don't know how to approach, when we want to be sure we've explored alternatives before committing to a particular direction, or when we aspire to do something significantly different from what we've seen or done in the past—it's an opportunity to cultivate and examine possibilities.

When we explore possibilities we are challenging our current or habitual thinking in order to explore new territory where different assumptions may present themselves. This type of conversation often starts with questions like, "What if...?" or, "How would it work if...?" or, "What else might be possible here, that we're just not thinking about?"

Brainstorming is what most people think of when it comes to generating possibilities, but it's certainly not the only approach, or always the best. Scenario planning and thought experiments (in which you set up extreme or seemingly impossible goals, policies or constraints, and then explore how they might be realized in perhaps previously unimaginable ways) are other common methods, and there are many more.

Whichever method you use to explore what's possible, be explicit about what you're doing (*We seem to be talking about possibilities, or Let's talk about what might be possible,* and so forth) and what the ground rules for the conversation are so folks know how to engage. This is especially important in cultures where having rational answers and "certainty" is rewarded— and where *not knowing* is avoided or punished. In these cultures, people will be reticent to take the plunge and let go of the known and familiar unless they know it's safe, because truly exploring possibilities can take you out of your familiar comfort zone.

Are We Talking What or How?

Some conversations for possibilities may be focused on the "What" — the future outcome, goal, target condition, or state of the team, company or world. Other conversations may be more focused on the "How" — possible strategies, tactics, mindsets, means, processes to realize or achieve the "What."

Either the *What* or the *How* are fair game for talking about possibilities — but rarely both at the same time. Be explicit about which you're focusing on, and then be rigorous about keeping the focus there until it's time to move on. Bouncing around between *What* and *How* is very common and it rarely yields good results — especially when folks aren't aware that they're doing it. Usually, because many folks have more experience and comfort solving problems, they default to *How* conversations, even if the *What* they're trying to figure out hasn't yet been fully baked. So, as a rule, don't move into the *How* conversation until you're clear about the *What* that you're trying to achieve. As author Peter Blocks tell us, going right to *How* conversations can be a way to avoid the more important and often less comfortable question of whether something is worth doing in the first place — which is a *What* conversation.

There's much more to explore on the theme of possibilities, but for the purposes of this book, keep in mind that *possibilities are declared*. They aren't facts; they can't be proven because they don't exist — they only exist in our imagination of the future. Remembering this may give you and your team more freedom to explore and declare new possibilities, to "make shit up," harnessing the power of *declaration* without the burden of needing to validate, evaluate, or justify it right away. That can happen later.

First and Second Order Learning

We've talked about meta-moves and First and Second Order learning several times already. Making a meta-move is one of the most powerful ways to amplify your collaborative learning. It's how you transport yourself to a different level of observing or thinking about things.

First Order Learning

When a child first learns to tie her shoelaces, it may seem to her like a fantastically complex learning challenge. Like when, a few years later, she begins learning to solve pre-calculus problems. Or, as an engineer later on, she must learn how to calculate the structural load factors for a new high-rise building her firm is working on.

These are examples of First Order learning. As challenging and complicated as learning these things may be, they are First Order challenges because they are clearly defined, and because the path to figuring out how to do these things is known and proven. They are part of a self-contained system of knowledge and know-how that will allow us to solve many different types of similar problems—even very complicated ones.

Learning to create a knot that will reliably hold shoelaces together for a reasonable period of time is a clear and well-defined learning task. As when learning to solve pre-calculus problems, the solution is well-known and proven, as are the means for arriving at it. Even determining structural load factors for a high-rise building involves First Order learning—as mentally taxing, complicated and time-consuming as it may be. The background conditions for solving these types of problems are well understood and reasonably consistent.

First Order Learning is what you do when solving most of the problems you encounter in your daily work. This is not to say that First Order challenges are mundane or trivial: Responding to many life-threatening emergencies is anything but trivial, but in most cases, these responses are also First Order responses, following well-known emergency procedures. The training, checklists, protocols, tools and thinking involved in learning and solving these problems will produce the desired outcome most of the time.

Second Order Learning

You already know how to tie a bow knot (the one you use to tie your shoes). But let's say that you want to find a different way of keeping those shoes on your feet that requires less dexterity, allows you to easily make adjustments, and can be managed when you're in a hurry...

How to tie shoe laces better?

The question, *"How to tie shoe laces better?"* reflects the **1st Order** you're operating within (of shoe laces). So any potential solutions you come up with will likely also reflect that **1st Order**.

After several attempts with all the various types of knots you can think of, you decide that what you've learned about knots to this point just isn't going to solve this new problem. You need to challenge your assumptions about knots—and perhaps laces altogether. You're going to declare a different problem.

How to more easily keep shoes on my feet?

A new question, "How to more easily keep shoes on my feet?" only occurs to you when you've left the **1st Order**. There might be many different solutions to this new problem that don't involve shoe laces.

If you were very clever—or perhaps had engaged in a very successful Learning conversation or two, you might have come up with an entirely different solution to the problem... and perhaps called it "Velcro." This would have been an example of Second Order learning, because to solve this new and different problem, you had to leave the original (First Order) system of knowledge and know-how you'd been operating in (tying shoelaces) and move to the next order. In this next order, you look around with new eyes and can see your previous assumptions more clearly. From this new vantage point, you could envision an entirely different way of solving your problem using different materials, different tools and different actions (pulling and pressing, vs. measuring, adjusting and looping, for instance). If you'd invented Velcro, you would have meta-moved your way into solving many additional problems beyond tying shoes, without at first even realizing the full extent of your invention's utility. But alas, that honor goes to a French engineer, Albert de Mestral, who invented the hook and loop fastening "solution" in the early 1940s. In actuality, it took many years—and probably many Learning conversations—before de Mestral figured out how to manufacture Velcro for commercial use, and many more before it was applied to shoes.

Conversationally, when we shift from a focus on the *content* of the conversation (say profit margins, quality issues, talent development, or some other topic), out to a new focus on *the way we are talking about that topic*, or *why we are talking about it in the first place*, we are making a meta-move—moving from one order of thinking to another, *meta order,* that encompasses but isn't limited to the previous (First) order. So, you can see that making meta-moves is not some specialized procedure or technique. You already know how to do it; you just may not have had a name for it or seen how powerful it can be for collaborative performance.

Moving from the First to the Second Order refers to two different focuses of learning: one that occurs *within* a given system — First Order learning — which leaves the overall system unchanged (such as trying to use string and knots to fasten two things together), vs. learning that is uncoupled from the concepts, practices and mental models of that First Order, so that new ways of solving a problem — or new problems altogether — might be declared.

The Dots Are Never the Problem

You no doubt know the popular puzzle of the nine dots in which you must connect all nine dots with only 4 straight lines, never taking the pencil off the page. (I realize it's a well-worn cliché, but I use it here to show how we all — even kids — already make meta-moves to the Second Order all the time. We just don't always do it consciously. By making this type of meta-move explicit, we gain more options when facing puzzling or challenging circumstances.)

Where's the box?

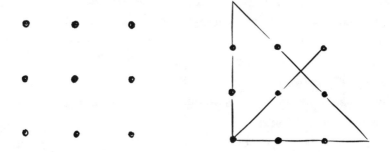

As you may recall, to solve the puzzle (spoiler alert if you've never tried it before), you'll need to extend one or more of the lines out beyond the imagined boundary comprised of the outside dots. The reason so many people don't solve the puzzle at first is because they mentally assume that the dots make a box, and they further assume that they're not allowed to draw outside that box (or even to think outside the box). Of course, the box doesn't *exist*—we just believe it exists because of how our brains tend to interpret the situation.

The imagined box and what's inside that box is the First Order, and you simply can't solve this puzzle from within that set of assumptions (Order). You can only solve it by stepping outside of the imagined box, into the Second Order—where it becomes clear that there never was, in fact, a box. The instant you realize that there's not a box, the solution becomes one of those no-brainers—*Duhhh!*

The problem is never the dots; the dots are simply circumstances (facts that we could assert). The *problem* lies in our assumptions and interpretations about those circumstances. This is another example of why Learning conversations are so valuable. Many of the vexing problems we face in our organizations (and elsewhere) are like the dot puzzle—our limitations stem more from how we're thinking about things than from the circumstances or facts themselves. No matter how clearly we're thinking *inside* the box, some problems will never be solved from this place. They can only be solved from outside of the system in which the problem was originally conceived. Although it can be difficult to examine our own thinking solely with our own thinking, it can be a lot easier to do with others.

We'll return to this theme of First and Second Order Learning in the next chapter when we look at designing problems together.

Reflection and Practice – The Learning Conversation
Four Ways to Have Better Learning Conversations

Following are four ways that you can help folks have more constructive Learning conversations. I encourage you to experiment with one or more of these when it feels right in one of your upcoming meetings...

1. *Make the physical setting comfortable and informal.* It helps when people feel physically comfortable and relaxed. If they're distracted by uncomfortable chairs, restrictive clothing, or if they must struggle to see the screen, whiteboard or other media, it's distracting and tiring.

2. *Ensure that everyone can easily see and hear everyone else in the conversation without straining.* Many conference rooms are designed for the opposite: to ensure that only the person at the head of the table can easily see everyone, and vice versa. All those seated along the sides have to constantly jockey and contort to see the others sitting on their side. When working with groups I make it a point, whenever possible, to meet in rooms with no tables at all, or at least moveable tables that can be arranged in the semblance of a circle so everyone can see everyone else. I also like to avoid separating people by large tables, which feel like barriers, blocking the flow of energy and impeding the connection between people.

3. *Especially when you want to focus on generating new possibilities for innovation or for challenging the status quo, it helps to have the conversation in a different, non-habitual location from the normal setting.* Meeting in the same room you always meet in can keep a group recycling the same conversational routines and thinking. Mixing it up by meeting in unusual places can help

to stimulate new thinking and fresh energy. When possible, go for places with lots of natural light, access to fresh outside air, and room for standing or moving around. Avoid long seated sessions. Inspiring views and beautiful, natural settings can be great, but they're not the only options. Sometimes meeting in the least likely place imaginable, where interesting things are going on that may have nothing to do with your business at all, can generate different thinking. I've led meetings with management teams on working farms, in homeless shelters, at outdoor high-trapeze schools, around late-night campfires in the woods, at the beach, and in martial arts dojos (training halls), among other places. Unexpected and transformative Learning conversations can happen when people take their bodies out of the normal routine.

4. *Finally, if the group is game, consider bringing in a qualified instructor or facilitator to engage them in simple, low-impact movement and/or awareness practices.* These might include yoga, stretching, meditation, breathing exercises, or martial arts-based practices. Just be sure that people have the opportunity to opt-out of anything that they truly don't feel comfortable or safe doing, and that the instructor is skilled and sensitive to maintaining physical, psychological and emotional safety and knows how to keep constructive conversations flowing.

We can't always plan for and set aside a special time or place for Learning conversations. They can happen at any time or any place, including in the middle of a Design or Fulfillment conversation. But when you know you need to have an important Learning conversation, make sure the conditions are as conducive as possible for people to make the most of it.

Chapter 14

The Design Conversation

The Design Conversation is where we make decisions and other declarations about the shared future we aim to create together. We are designing every day. When we decide which route to take to work this morning or how to create the agenda for tomorrow's meeting, we are designing. Your team's values, vision, mission, goals, strategies and metrics—even culture— are all products of design. Whenever you declare that you want something to look this way or to function that way, you are designing. All of the things you care about are opportunities for design—from your career, relationships, home, hobbies, and health, to the organizations you start, work in or want to transform. Even your personal identity or "brand"—the way others see you and relate to you—is a domain of design (via actions that generate assessments, as we saw earlier).

This isn't to suggest that all of this is the result of well-considered and deliberate design, or that everything we design comes to fruition and is successful. Many aspects of an organization, for instance, arise ad hoc, "designed" by default, reflecting the habitual and often unconsciously held values, conventions, practices and processes that the founders and their employees have brought to it over time. But whether things were designed deliberately or not, any of it could be up for redesign. When we talk about design (or redesign) in this context, we're talking about *declarations*.

Let's assume your team has had fruitful Learning conversations and you all feel ready to move forward with the decision, goal, or solution you've been pondering. You're aligned on the relevant data and what it might mean and you've actively drawn out and examined dissenting views and explored

225

alternative possibilities. You're probably ready to move into a Design conversation.

Good Design Conversations

The output of a good Design conversation is one or more clear and shared declarations. Recall that declarations create or set the context for the future. Same with good Design conversations. They remind group members and inform others about what's important to pay attention to, how to think about things and what to commit to.

A good Design conversation will usually include one or more clear directional declarations that express the speaker or the group's intent, clarifying or affirming some decision or choice the group has made. Design conversations plant the flag, paint the picture, create a sense or story about some aspect of the future and how the group wants to relate to that future.

Clearly, Design conversations cover a lot of territory. For our purposes, we'll focus on one particular type of Design conversation: *Designing problems and solutions*.

We'll focus on designing problems and solutions because whatever else we may choose to design—whatever decision or declarations we aim to make—it will usually involve solving some problem or another. It may be the "problem" of what mission, goals or objectives best reflect the team's aspirations. Or how to design a coherent strategy to realize the mission, goals or objectives. Or which metrics to use to guide behavior and track progress. Or infinite other possibilities.

Designing Problems

He's a real problem…
Look at these numbers—that's where our problem is.
This new pricing policy is creating huge problems.
I don't see what the problem is…

The list of problems we humans design and contend with is infinite. We have money problems, relationship problems, career problems, health problems... Our organizations have revenue problems, margin problems, branding problems, customer service problems, quality problems... Our communities have housing problems, clean water problems, traffic problems, public safety problems. Our countries have national security problems, trade problems and problems of corruption, injustice and social inequity. As a species we have environmental problems, hunger problems, public health problems...

But wait a minute. Are all of these problems really problems? Most dictionaries describe a problem as something that causes difficulty or that is hard to deal with; a situation that is unwelcome or harmful that we need to address, eliminate or overcome. Some problems are defined as questions to be answered or solved through reasoning or calculation, as in math or science problems, for instance.

But what really makes a problem a problem? And where do problems really live? If I were to ask you to show me, literally, any of the problems in your own life, where would you point?

You would probably point to circumstances or behaviors. You'd tell me a compelling story or perhaps show me some data. And I might look at you and agree, *"Yep—you do seem to have a problem."* But you couldn't really *point* to the problem. You couldn't take a picture of it or make an audio recording of the problem. All we'd see would be some object or scene; all we'd hear would be some sound, conversation or situation. While we might all agree on the serious nature of many of these problems, the problems themselves would remain invisible. Like a ghost in the mirror, we know there's something going on... but *what is it* and *where is it?*

Once again, our old friend and Stoic philosopher Epictetus, provides us with a clue when he said, *"It is not the things themselves which trouble us, but the opinions that we have about these things."* Our everyday language suggests that problems are as tangible as tables, chairs, figures in a spreadsheet, or people doing certain things (usually doing things that disturb us). As if problems were *in* the things or behaviors themselves. But we know—as did Epictetus—that facts themselves are empty of meaning or value. Just as Pet Rocks had no intrinsic value, there is nothing inherently *problematic* in life's circumstances or in our assertions about those circumstances. The "problemness" of something—anything—including concepts, arises in our assessments about that thing or concept. Problems, like so much else in our lives, are born of language.

They are uttered into being through a declaration.

Until a problem is declared, it doesn't exist.

No Ferry Today

A friend recently told me about a trip her parents made to one of the outer islands of Greece. On this beautiful island her parents would stroll down from the hotel to the dock each morning and ask the ferry operator if the ferry would be working today. And each day, he'd shake his head, sigh, and say in his broken English, *"Is problem—no ferry today."*

My friend's parents found this amusing and charming. At least for the first few days. But as their eagerness to move on (via ferry) to their next destination grew, their good humor turned to frustration and impatience.

What had been an endearing experience became *a problem.* The circumstances didn't change—the Ferry captain's behavior didn't change—only the couple's perspective changed, which changed everything. When they returned home, they told my friend this story, describing their problem over a good laugh.

Why does this understanding about problems matter? Because every day, in every organization, people spend a ton of time, energy and money trying to solve problems. Some of those problems are easily solved. Some take longer to solve, while others remain stubbornly resistant to solutions.

When important "problems" don't get solved, they may get ignored, covered over, fester—or they may evolve (or erupt) into more challenging circumstances. This is especially common for those problems that pertain to getting important things done with other people—to collaboration. In fact, many of the "solutions" people try to implement for their collaboration problems actually perpetuate the problems or make them worse.

How does this happen? It happens when the problems themselves are designed (declared) in ways that make their solution impossible. Here's an example from a workshop I was leading for managers gathered in a large, window-framed conference room on the fifteenth floor of the company's Manila office...

They don't want to change. (When the stated goal is the problem.)

Early on in the workshop, one of the participants, Robert, described the following scenario to his fellow participants: *There's a group in our organization that never wants to change the way it does things. Every time a new challenge comes up and we try to discuss the best way to approach it, this group always falls back on old and ineffective solutions. This leads to the same exhausting arguments in every meeting. Ultimately, everyone just gives up and withdraws back into their own bubble to do it their way—which means duplicated work and wasted time.*

Robert's stated goal was to get this recalcitrant group to adopt his thinking about the change needed in the organization. When I asked him how he might approach an upcoming meeting with the group, Robert thought about it and then shared the following conversational strategy: "I'll approach this personably, so they don't start out defensively. I'll do my best to debate the merits of the change we need. The optimal solution is for them to accept my suggestions based on sound reason and not just appeasing or accommodating us. I don't want them to feel forced into it..."

On the surface it sounds pretty sensible, doesn't it? But let's look at this from a different angle... First of all, how do you think *you'd* respond to someone who approached a conversation with you based on the above strategy? Do you think you'd feel open, eager to change your outdated ways and—after debating the merits—happily adopt that person's suggestions because those suggestions are based on sound reason (as opposed to your own, poorly reasoned approach)? Me neither.

While Robert recognized the downside of defensiveness and the undesirability of appeasement or rote compliance, the way he described "the problem" almost ensured that his strategy *would* create defensiveness, appeasement or compliance—the very opposite of what he really wanted. Rather than attempting to learn more about what may be going on with the folks in the group, or examining his own assumptions, Robert's strategy starts right off with "debate," and with the clear presumption that his suggestions are the only sensible ones.

By framing things in terms of what's "reasonable," (i.e., what constitutes sound reasoning *to him*), the other group's views and reasoning must be inferior—which, naturally, turns *the group* into the problem Robert must solve. And the group's likely responses to Robert's strategy will probably only confirm their unreasonableness and obstinance in his mind. In other words, his solution is likely to perpetuate, if not worsen, the problem he has declared. His story about the group contains the seeds of his own collaborative failure.

Robert didn't yet realize that his problem was designed (declared) *by him*, that it reflected his own assessments and story about the group. He assumed that he was making a factually accurate observation (a true assertion). This confusion about what he was really doing—and how the problem he was trying to solve actually came to be— naturally led him to focus his attention on trying to change *those folks out there*, because that's what a reasonable person would do when confronted with a problem designed like this. Because *"the group never wants to change the way they do things"* appeared to Robert as a given, it wouldn't occur to him to refocus his attention and creative problem-solving skills anywhere else. (Remember, our attention generally goes where we believe the problem or threat lies.)

Robert's internal story contained the "operating instructions" for his conversational strategy, his attention and his subsequent behaviors, which were aimed at getting that group to behave in accordance with his desired outcomes.

And there's still more going on here: Throughout all of this, Robert's approach was to keep his internal story to himself and his close allies; he wasn't going to share his assessments or his story about the group with the group itself. This makes sense because to share this openly with the group could easily invite overt conflict (that "defensiveness" which Robert hoped to avoid). But withholding his honest assessments and stories also has consequences: For one, it doesn't help to foster learning in the form of honest and transparent dialogue (because it isn't honest and transparent in the first place). Secondly, it makes it impossible for collaborative examination with that group of his assessments and stories about the group (because he's not making those available to examine). So not only will Robert's actions likely fail to achieve his intended outcomes, they'll also make it difficult for him or the group to learn more about how his story led naturally to his proposed solution.

Robert's body was of course also a part of all of this, as our bodies always are. As he was outlining his conversational strategy and describing the group he was struggling with, Robert's body became perceptibly more tense, his face hardening and voice rising as if preparing for confrontation. Describing how the imagined conversation would likely unfold, his words became clipped—he had already entered "debate" mode—and it wasn't friendly debate.

Later in the workshop, when debriefing the exercise, Robert commented on his sense that, "although it was just an exercise in a safe workshop environment—it felt real." Just envisioning the encounter triggered emotions and reactions in his body and his thinking similar to what he'd experience if he were engaging in the actual conversation with that "problematic" group. This is true for all of us; our body is always with us, and is always interconnected with our thinking, imagination, feelings. And, although our bodily experience can reinforce our unquestioned beliefs about where a problem lies, with practice we can learn to notice these bodily feelings so they have less sway over our thinking and behavior. (Again, we'll look at some simple ways to do this in Part III.)

Robert's example reveals a lot about how we tend to approach our collaborative challenges. One particular point to highlight is how our stories and declarations set the stage for all that follows. As we saw, it started with the way Robert assessed and characterized the "problematic" group, which led to his declared goal to get the group to change. This declared goal then seamlessly shaped where he focused his attention, his conversational strategy, and his physical and emotional reactions to the conversation he imagined having with the group in pursuit of his goal.

Here's another example...

He's being stubborn. (When my ignorance is the problem.)

Not long ago, a business friend, Justin, told me about a problem he had been grappling with regarding Thomas, one of his direct reports. Thomas had been repeatedly unwilling to commit to a date for the team's next quarterly business review. It was an important meeting and Justin wanted the entire team to be there, yet Thomas continually hedged about each date the team proposed. For Justin, the problem was "getting Thomas to commit to a date," so that the team could move forward with designing the meeting.

With this problem in mind, Justin had been brainstorming strategies to get Thomas to commit. The strategies ranged from *insisting* that Thomas provide the date for the meeting, to offering Thomas subtle incentives to commit, to levying unwelcome consequences if he continued to avoid committing himself.

By the time Justin told me about this situation, his frustration had been amping up and he was leaning strongly towards the "unwelcome consequences" scenario (a "Performance Improvement Plan" in corporate-speak). Curious, I asked Justin why he thought Thomas was having such a hard time committing to a date. The question was simple and would have occurred to many people, but somehow it struck Justin like a thunderclap. He shook his head and confessed, *You know, I can't tell you why, but that question never even occurred to me to ask. I've just been so busy feeling annoyed with Thomas and assuming all sorts of negative reasons that I haven't even asked him what's going on.*

The next day, Justin called to tell me that he had called Thomas right after our conversation and simply asked him what was going on and if everything was alright. Unexpectedly, Thomas teared up and confided that his mother had just entered hospice and they had no idea how much longer she would be alive. Thomas had been feeling really torn up inside about wanting to be fully available to his mom, while also being fully engaged with the team. But he hadn't felt comfortable talking about it with the team and just found himself stuck, not knowing how to commit himself to any date—so he just kept hedging. As Justin listened, he realized several things: That although the problem he'd been trying to solve had seemed critical up to this point, he now knew that there was much more at stake than simply getting Thomas to commit to a meeting date. Simply by getting genuinely curious about Thomas *the human being*, Justin realized that it was far more important to support Thomas at this point in his life (and his mother's life) than to insist on committing to a date. Thomas thanked Justin for asking about him and not holding this situation against him. Justin in turn thanked Thomas for confiding in him, and was genuine when he told him that being there for his mom was more important than any meeting. If Thomas could make it to the team meeting they scheduled, great, and if not, they'd figure out how to keep Thomas in the loop and get his input on important issues.

What had Justin done to "solve" this problem? He had simply shifted his attention, gotten curious and made human contact with Thomas. In addition to strengthening his relationship with Thomas, this simple move allowed Justin to gain new insight which allowed the "problem" of Thomas' hedging to simply evaporate. Now, he and the team (including Thomas) could declare a new and better problem: *How to keep Thomas in the loop with the team while he took care of his family*. This new problem brought the team together far more powerfully than the previous problem had done—which had been premised upon one of their team members' shortcomings, rather than their shared human concerns.

Okay, now it's your turn: *Please show me a problem.*

No, that stack of emails piling up in your inbox isn't a problem. And neither is the complaint you've just received from someone on your team about the guy in Finance who never responds to her emails. And, by the way, the fact that your parents haven't called you from their vacation in the Greek Isles isn't a problem either (although you may be wondering how they're doing).

You know where we're going with this, right? You're anticipating my response: *No, that's not a problem, either.* You'd be right of course, because *factually* not one of those things you might describe actually *is* a problem—no matter how inconvenient, annoying, stressful, or even catastrophic they may feel to you. The circumstances you describe may well all be factually true, and they may feel extraordinarily problematic for you and for many others, but they're not problems that exist independently of you or anyone else (including anyone else who may also declare those circumstances to be problematic).

You can't point to problems because they aren't *out there.* Problems and every other scenario we've declared into being are only *in here*—in our thinking (assessments) and feelings. Circumstances—no matter what they are—have no intrinsic *problem-ness.* Problems are built of words and perhaps mental images, not of sticks or stones; not of people or their behaviors. Although problems seem to reside in the circumstances of our lives or in the behaviors of our annoying colleagues, problems aren't "properties" of anything or anybody. And neither are solutions.

This might seem like some cheap linguistic trick, or just outright lack of empathy on my part towards the circumstances in your life (or both), but stay with me, here. I have seen, time and again, how the belief that *problems live in our circumstances* (rather than in our interpretation about those circumstances) keeps individuals and teams trapped in their own imagined box of dots, doomed to continue to impose solutions that can't possibly work and which often make things worse. I've seen this in myself and my own teams as well.

Please understand that I'm not saying that problems *don't matter* just because they are declared. And I'm also not saying that what we call problems are any less important or less demanding of our attention than if they *did* exist independently of our assessments. I'm saying that *the way we understand problems and where they come from matters* because it determines how we will likely focus our attention, energy and resources. And it determines how we'll attempt to solve our problems.

So, do problems exist? *Yes*, they "exist" in language and in our personal thoughts and feelings, and *No* because until someone declares a problem, there isn't one. And once we no longer consider something to be a problem, that problem disappears, even if — like the Greek ferry captain, that group Robert was trying to fix, or Justin's direct report — the circumstances haven't changed one bit.

Problems or Semantics?

When corporate groups invite me to help them solve some complex organizational problem, I sometimes start out by doing what I just did with you — I ask them to *show me the problem*.

They might show me PowerPoint slides or Excel charts that show how customer satisfaction scores are lower than the industry norm, or how sales have been slipping. Or they describe how they aren't working together as a team as well as they could be, or that the Marketing Department needs to transform itself and rebuild the company's brand. Or whatever it may be.

I'll then say, "Okay, but *where* is the problem — I see numbers, words, diagrams on a slide, and descriptions of people's behavior or circumstances." To which they usually respond, with growing impatience — "Look, it's right *there* where that dashboard indicator is red, instead of green!" Or "We really need to change the culture on this team." Or "If Marketing doesn't get its act together, we won't be in business in two years." They rarely just come out and say, "Who invited this California Consultant here, anyway?" But I know some of them are thinking it.

Before they blow a fuse, or I blow the consulting gig, I'll concede that I do "see" what they are talking about, and I do understand how it might be a problem for them. And then I'll walk them through what I've been explaining in these last several pages: That there is nothing inherently problematic about anything they're showing or describing to me, blah, blah, blah.

This can trigger some vehement discussion: "Don't play games here—that's just semantics. Of course, this is a problem—anybody who understands business knows that low customer satisfaction scores [or weak sales, or confusing brand positions, etc.] are problems!"

But I know that no matter how many of us in a relationship, room or company agree that something is a problem, it doesn't imbue those circumstances with the property of "problem." It can't, because that's not the world that we linguistic beings live in. As individuals, teams, companies, industries and markets, we "declare" problems into existence. And we can use this fact to help each other more effectively solve these declared problems together.

Circumstances are circumstances regardless of our assessments about them. We may be successful at changing them—at making certain circumstances go away or become more or less acceptable to us. We may, in other words, solve many "problems," like shrinking profit margins, polio, social inequality, or climate change. But we will solve them all the same way we created them—with our declarations.

Solutions live where problems live—in our declarations.
Just like problems, solutions aren't *discovered* as we might discover a new species of dinosaur, a new planet, or gravitational waves. Although we can hunt around for circumstances, objects, tools,

strategies, or ideas that we can apply to our declared problems, not one of those problems will be solved until someone declares it to be solved.

This understanding about the nature of problems and solutions is central to our ability to think well together and collaborate. In many respects, collaboration is all about the kinds of problems we declare together and the solutions to those problems (which we also declare). It's about how we *connect the dots* (which, as we know, are *never* the problem).

Good Problems, First Order Problems & Second Order Problems

A *problem* is a declaration about a future that someone cares about and may not know how to bring about. It may be an ideal, a behavior, an objective outcome, a future condition to achieve, or a new possibility to realize.

Not all declarations are problem statements, but all problems are declared. For instance, *I love chocolate ice cream* is a declaration, but it's not a problem. *I want chocolate ice cream and I don't have any* may be closer to a problem statement (a First World problem statement, but a problem statement nonetheless).

While declaring and solving this type of problem may lead to immediate personal gratification and even a short-term sugar high (which could *feel* like a good solution in the moment), it may not generate sustained improved performance, stimulate new thinking, or result in any meaningful long-term change — all potentially helpful criteria for assessing whether a problem is good or not. To stretch the slightly absurd ice cream example further: from a personal perspective, getting that fix of chocolate ice cream may actually create more problems than it solves — which can point to additional possible criteria to consider in assessing the "goodness" of a problem.

So, what is a good problem? As we know, the answer will be an assessment we make and it'll depend upon the factors that go into that assessment (which the five grounding questions for assessments help us think through).

The problem of that obstinate group that Robert was trying to solve was not a good problem because it was causing Robert to focus all his attention and energy onto trying to change that group and not onto his own thinking that led him to believe the group was the problem in the first place. That problem was bound to be unsolvable. Same for Justin when he was trying to "improve" Thomas' commitment. In both instances, the problems, as originally declared, were not "good" problems because they were unlikely to yield particularly good solutions. That is one criterion for how good a problem may be.

From an organizational perspective, I would say that a good problem is one that could be solved in a way that is satisfactory and valuable—in a sustained way—to the person or team that has declared the problem. In simple terms, this just means it will advance some aspect of the business without creating further problems elsewhere or later.

To assess what is a good problem for you or your team, you can ask, *where does this problem focus my/our, attention energy and behavior?* If it focuses you in a useful direction, it may be a good problem. And this may be true even if the solution appears impossible to achieve.

Some of the most inspiring mission and vision statements point to problems without known or imminent solutions, to future states that seem purely aspirational, like Toyota's long-standing vision that includes achieving zero-defect production. This is an ideal, a problem that has—for over six decades and counting—no visible solution in sight. Yet it has driven relentless, continual learning, improvement and innovation throughout the company. I'd call that a good problem, even if it might never get solved.

So a good problem focuses our attention and guides our thinking and action in useful ways that will address some

240

concern, create value, fulfill an ideal or realize an outcome or possibility that someone cares about. Not all problems will do this for us, even though they may appear to be very "obvious" and widely accepted.

First Order Problems and First Order Solutions

In the last chapter, we looked at First Order and Second Order learning. Now, let's apply this concept to designing and solving problems, starting with First Order problems...

Most of the everyday problems you deal with at work probably yield to fairly well-established solutions. They are *First Order* problems. As I said earlier, although some of these problems may involve complicated solutions, these problems may involve complicated solutions, sophisticated tools and/or highly skilled people to solve them, they are First Order problems because *they are solvable within the same system or Order in which they are conceived.* In other words, they are solved by First Order solutions — even if some of these problems may still require Herculean effort. Here are a few examples of First Order problems we're all familiar with...

Financial Accounting– While in large companies, financial recordkeeping and management may be extremely complicated, most of the problems encountered can be solved within well-established frameworks and using principles, tools and know-how already known and understood by financial professionals and executives. The basic system of bookkeeping that organizations everywhere use has its own set of rules, assumptions and logic that enables managers to account for money (i.e., solve the problem of accounting for and managing the company's performance) in a systematic and predictable way. Going outside this system will likely lead to books that don't balance, poor management decisions, government audits, or worse (which may lead to the declaration of a different type of problem).

Learning (or designing) New Software – There are some extraordinarily complex software apps out there, many of which we all interact with on a daily basis. These apps are designed to solve specific types of problems consistently based upon established user interactions. Although they may be built upon unfathomably complex programming scripts, the problems these apps can solve are still "simple" in the sense that they will always and only operate within those programmed parameters. This might be changing with advances in artificial intelligence, but at this point, most apps still have their own set of rules, logic and assumptions coded into them, so that if we enter data or commands the program isn't designed for, we'll get an error message, a spinning icon, or the program will just crash.

Operating Machinery – Machines are designed to complete specific tasks by operating in specific ways. Most machines will either not work or will break if we try to use them in ways they aren't designed for. We're talking about transportation vehicles, manufacturing machinery and so forth. In most cases, neither the machine nor the machine's users need to think beyond the established operating procedures to effectively run or fix the machine.

Procedures and Checklists – We should all be grateful for these First Order tools (and for the First Responders and others that often employ them). As we saw in the last chapter, these First Order solutions help keep us healthy and safe, whether its emergency first aid procedures, protocols for performing brain surgery, or bringing a jumbo jet safely to the ground when an engine has cut out.

Restructuring your R & D Department (or any team, department or organization) – While there may be many different roles and skill sets involved, multiple cultures to engage, a variety of systems and tools to juggle, and a host of different personalities engaged in solving this type of problem, there are also many models and best practices out there to draw upon. There are case studies, articles, books, process design experts and other resources to assist in solving this type of problem. Although you could, you don't necessarily need to invent an entirely new way of thinking about organizational design or challenge commonly held assumptions in order to successfully restructure your team.

As some of the above examples indicate, most repetitive business processes are First Order activities, as are most incremental improvements we make to those processes. Even highly complex projects like constructing a skyscraper or building an airliner consist primarily of First Order problems, solved by known types of solutions.

A friend of mine, Ben, is a successful architect who designs skyscrapers with one of the big firms on the West Coast. I asked him what goes in to designing a new cutting-edge skyscraper and he rattled off a long list of the types of expertise, resources and coordination needed. It sounded super complicated, with lots of different professionals involved, and lots of collaboration required.

I then asked Ben how much of what goes into the design of a typical modern skyscraper was truly innovative. After thinking it over for a few minutes, he mused that one or more aspects of the design concept may actually be innovative and involve rethinking the basic rules of the game (moving to the Second Order). But, he continued, even for the most innovative concepts — most of the thinking that goes into the actual design of the building will be devoted to solving fairly routine, though perhaps complex, problems which are already well known and understood by the design team.

The tools you need to solve most First Order problems are those that are already in your First Order toolbox.

But when the tools, perspectives, or techniques that have worked before aren't working, it may be time to move to the next Order, because you're probably dealing with a Second Order problem.

Obviously, the above examples are just a few of the infinite types of First Order problems that are designed and solved in organizations all the time and they are primarily technical or process-related. Although they're not specifically collaboration-related, they do provide a contrast with the Second Order examples we'll look at shortly. But before we move on, let's look at some First Order Solutions...

First Order Solutions

How do we know whether a problem is a First Order or a Second Order problem? Sometimes, we can only know by its solution. If we find a rational, "common-sense" solution that resolves or eliminates the problem without creating new problems or pushing the problem underground to surface later, it's likely a First Order problem. If various common-sense solutions have been attempted but the problem persists or pops up somewhere else, it could be a Second Order problem that requires Second Order thinking and solutions.

With respect to collaboration problems, the shift to Second Order thinking doesn't usually need to focus on technical or process-related solutions—it instead focuses on the assertions and assessments people are making, the beliefs and stories they're telling themselves about themselves and others, the quality of listening, emotional awareness and contact that people are making together.

Here are a few signs that may indicate you're dealing with a Second Order collaboration problem:

- Individuals or groups remain polarized from one another, strongly believing that "the problem" is the other person or group—that those others are somehow deficient, unhelpful, uncollaborative, unwilling or incompetent. This may show up in one-on-one relationships or with respect to other teams or departments, as when employees blame management, management blames employees, field or regional people blame corporate (and vice versa), or one department keeps blaming another.

- People continually design their conversational strategies (to try to solve the problem) in ways that attempt to get the others to change without attempting to learn more about how the others are thinking, feeling or seeing things.
- Distancing behaviors – often characterized by statements like "We need management's support to solve this problem," "That's not my/our area," "I'll go along, but I don't think this is going to work," or behaviors like disengaging from conversations that don't go the way someone wants, or consistently poking holes in proposed ideas or solutions without seeking to better understand or explore the ideas/solutions.
- Continually repeating the same idea or proposal over and over, even when that idea/proposal has already been discussed or explored.
- People keep trying to relate the current problem to past problems they've experienced, without considering how this problem might be different and require a different approach or new way of thinking.
- People continually avoid or ignore critical issues that might cause discomfort or embarrassment if talked about openly.
- Continual happy talk, cheerleading, cajoling people to feel good, and other socially upbeat behaviors (especially when they're performed by the boss or other influential colleague) that tend to downplay or minimize issues or discomfort around issues, thereby inhibiting close examination and self-reflection.

These are just some possible indicators that you might be stuck in a mental (First Order) rut and need to make a meta-move to the Second Order. (Of course, these behaviors may also have other causes as well.)

Second Order Problems

In contrast to First Order problems, addressing Second Order problems requires new perspectives because they are *systemically complex*, or they are *socially complex*, involving complex social dynamics (or both).

Systemically complex problems are part of a larger system with multiple, interdependent variables in which changes to one part of the system will exert changes on other parts in ways that we can't always anticipate. In these problems, a single change (a cause) and its effects may be so distant in time or space that we don't experience this causality directly.

For instance, many companies are very concerned with customer experience ("CX," which may be measured by various customer satisfaction or customer experience survey tools). The companies invest lots of money, resources and training for employees so that customers or prospective customers feel good about their interactions with the company. While many of these efforts yield positive improvements to CX, they sometimes do just the opposite—especially when they are approached piecemeal, as a series of separate, piecemeal efforts. One company for instance, put their entire customer support department through rigorous and expensive training aimed at helping their support agents be more empathetic with customers, and keeping the customers updated frequently while their issues were being worked on. Both of these behaviors were appreciated by customers, who responded positively in their satisfaction surveys about their experiences interacting with the support agents.

What the company didn't anticipate, however, was the sharp drop in satisfaction ratings by the same customers regarding their experience with the company's products and policies. By lifting the bar in one area, the company unwittingly raised the bar for customers in other areas. Customer experience is generally multi-faceted, with a customer's experience in one domain influencing her experience in another. It's a complex system which means that solving problems within this system must be approached from a system-wide perspective. This entails identifying and understanding as many of the variables at play in the system as possible, and how they each interact and affect the whole. A less linear and rational approach and a more intuitive, non-linear and exploratory orientation is often what's needed. For many teams or individuals, this non-linear way of thinking is a big (Second Order) stretch.

Socially complex problems are those in which the people involved see the circumstances, problem and/or possible solutions differently, or operate in entirely different cultural contexts. Often, they (like most of us) also have strong feelings or attachments to their own views and may feel confused or threatened by radically differing orientations. Socially complex problems may also be systemically complex in that each person's views, feelings and behaviors are bound up with and trigger others' views and feelings.

To further complicate things, many of the circumstances in which systemically or socially complex problems are declared are also characterized and made more challenging by rapid change, uncertainty and/or ambiguity. This increases the pressure people generally feel as they grapple with the underlying challenges.

Many organizational "problems" include all the above characteristics, and attempts to address them often feel messy, emotionally charged, and/or unfocused. Many of these problems can't be solved within the same thinking in which the problem has been declared, even with "solutions" that may have worked well in the past for other problems that appeared similar. When the company I just mentioned realized their Customer Satisfaction challenges involved a more complex systemic issue, they convened a series of meetings with various department heads to figure out how to shore up the areas that were now garnering negative customer ratings. These meetings were challenging for social reasons: The leaders of the departments with the negative ratings came in on the defensive, feeling blamed for their relatively "poor performance," while those from the customer support department initially held themselves aloof, believing that they had already solved "their" part of the problem and now it was up to the others to get their act together.

Many types of otherwise simple organizational problems are also socially complex because their solutions can't be implemented by any one individual or team, no matter how gifted or productive that individual or team may be. They can only be addressed in collaboration with others. Addressing these problems often requires good listening, candid reflection, inviting insights, concerns and dissenting views from different perspectives, along with a strong willingness to commit to the solutions the group finally arrives at. (Sounds like a Learning conversation, doesn't it?) They might also require that the group make a meta-move to the Second Order to identify and examine underlying beliefs and assumptions.

Making a meta-move to a new Order can sometimes feel disorienting to a group, as if the ground has moved under their feet, but this can be a good thing—it's what it takes to step beyond the familiar First Order into new territory. It's how you can gain access to what lies beyond and how you can see what may have been hiding in front of you in plain sight all along.

First Order problems don't require us to ask, "for whom is this a problem in the first place, and why?" Or "what might be

going on with that person or group—or with me or my group—
that may be perpetuating this dynamic and rendering all of the
obvious solutions we've tried ineffective?" But Second Order
problems do.

The following examples can illustrate what often happens
when we attempt to solve Second Order collaboration problems
with First Order solutions...

When First Order Solutions Meet Second Order Problems

Recall that when a problem we've declared arises out of the rules,
thinking or behaviors of the individuals or groups involved, we
call it a Second Order problem, and we'll need to go "meta"
to move beyond that First Order to solve it. If we don't—if
we remain at the same level of the problem, viable solutions
will elude us, the problem itself will often get worse, and the
social dimension—the interactions between people—will often
also become strained or polarized. A common response when
we face elusive problems is to attempt to solve the problem by
applying its opposite. Here's what I mean...

The Boss as Cheerleader

Remember that email from my health care provider about *feeling
bad about feeling sad*? Let's say you have a friend who is feeling
depressed. First Order thinking (and common sense) says that
to help someone who feels depressed, we should counteract that
depressed feeling (or any painful or disturbing fact or thought)
by introducing its opposite: *happy thoughts*! So, we try to cheer
the person up by telling them all the reasons they should feel
better than they do. Sometimes it may help for a while, but very
often it just reinforces the person's discomfort, because now, on
top of their feelings of depression, they experience our efforts to
cheer them up as thinly-veiled judgments that their feelings are
somehow wrong; that they need to be fixed or eradicated—and

then they would feel happy (but how do you do *that*?). What may have started out as a short-term mood dip may get piled onto by feelings of inadequacy, resentment, or even despair. And we were only trying to help! This tendency to try to solve a problem with its opposite is a common and natural tendency, and it often works for simple, First Order problems. But it can do more damage than good when we apply this logic to Second Order problems.

It's similar in organizations. Take the familiar performance review or "feedback" conversations that take place (or are supposed to take place) in most organizations. When the manager must deliver feedback to the employee that could be considered "negative" (meaning it may cause the employee to feel discomfort, anxiety or uncertainty), managers often attempt to counter the negative messages with positive, upbeat message (the office version of cheerleading). Similar with company "all-hands" or other corporate updates that must convey potentially negative or anxiety-provoking news or information.

By cheerleading, the hope is that the positive, upbeat messages will, like a seesaw, balance out the negative messages, thereby saving the listener(s) from discomfort. While well-intended and often espoused as a "best practice" for delivering difficult feedback, it frequently doesn't work and often backfires because, as soon as the boss starts cheerleading, many people (especially those who have been recipients of this strategy before) know that the other shoe is about to drop. So they begin girding themselves for it—tensing up, tuning out, and/or discounting or disregarding the positive stuff. In my experience, the tendency towards cheerleading is driven as much by the manager or leader's own discomfort delivering the negative feedback as by the actual impact on the recipient. Even when this strategy may lift the other's spirits temporarily, the hoped-for happy feelings rarely overcome the discomfort. And frequently, the trustworthiness of the boss may come into question: *Were those positive statements really genuine, or was he just trying to cushion the negative stuff?*

This strategy of trying to solve a problem with its opposite takes many different forms both within our organizations and beyond. And just as it doesn't work for Second Order problems, it also fails for many First Order issues. Like trying to force yourself to fall asleep when sleep just isn't happening—the effort itself often just adds to the anxiety about not getting enough sleep. Or like trying to overcome the "problem" of laziness with working harder. Or solving the "problem" of falling behind on a project by shortening meetings and eliminating conversations. Or trying to foster stronger internal engagement by offering employees external incentives or threatening consequences (sometimes both). I could go on, but you get the point.

First Order thinking often assumes that introducing what seems to be the opposite of the problem should automatically lead to significant change: If we replace or remove something undesirable, then its replacement or outcome must be good. Yet, if this were true, then most of our collaborative problems would quickly clear up (they don't), most revolutions would be successful (they aren't), divorcees would *not* routinely end up in similar relationships later on (they frequently do), and most organizational change efforts would be successful (they're not). Instead, by trying to "solve" First Order problems by introducing or increasing their opposites, those solutions tend to cancel each other out, leaving the problem the same, or— in the case of many organizational problems—worse, because people tend to get fatigued, cynical and resigned when new solutions repeatedly fail.

Following are two more examples in which First Order thinking—and an outward focus on other people as the source of the problem—kept two different leadership teams spinning their wheels before they made a meta-move to the Second Order...

Our Employees Don't Get It

The first signs of spring are budding at this beautiful New England coastal resort where about 40 global leaders of a services department have been meeting for the past two days of this three-day offsite.

A recurrent theme so far has been "complexity." Folks have expressed an urgent need to simplify how things are done in the company—from business processes to decision-making, to customer interactions. Every time the theme was raised, heads started nodding around the room.

Today's meeting was with a smaller subset of the team, about 17 leaders. The conversation started off with a statement by the head of the department about how the employees reporting to the leaders in this room were not, in general, performing as expected. About 18 months ago, this leadership team had put in place a new framework for customer engagement, along with new role definitions for the team. But as of today, less than a handful of the hundred or so folks in the new role were using the new framework and performing to the new standards.

I asked the group why they thought this was the case. I took notes as they explained...

- *There's just too much work to do, both for our people and ourselves, to focus on the right things*
- *Things are too complex—we need to simplify things*
- *People lack training and skill*
- *People lack practice opportunities*
- *We don't model the right behavior enough*
- *We don't spend enough time coaching and leading*
- *Our people lack clarity about the framework and the role itself*

- *They don't know how to prioritize*
- *If we push them harder, they may decide to leave*
- *They lack confidence*
- *Some employees are perfectionists—if they can't do it perfectly, they just stop trying*
- *They have too much empathy—they want to help the customer so much they don't always make the right decisions*
- *They don't know how to say no, so instead always say yes to new requests by customers and internal colleagues*

At this point, I interrupted: *I've counted 13 explanations for why your people aren't performing well. Why do you think there are so many explanations?* They struggled to find a cogent answer.

Rather than trying to force it, we hit Pause and shifted into a role-playing exercise to see what might show up. The role play was simple: one person would play him/herself (the boss) and another would play the employee. The boss's job in the role play was to have a conversation with the employee to try to get the employee to understand the behavioral changes needed and to commit to making those changes. Three different pairs did this role play in succession, while the rest of us watched.

After the third role play, it started dawning on the group that the problem wasn't actually with the "employees." The leaders themselves (the bosses who were playing themselves) had very disparate understandings about the new program they themselves had put in place 18 months ago. It was evident from their words and their body language that these leaders were unclear about the behaviors they should be expecting and the standards to

Full Contact Performance

use in assessing those behaviors. And they were visibly uncomfortable.

No wonder their people were confused. How could those experienced, professional employees possibly behave any differently, if their own bosses (who came up with the new program) couldn't clearly articulate it or tell them what behaviors they expected to see? Seeing this so clearly had moved the group into Second Order thinking and it was a pivotal point in the meeting.

Along with some sheepish laughter acknowledging their own role in their employee's problem, there was also tangible relaxation around the room. Someone remarked, *How could our people help but perform fuzzily, since we—their leaders—were daily reinforcing that fuzzy thinking?* Things had suddenly become more "real" for this group, which allowed them to become fully engaged participants in the "problem" rather than simply hapless victims of their employees' poor performance. Shifting their focus away from their employees and back to themselves and their own role in the situation opened up a new avenue of conversastion, along with very different potential solutions—which simply weren't accessible from the First Order they'd been operating in previously.

Another insight followed quickly for the group: That much of the complexity they'd been complaining about was inside their own heads. Sure, the processes and systems used to manage the employees' work were complicated, but this was a large, successful global tech company—they routinely solved these types of problems.

The difficulty arose because these leaders had not been clear about the problem they were trying to solve and where it resided (in their own confused thinking). *They had been looking for simplicity in all the wrong places.* They could have spent the next ten days trying to strategize how to change their employees' behaviors, but it still wouldn't have worked. Instead, by moving to the Second Order, they could see their own thinking with new clarity, which brought renewed energy, confidence and humor to the rest of the meeting.

For the remainder of that offsite, they referred to this new orientation as their "contextual shift" (another way of referring to the meta-move to a new Order) and were soon correcting themselves and each other whenever someone fell back into the earlier explanations for their people's performance (which they now dubbed "excuses").

For many complex problems, the solution won't be found in the behaviors which *appear* to be causing the problem, but in the source of that behavior: the way we are perceiving things. This involves a new level of awareness about what we are really doing. If we don't go *upstream* to the source of our problems (to our own assumptions, stories, assessments, and even our bodies and attention) then many of our most critical "problems" are destined to perpetuate themselves.

In the next example, the "problem" isn't the employees, but the company's senior leaders—the people who oversee the seven members of this Professional Services leadership team within a global software company.

Our Leaders Don't Get It

The team was assembled in a windowless training room in the company's West Coast headquarters. They'd asked me to help them turn around their department's performance, as they were consistently missing their targets and aggravating their customers. Prior to this meeting, they had detailed for me the specifics of the performance issues they were concerned with. I was curious to learn more about how they were thinking about these issues, so we started with a simple question: *Why do you think this department is where it is right now—how did you get here?* I then wrote down their responses on a flip chart exactly as they said them...

- *We missed environmental cues and changes—we lacked awareness.*

("Great start," I thought to myself, "they seem to be looking at *themselves* rather than blaming others for their problems..." But my optimism was premature, as they continued with their responses...)

- *Our numbers—the quotas we get from our bosses—are unrealistic.*
- *There is a lack of confidence in our department to make change.*
- *We're not empowered – saying no to requests from other departments is futile, someone higher up will just override it.*
- *We lack information and solid management practices to get and use this information well.*
- *Our metrics are always fluctuating, depending upon which executive is interested.*

- *We're always making concessions to whichever customer our bosses tell us is more important that day.*
- *Our colleagues in other departments (i.e., Sales, Marketing, R&D, Finance, etc.,) are not in alignment with our goals and strategies.*

The rest of their responses were variations on these same themes.

Once I'd listed all their explanations, I gave them a few minutes to reflect on them. I then asked them to explain how they—the senior managers of their department, with many years of experience in their roles—would explain the list of explanations they were looking at. In other words, how is it that they "lacked awareness and missed the environmental cues?" "Why were their numbers/quotas unrealistic?" "Why do their senior leaders lack confidence?" And so on.

I started a new flipchart sheet right next to the first one, and titled it "2 – Our Explanations for our Explanations," and waited. After a minute or so, they got going, and once again I captured their responses verbatim...

- *Lack of maturity by senior leadership (our bosses) to remove obstacles.*
- *Lack of consideration for our views by senior leadership.*
- *Our opinions don't matter—we don't get a lot of credit or respect for our work.*
- *Senior leaders place demands on us without understanding what those demands really mean for our department—like utilization rates, gross margin, etc.*
- *Our senior leaders don't listen well. They just want what they want.*

And more variations on the same themes.

After this round of explanations petered out, several folks seemed to be squirming around in their seats, with lots of nervous wise cracks and uncomfortable chuckles. I asked folks to take a mental step back for a moment, take a few deep breaths and again reflect on what they had just listed—their explanations for their explanations (yes—this was a meta-move I was asking them to make). Meanwhile, I readied a third blank flipchart sheet and titled it, "3 – Our Observations & Thoughts about our Explanations."

I now asked them to share any observations or thoughts about the previous two flipcharts. Once again, I captured their answers in their own words, with no added commentary of my own.

- *I'm embarrassed by these lists.*
- *It's all outward focused!*
- *I think we need to make some fundamental changes in our own minds.*
- *Yes, but some disconnect and misalignment is healthy.*
- *Yeah, but it just sounds like excuses backed up by excuses.*
- *There is clearly confusion and frustration.*
- *It's all whining—we sound like a bunch of victims, and we're supposed to be leaders of this department.*
- *I hate this list!*
- *This must become a turning point for us—we can't just remain victims! What can we own and control ourselves, and what do we need to work with others to change?*

As I was recording their comments, it was clear that the mood in the room was starting to shift. Folks were relaxing and the nervous titters, joking and squirming began to subside. Their comments were no longer reflecting feelings of impotence, resentment and righteousness, but now started to express curiosity and even humility. The energy in the room began to rise, but it was a more grounded energy driven by a sense of possibility, rather than by frustration or discomfort. By stepping outside of the First Order system in which they'd been operating, they were gaining a new perspective on their own thinking and on their own roles in perpetuating the "problems" they had been struggling with. And, equally important—they were finding "the ground" under their feet.

This conversation *was* a turning point for the team. They had started by "honestly" stating what was on their minds—all their grievances and frustrations about their situation—all of their First Order thinking. But that honesty wasn't enough; they'd been venting "honestly" with each other for months and years with no apparent benefit. It was only when they stepped back to examine their own thinking and their behaviors—from beyond that First Order—that they were able to see how the "problems" they'd been trying to solve were fundamentally unsolvable. They'd inadvertently been victims of their own blind spots (which happens to all of us), which kept them perpetuating the very problems they so desperately wished to solve.

Having brought themselves to this new vantage point, this new Order, the team's conversation shifted dramatically. In a light-hearted mood, these executives started listening to each other—and to themselves—with interest and curiosity, finding it much easier now to challenge each other's thinking and to let others challenge their own thinking without getting defensive. They'd stepped down from the self-righteous pedestal they'd been standing on in which their problems all lay elsewhere. Now, they were just a team of thoughtful, curious leaders taking responsibility for themselves and their circumstances, earnestly exploring how to move forward together in a new way.

Before we leave this example, take a moment to return to their comments from Flipchart #2—the one in which they listed the problems and deficiencies with their own bosses, the company's senior leaders. What types of solutions would you come up with, if you took those explanations (problems) at face value? What would be some of the obvious solutions to "the problem" of their senior leaders being *immature, inconsiderate, lousy listeners,* and *unrealistic*? Perhaps, solutions like...

- *Replace the senior leaders (their bosses) with more "mature" and "considerate" ones, or perhaps send them all to executive charm school.*
- *Ask their bosses to take listening skills workshops.*
- *Have their bosses "be more realistic" with their sales quotas.*

How well do you think those solutions would work? How receptive do you think their bosses would be to those solutions?

In case you're wondering, by the end of that meeting these leaders were able to leave with a clear and cogent set of new actions they each committed to, to turn their organization around. These new actions didn't require that their bosses change in order for the team to be successful. And over the next 12 months they were successful at bringing about major change in their organization.

I'm not suggesting that we should never declare problems focused on other people or circumstances—of course we should when it makes sense to do so. We just need to remember where those problems really live—in our declarations and our thinking—which is always occurring within a given context, a given set of assumptions that we are operating in. Unless we know how to shift our focus, it will be easy to remain trapped in that First Order thinking, beating our heads against the wall trying to solve problems that are fundamentally unsolvable.

Every problem is declared within a particular context

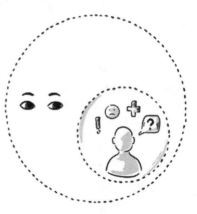

The context of a problem includes social and cultural factors, our emotional state, our body, how we're using our attention, our beliefs, assumptions and preferences, and much more, which lead us to assess a situation's **"problem-ness"**

Context matters, and becoming a better observer of the contexts within which problems are declared is a powerful way to approach problems—especially when they are "social" problems.

Being Lost and Getting Present

Author Lawrence Gonzales describes what happens when people discover that they are lost in the wilderness or stranded in deeply unfamiliar terrain. Their responses tend to fall into two categories: Some find a way to come to terms with the new and unfamiliar world they find themselves in (their "new world order"). Others don't—they remain attached to their familiar mental models (their First Order) and their expectations about how things are *supposed* to be, which causes them to resist what's actually happening. It's well documented that those in the first category tend to survive much better than those in the second category.

Those who can come to terms with where they are in real time (who become Second Order observers of themselves and their circumstances) are able to let go of the world they *had* been living in just moments before in order to fully inhabit the new one they now find themselves in—however unfamiliar, unpleasant or undesired it may be. It appears that, for survival, the act of letting go of what *was*, to align with what *is*, allows you to learn and operate more effectively. That's another way of describing the shift from First Order to Second Order learning.

Getting lost in a conversation or amidst fast-moving organizational change isn't so different from being lost in the wilderness, even for very successful, seasoned executives. Our nervous system responds similarly to perceived threats, whether physical or cognitive, real or imagined. Our well-oiled and thus-far mostly successful mental models, expectations and beliefs about what should be happening and how to succeed in the world, cause us to override environmental cues about what's happening, here and now. It often doesn't even occur to us to question our own assumptions.

The group of leaders on Cape Cod had been lost but didn't realize it. They hadn't been able to understand why their people's performance wasn't meeting expectations until they experienced firsthand, through those role plays, how they themselves were not living in the world they thought they'd been living in.

The Professional Services leadership team in the last example was also lost in their own thinking. They couldn't begin to solve their organizational problems until they first recognized how their thinking was keeping them locked in a cycle of blame and impotence. In both these cases, and in most others, we simply can't find our way out of the quagmire we are in until we first recognize that we are in it. Where we are is always the place we start from, but we can only know where we're starting from by making a meta-move, which reveals the topography of our inner and outer conversations and how they are influencing us. From that new Order, different routes out of our predicaments and new solutions present themselves.

Designing good problems is one of the most important jobs for leaders who wish to transform their personal and organizational performance. It's a cornerstone of good collaboration.

Reflection & Practice – The Design Conversation

1. *Following are some statements made by other executives. Choose one or two and take a moment to infer the declared goals behind the statements and the conversational strategies you think might follow from those goals. Then imagine how these conversations might play out in the "real world."*

   a. He doesn't bother to copy us on important messages because he's self-centered and lazy.

   b. Because the VP of finance has no "real-world" understanding of what it takes to run a business, he is always pressing us to cut our budget, even though sales are growing and we need more people to handle the demand.

   c. That team always tries to shift responsibility for the problem onto somebody else.

   d. They're more interested in checking the boxes than satisfying our customers.

   e. He's just not a team player.

2. *Now think of a problem that you or your team are grappling with. It could be your Case Study example or something else. Reflect on the following questions and write down your answers...*

   a. What is *the problem*? Write a brief description of the problem, as you see it.

   b. For whom is this a problem?

   c. For whom is this not a problem? The answer will often be many other people, teams or other groups. Just list a few of them. (One point of this question is to remind you that every problem is a problem for someone—and not necessarily for everyone. There may be multiple ways of relating to the problem.)

   d. What's already been or being done to solve the problem, and how has this solution (or these solutions) been working? If multiple solutions attempted thus far have failed, it may indicate that you are attempting to apply First Order solutions to Second Order problems.

   e. So far, is the interpretation of the problem you've written down shared by everyone else involved (for whom it's a problem)? If No, or if you're not sure, then a next step might be to have a conversation with the others so that everyone can share their various interpretations about the problem. Until you arrive at a shared story about the problem you're trying to solve and how attempted solutions have worked thus far, you're unlikely to solve it.

Chapter 15

The Fulfillment Conversation

The Fulfillment Conversation is where we make and manage promises that deliver value to customers — inside and outside of the organization.

If you work in an organization, you'll notice that there's often a strong pull to get into the Fulfillment conversation as quickly as possible. Because this is where, it seems, the action is.

As compelling as it can be to nail down concrete promises, however, rushing to the Fulfillment conversation is one of the most common ways that collaborations flounder. The siren song of the Fulfillment conversation lures us in with the prospect of "concrete action" — only to later reveal that we might not have taken the right actions, or that those actions didn't really create value for the customer. Or they may create new problems downstream which nobody anticipated. Rushing into promises before the group has taken the time to learn together and arrive at clear and shared decisions (design) often produces weak organizational performance — even when the promises made are fulfilled perfectly.

The Fulfillment conversation covers everything that happens throughout the lifecycle of the promise, beginning with a *request* by the Customer or an *offer* by the Promisor and ending with the Customer's declaration of satisfaction (or dissatisfaction). Let's look at this conversation in more detail...

The Promise Cycle

Recall that the whole point of a promise is to create value for the Customer. Earlier we showed how promises are cycles that are designed to deliver outcomes (goods, services, conditions or information) that the Customer values and wants the Promisor to deliver. The promise cycle begins with a clear articulation of those outcomes and (ideally) ends with the Customer declaring her satisfaction with those delivered outcomes.

Promises are cycles that begin and end with the Customer

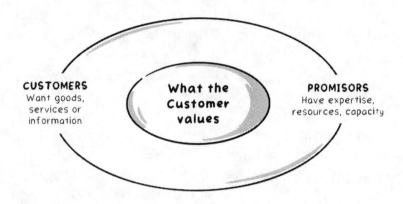

CUSTOMERS
Want goods, services or information

What the Customer values

PROMISORS
Have expertise, resources, capacity

In the middle of the cycle, the Promisor—who has the expertise, resources and/or capacity to deliver the outcomes—is busy doing what it takes to fulfill the promise and satisfy the Customer. Once the promise cycle is underway, both the Customer and the Promisor are bound together in mutual obligation to (and mutual reliance upon) one another.

In organizations, a promise is about performance. You can think of it as live theater. There are actors (Customer, Promisor, and often a supporting cast), three distinct acts, continual action, plots and subplots, and all sorts of potential twists and turns. Also, because it's happening in real time, you can't ever really know how it's going to come out at the end or what may happen in the middle. As in many live theater performances, the actors perform with their words (specifically their speech acts), their bodies and, of course, their attention. As the diagram below illustrates, there are specific actions featured in each Act.

Key Actions in the three acts of the Promise Cycle

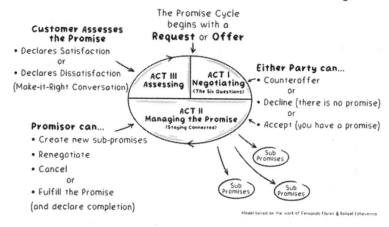

This model is based on the work of Dr. Fernando Flores and Dr. Rafael Echeverria.

Act One begins with a request or offer, initiated by either the future Customer or future Promisor, respectively. In this act, the two parties negotiate the terms of the potential promise, essentially designing a meaningful promise to enter into. This is where the actors go through the Six Questions for a good promise, and then opt to either go forward with the promise or not.

The Six Questions

1. Who is the Customer?
2. Who is the Promisor?
3. What outcomes will satisfy the Customer?
4. How does this promise align with and support the other important promises the parties are managing or know about in the organization?
5. Due Dates—When will the promise be fulfilled?
6. How do the parties want to be kept informed?

The Customer and Promisor work through the Six Questions together attempting to reach agreement and kick off the promise, which would be declared by some form of *Yes—I accept* (the request or offer).

For any number of reasons, however, either actor may not be ready to make the commitment. Instead of *Yes—I accept*, either person may make a *counter-offer*, *defer the decision* to another time, or they may *decline*, in which case there is no promise.

Once the request or offer is accepted, the deal is sealed, the promise has been made and the curtain opens on Act Two. This Second Act prominently features the Promisor, who goes about doing what it takes to fulfill the promise, often spinning off new subplots (sub-promises), in which she will be playing the role of Customer to *other* Promisors.

In a perfect world, Act Two would always go well and the Promisor would always deliver exactly what the Customer wanted (or more), right on schedule. But this is real life, and things don't always go as planned. Regardless, the Promisor still has moves to make to deal with any eventuality and to stay in Full Contact with the Customer.

The Promisor may *renegotiate* one or more terms of the promise (outcome, action or date, for instance), if the promise doesn't appear fulfillable as originally agreed. Or, the Promisor might need to *cancel the promise* entirely if she assesses there is just no way to fulfill the promise to the Customer's satisfaction. This sometimes happens, and when the Promisor assesses that things have reached that point, it's usually good practice to let the Customer know right away. Keeping the other party informed, no matter what, is one of the fundamental practices of managing promises well.

Let's assume that the Promisor fulfills the promise and closes Act Two with a *declaration of completion* to the Customer. The spotlight now shifts back to the Customer for Act Three of the promise.

As the curtain rises on the Third and final act, the Customer will do one of two things: Either *declare the promise to be fulfilled to her satisfaction* (value provided), which brings this promise cycle to a close; or, the Customer might *declare the promise to be unsatisfactory*, which should trigger another conversation: The *Make-it-Right* conversation, which we'll look at shortly.

That's the synopsis of the three acts of the promise cycle. Before moving on, however, let's zoom in on Act Two, where many new subplots might be introduced because the Promisor can't fulfill the promise alone—which is the case with many organizational promises. We'll use another example to examine Act Two in more detail...

Alain's Promise

Alain is the new Chief Information Officer for Acme, a large global manufacturing company with a complex and far-flung supply chain. Alain's first major deliverable—his most important promise to his new boss (the CEO)—is to replace the company's outdated inventory management system. The old system was installed over ten years ago and hasn't been able to scale with the growth and increasing complexity of the company. The old system is costing the company millions of dollars a year in inventory errors and inefficiencies, so getting a new system installed as quickly as possible is a real priority for Alain's boss.

Alain did his homework researching new systems and has decided to go with the system that Natali is selling. (Natali is the Account Executive with the software company that makes the new cloud-based inventory management system.) On her way home from an intense day of negotiations with Alain, she called her spouse to announce that she finally closed the huge deal.

As challenging as the negotiations were with Alain, Natali knows that delivering on the promise to Alain—on time—will be the trickiest part, because it's very sophisticated software. It will require significant customization and handholding by her company to get the system installed and configured, get the data from Acme's old system migrated into the new system, and get everyone in Alain's company trained to take full advantage of the new system. Natali is going to need several important promises (sub-promises) from her colleagues across the company in order to keep *her* promise to Alain, and all of those promises will need to go *very well*. Here's Natali's promise to Alain, in a nutshell...

The primary promise in the web of promises

CUSTOMER

To get the new software
system up and running

PROMISOR

Alain
(CIO)

Natali
(Account Executive)

The next morning, when Natali returns to the office, she begins contacting all the key players in her company whom she expects to handle the various sub-promises needed to deliver on her promise to Alain. Fortunately, Natali had already involved several of these folks in the pre-sales conversations with Alain and his team, so they were familiar with the basic terms of the deal. Natali's first call is to Paolo, the Professional Services manager who will be overseeing the team that will install the new system and work with Alain's team to get the data migrated. Natali has a lot of trust in Paolo's ability to get his team focused wherever needed. He has always delivered on his promises, even on very tight timelines, and is good about letting her know if any issues arise that may delay a particular promise. In this sub-promise, Natali is now the Customer, and Paolo is her Promisor.

Sub-promises in the web of promises

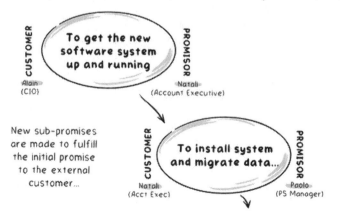

CUSTOMER

To get the new software system up and running

PROMISOR

Alain (CIO)

Natali (Account Executive)

New sub-promises are made to fulfill the initial promise to the external customer...

CUSTOMER

To install system and migrate data...

PROMISOR

Natali (Acct Exec)

Paolo (PS Manager)

For Paolo's part, he is relying on two other people, Josh and Alexis, to create the "sub-promises" needed to fulfill his promise to Natali. These two sub-promises involve looking into the quality of the data in Alain's company so they can begin designing the system configuration requirements needed to fulfill Paolo's (and in turn, Natali's) promise. As you would now guess, Paolo is the Customer to these new sub-promises with Josh and Alexis.

Natali's next conversation is with Leon, who heads up the Onboarding team that will prepare Alain's company to use the new system effectively, providing the documentation, training and additional support they may need.

In Natali's experience, Leon is quick to make big promises but isn't always so dependable when it comes to fulfilling them. He means well and wants to please, but he often says *Yes* before checking to be sure his team has the bandwidth to deliver. Not wanting to be the victim of a bad promise from him, Natali schedules a meeting with Leon and his team to walk through the entire onboarding process together, to ensure the key resources and people will be available to make it happen. Because another very large deal just closed a couple of weeks earlier, it appears that there may be a bottleneck with the Onboarding team, which could delay Natali's project. After Leon checks with one of his Onboarding Specialists, Deepak, he confirms with Natali that her project will be completed on time. Just to be safe and to keep her Customer informed, Natali adds another week into her own schedule as a buffer and gives Alain a call to run it by him. Alain appreciates the heads-up, and a week or two won't be a problem for a project this big.

Finally, Natali walks over to visit Becca, in the customer training organization, to make sure that Becca's team schedules the instructors and documentation needed to fully train all the system users in Alain's company once the new system is installed.

You can see now how Natali's primary promise to her Customer, Alain, has spawned a network—or *web*—of many new promises throughout the organization.

More sub-promises in the web of promises

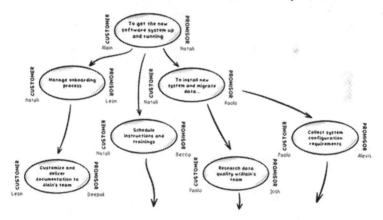

This series of interdependent promises—this web of promises—is held together by the mutual obligations, mutual reliance and expectations of each person in each of the promises that make up the web. For this example, we kept the number of sub-promises intentionally small, just to make the point. In many real-life scenarios, there are scores or even hundreds of interlinked promises—all of which must be managed well in order to fulfill a promise like the one Natali made to Alain.

The web of promises

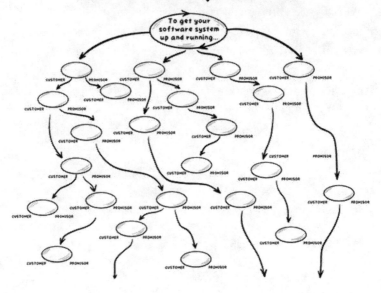

The Customer Must Also Stay Connected

Although most of our focus so far has been on Natali's role as Promisor to Alain, the Customer (Alain) also has responsibilities in the promise. Customers may encounter circumstances that directly impact their promises, such as changing business priorities or strategies, shifting resources, or other factors that might make it difficult, impossible, or no longer desirable to continue with the promise. When this happens, the Customer needs to keep the Promisor informed. Alain could also ask to renegotiate one or more terms of the promise with Natali, or even cancel the promise entirely, if necessary. Just as with the Promisor, there will be consequences when this happens (financial, reputation, relationship, performance, and so on) but it will be much easier to maintain trust and accountability (and minimize the fall-out) when the Customer keeps the Promisor informed as soon as circumstances change.

Before we leave this example, let's fast-forward. We'll assume that Paolo's promises about the data migration and configuration have all gone well. It also appears that Becca's promise is on track and that her team of instructors is already scheduling training sessions with folks from Alain's team. Unfortunately, however, Leon's promise to Natali hasn't been delivered as agreed. Although Leon declared completion of the Onboarding process, Natali has heard from Alain that there seems to be critical gaps in the onboarding process that are creating confusion and frustration for Alain's team. Natali listens carefully to Alain's concerns, taking detailed notes and then promises to get back to Alain with her proposed steps to get things back on track (yes, that's another promise). As soon as she gets off the phone with Alain, she contacts Leon to have a *Make-it-Right* conversation.

The Make-it-Right Conversation

This is a conversation about what to do when a promise is broken or not fulfilled to the Customer's satisfaction. The Make-it-Right conversation is sometimes referred to as complaining (or even whining), but it's much more than that. It's the conversation you have when a promise made to you, as Customer, doesn't meet your satisfaction and has instead created *problems* for you. While it does involve a complaint, the point of this conversation is to negotiate a new promise—or at least a new understanding—that will clean up the mess created for you by the unfulfilled or broken promise.

The Make-it-Right conversation is critical because when promises are broken or don't satisfy agreed-upon expectations (those you addressed with the Six Questions), the consequences for the Customer can be significant: It can make it impossible for the Customer to keep other important promises to his own Customers; it can cost the Customer (and the team and entire organization) time, money and other resources; and, it can prevent the Customer (and team or organization) from realizing valuable opportunities or avoiding major risks. Because the Promisor took personal responsibility for fulfilling the promise to the Customer's satisfaction, it falls to the Promisor to do what it takes to "make it right."

Hopefully, when one of *your* Promisors realizes or suspects that she hasn't fulfilled her promise to you as her Customer, she'll initiate the Make-it-Right conversation with you. But when the Promisor doesn't initiate it, it's *your* job as Customer to have the conversation.

In the Make-it-Right conversation, you and your Promisor will review together the original terms of the promise—what you'd agreed upon in Act One (those Six Questions again). Then, you can share your observations (assertions) about what happened, what was delivered, and the mess that was created by not fulfilling the promise (assertions and assessments). Many times, you'll be able to see eye-to-eye about these things and agree on a new promise to clean things up. But for whatever reasons, you each might also decide to just move on and not enter into another promise (for instance, if the trust is so weak that it just doesn't make sense to expose yourself to the risks of another broken promise, or it's clear there isn't enough time or enough resources).

If you're not able to reach agreement about whether the promise was fulfilled or not, it could be time for a *meta-conversation*. The meta-conversation might about what is important to each of you in this situation, and what the consequences might be for each of you if you fail to agree on the next steps to make things right. This could include the likely impacts of this impasse on your other promises, the impacts to your relationship and future collaboration, your respective reputations, and so on. These are not things we always talk about with people, even when things are difficult between us, but having this type of meta-conversation at these times can often be transformative, especially when you're doing it with a genuine intention to understand what happened and chart a path forward that works for you both. It might mean agreeing on more time needed to fulfill the promise, different quality standards, different pricing, or whatever. You want to get back into a promise, but this time hopefully with more clarity about how to bring it to a successful and satisfactory close.

Through the Make-it-Right conversation, you might discover (or be reminded) that the Promisor may have all sorts of challenges to fulfilling the promise, from incompetence or inexperience, to personal distractions, to poor work practices, to them not knowing how to be a good Customer to their sub-promises, to having too many other competing promises they're trying to manage, and so forth. Many of these could be good for you to know about, for the future.

Even if you're not able to reach agreement about how to make this promise right, you might be able to at least agree on what you *won't* expect from each other going forward.

Having a Make-it-Right conversation whenever a promise isn't fulfilled as expected is how you build a culture of high-performance and accountability. Without this conversation, promises lose their value, performance wanes and resignation can easily set in.

As awkward as it may feel the first few times, the Make-it-Right conversation is an important opportunity to build trust with your Promisor or Customer. Hopefully they'll get to experience you initiating a potentially difficult conversation while you maintain open and respectful contact with them in the process.

Putting It into Action
Every one of us is both a Customer and Promisor for many different promises in our organizations, small or large. We

are all part of our organization's *web of promises*. Our own success and the success of our team hinges on how well we are managing our part of the web—which means how well we are managing ourselves as both Customer and Promisor for each of the promises we are involved in.

When people on your team and in your organization are making and keeping good promises that are aligned with all the other promises being made and managed, you'll have a strong web of promises, which means strong execution and clear accountability. That's the simplicity and beauty of the *promise*: Every promise is personal—it is created and managed by a human being with a personal stake in the outcome and clear visibility into what it takes to make and manage good promises.

> *One benefit of seeing organizational execution as a personal promise is that we always know who to have a conversation with when things go well—or poorly.*

You can hopefully see how central *words* (and the action in those words) are to organizational fulfillment. The entire cycle of the promise from identifying a problem or goal to be realized to negotiating terms, to assessing fulfillment is rooted in the actions of assertions, declarations, requests and offers.

Promises also involve our attention. How am I paying attention and prioritizing this promise relative to all the other promises I'm managing in my web of promises? How am I continually keeping the Customer's satisfaction in mind throughout the cycle? Where does my attention go when things get problematic—do I get fixated on the other people, circumstances or problems out there, or can I remember to check in with myself and my own thinking as well?

And, like everything else we do, we make promises with our body. Our sensitive nervous system is present throughout the promise cycle—giving us constant cues about how our promises may be going, whether we may need to rethink or renegotiate to maintain integrity with our Customer or Promisor, and so forth. And our body also perceives and interprets signals around us that may point to challenges or opportunities related to our promises—opportunities to create more value for our Customers, or perhaps challenges that we need to attend to in order to keep our promises on track. Finally, our nervous system is going to let us know when we've taken on too many promises, which usually means we start to feel anxiety, frustration or overwhelm (or any other emotions that fall in the "stressed out" category).

Even a small organization has a significant web of promises— hundreds and often thousands of promises constantly being made, managed, kept or broken (and perhaps renegotiated, ignored, or fretted over). Multiply this exponentially and you're describing any mid-sized to large organization.

A Map and a Diagnostic Tool

This way of looking at promises—as an interrelated web—is also a map and a diagnostic tool. You can use it to pinpoint weak promises in your business processes or projects, and also to diagnose recurring performance issues. Look at the promises surrounding any chronic performance issue (and acute ones), and you'll find a weak or poorly managed promise or group of promises.

The web of promises shows you how interrelated every promise in your organization is with every other promise. It also shows you how every promise should directly tie back to one or more key promises made to your company's external Customer(s)—the ones who pay for your company's goods or services. If you can't trace every internal promise back to an external Customer promise—or some future planned promise to Customers, then you're probably looking at wasted energy, time and money. You'll also likely find a lot of stress, because people are working hard to deliver on promises that others may not support or see as valuable.

At the start of a consulting project I took on with one company which had recently brought in new leadership, virtually the entire management team told me that under previous leaders, there were absolutely no consequences for failing to deliver on promises. People could do whatever they wanted and there was never a conversation about it. They told me this almost apologetically, and it was clear that they wanted to break out of this pattern, which still persisted in some teams. This new management team had not yet learned how to have effective Fulfillment conversations, so it was no surprise accountability would be weak.

In this approach to promises, accountability is very simple: Either the Customer is satisfied with how the promise is fulfilled or she's not. The purpose and the power of an effective Fulfillment conversation is that it generates a shared expectation about the future that everyone can rely upon, and confidence that for every promise there is a specific human being committed to realizing that future and managing their promises well.

Managing Ourselves

Managing promises well means maintaining Full Contact with your counterpart (Customer or Promisor) throughout the promise cycle. But we know that managing anything or anyone is really about *managing ourselves* — our words, our focus, our bodies and our capacity. Before saying *Yes* to a Customer's request, or before making that offer, ask yourself: *Do I (or does my team) have the personal and organizational bandwidth to take this promise on and actually deliver?* Don't take on more promises than you can manage well. In addition to the stress of exceeding your capacity, this will compromise your performance, your reputation, your relationships, and your self-confidence.

Before we move on, it's helpful to remember that—as important as the Fulfillment conversation is—action taken in the Fulfillment conversation isn't the only type of action needed for strong organizational performance. The kinds of actions you take throughout the Learning and Design conversations are no less important than the promises you make in the Fulfillment conversation, although the Fulfillment conversation often seems more "actiony." All three of these conversations are necessary for sustained Full Contact Performance.

Know the Type of Conversation You're Having

As I stated earlier, in concept the three types of conversations we just looked at would seem to follow a fixed order—first we learn, then we design based upon what we've learned, then we execute to fulfill on what we've designed. But it's not so linear.

We usually move back and forth through these three conversations, often cycling through them many times even in one meeting, especially for complex or challenging collaborations.

So don't be too dogmatic about staying in the particular conversation you're in at all costs. If you need to shift gears and cycle through one of the other ones, then do it. The main thing is that you all do it together and intentionally. It's easy to inadvertently slip into one type of conversation before you've really completed the other one, or for one person to think you're having a different type of conversation than others think you're having. The point is to know which conversation you're all having when you're having it, so you can have the conversation you want to have.

Reflection & Practice – The Fulfillment Conversation

From your case study or other collaborative challenge, reflect on the last meeting or conversation you had—or imagine an upcoming conversation...

1. *What type of conversation would you say you were having? A Learning conversation? A Design conversation? A Fulfillment conversation?*
2. *Was it clear to everyone (including you) the type of conversation you were having?* If you think folks may have been assuming they were engaged in one type of conversation, while it really appeared to be different types of conversation, how might clarifying the type of conversation you were in have been helpful?

For example, if people were driving hard for commitments or promises (fulfillment), but those commitments weren't forthcoming, what might have been missing? Was the group truly ready to move into fulfillment? Had sufficient learning occurred? Were the objectives or strategies clear and shared (design)?

For the next week or so, keep a log of all the promises you make or ask someone else to make to you—even the trivial ones. Use the Six Questions (repeated below) and write down brief answers to each question for each of your promises. Just doing this for a week or two will get you thinking much more precisely about the promises you're involved in and the strength of your own *web of promises*.

The Six Questions

1. Who is the Customer?
2. Who is the Promisor?
3. What outcomes will satisfy the Customer?

4. How does this promise align with and support the other important promises the parties are managing or know about in the organization?
5. Due Dates—When will the promise be fulfilled?
6. How do the parties want to be kept informed?

Chapter 16

Building Trust in Conversations

I wouldn't trust him with a nickel.

I could never trust her again after what she did to me.

We have a lot of trust on our team; we just lack accountability.

He knows his stuff, but he always comes in late and over budget, which makes me lose credibility with the board.

I'd trust her with my life.

Yes, he's smart and he really wants to do well, but we're constantly having to make up for his missed deadlines and unexpected breakdowns.

In the last few chapters, we explored the three different types of conversations that are at the heart of collaborative performance. When these conversations are well managed, they build trust, which enhances your contact with your colleagues. When these conversations aren't well managed, trust will likely erode.

Trust is one of the pillars of collaborative performance and it's central to everything we've been exploring throughout this book. The way we speak, listen, use our attention, show up in our bodies and manage our conversations all impact the trust that others have in us, as well as the sense of trust we have in ourselves and others.

Researchers even tell us that trust is one of the strongest predictors of a country's wealth. Countries with "low trust" tend to be poorer due to less investment in long-term initiatives that could create jobs and raise incomes. Where trust is low, there is little confidence that the investment will be handled properly to generate the desired social or economic benefits. Mega-scale social investments, just like the much smaller investments we make every day in our business interactions, require trust that our time, energy and resources are worth betting on.

In organizations where trust is low, communication problems are a sure thing. When people complain about a lack of accountability, they're talking about trust. When gossip is rampant but the "elephants in the room" are never openly discussed—trust is the reason. When the same problems keep resurfacing, trust issues are at play.

As important as it is to our organizational performance and so many other areas of our lives, when you ask people *what trust actually is*—the answer is often pretty vague: "It's just a feeling I have." But, as we know, the more specific we can get about just what Trust is, the easier it'll be to observe it, talk about it and build it. So, just as we've been doing throughout this book, we'll break Trust down into finer distinctions. But first, please do the following brief exercise...

On a sheet of paper or device write down the names of three people you trust, and three people you don't trust. Next to each name, describe in a few words or a short sentence what it is about them you do or do not trust. Leave space after each name, as we'll come back to this exercise a little later...

An Action, a Feeling, a Molecule

Although we all have a general sense of what we mean by trust, it isn't just one thing. It's three things: Trust is an action, a feeling, and a molecule.

Trust Is an action

When we say things like John is trustworthy, we are treating trust as if it were a property or attribute of John, just waiting to be observed by anyone who passes by (similar to how many people think about value, as we saw earlier in the book). But treating trust in this way limits our relationships and can lead us to believe that we're just passive observers of this thing called trust. Extending trust or distrust is an assessment we make—an action we take. Like other assessments, we assess trust to help us place our bets about the future. What we trust someone to do or not to do determines how we'll commit ourselves going forward. Assessing trust is an action we take in the present, to guide our future actions. Other than that, we'd have little reason to think about trust.

As we saw earlier with the concept of *value*, when we treat trust as a property of someone or some group, our view of them becomes static. It's difficult to change or update our view of them when we believe that what we're viewing is an intrinsic part of them. That belief proscribes the boundaries of our relationship, locking us into an all or nothing view of them, which limits our relationship and the types of things we might do together.

Sometimes, our assessment of trust seems to just *happen* to us—when someone does something we really appreciate, or that really disappoints us. In these moments, it's as if trust were happening "out there," and we are just recipients of it. But trust can be a choice—something we actively do, build, create, sustain or diminish through our awareness and actions, including actions we might only take with ourselves as we observe our thought processes and feelings. Recognizing trust as an action we take can free us from becoming passive victims of what happens to us.

Fernando Flores, in his book *Building Trust*, distinguishes *responsible trust*—which recognizes the possibility of betrayal and disappointment, from *blind or naive trust*, in which we just hand ourselves and our future over to another person without examining and grounding our assessment of trust. Our willingness to enter into a promise with someone, or even make a simple request of them, is rooted in the trust we assess in that person to protect our interests and well-being.

Trust plays a critical role in the quality of the conversations we have every day. In their article "The Neuroscience of Conversations," Nicklas Balboa and Richard D. Glaser, affirm that "Conversations are not just a way of sharing information; they actually trigger physical and emotional changes in the brain that either open you up to having healthy, trusting conversations or close you down so that you speak from fear, caution, and anxiety." Here again are those circular themes of *connection* and *reciprocity*: When we have respectful and healthy conversations, we increase our capacity to trust, which helps to improve the quality of our conversations.

Trust Is a Feeling

In addition to an action, trust is also a *feeling*, an emotional experience. It's associated with a sense of *security*, which—like all emotions—has a bodily dimension. One storyline for trust is that the other person is looking after me and my interests. It points to my sense of confidence in the other person, that what this person will likely do corresponds with what I hope and expect them to do.

Trust is linked to emotions in another way as well. As we saw earlier, just as emotions predispose us to notice and perceive things in certain ways, the particular emotion and its degree of intensity can influence how much we may trust in someone or some circumstance, or even if we'll trust at all. Anxiety, for instance, which is a "low-certainty" emotion, has a well-recognized dampening effect on trust, whereas feelings of happiness or gratitude tend to encourage us to trust.

Trust Is a Molecule

The emotions and bodily sensations of safety, security and being well cared for closely correlate with a chemical in the body called oxytocin, which is sometimes referred to as "the love hormone." Oxytocin is produced in the brain, where it carries its message of bonding, intimacy and well-being across neurons. It's also released as a hormone into the bloodstream, coursing through our veins when we are with people we trust and feel trusted by. Oxytocin is abundant in breast milk passed from mother to her nursing infant, which may help to explain the deep bonding that takes place between mothers and their children.

Paul Zac has spent years designing and conducting clever studies to better understand the role that oxytocin plays in generosity and trust. He and his colleagues have found that when subjects inhale a nasal spray infused with oxytocin, their generosity increases as much as 80% over a control group that received a simple saline nasal spray with no oxytocin. And when participants were recipients of another person's generosity, they tended to reciprocate with generosity in return.

In other studies, Zac has demonstrated how understanding and empathy can be a catalyst for oxytocin production, and the generosity and selfless behavior that goes with it. In one experiment, participants watch one of two short videos, each featuring a father with his four-year-old son. The son is bald from chemotherapy due to terminal brain cancer.

In the "emotional" video, the father discusses how it feels to know his son is dying, but in the "neutral" video, the father and son are having a day at the zoo and cancer and death are not mentioned.

When showing the emotional video to a group of lawyers at a conference, Zac had to stop his lecture because fully one-third of the attorneys were crying so much (this should put an end to those bad attorney jokes).

Zac's researchers also drew blood from the participants before and after they watched either of the videos: Those who watched the "emotional" video showed a 157% spike in oxytocin levels, while oxytocin levels actually dropped for those who watched the "neutral" video.

As a kicker, as participants were leaving the experiment, Zac's team gave them all a chance to donate to charity. One-third of the participants donated... and it was those same folks who were empathically engaged by the "emotional" video.

If there is a Full Contact molecule, it would probably be oxytocin, as it enhances our sense of connection with others.

Oxytocin may be a primary driver in our tendency to reciprocate with one another and to identify and feel bonds with those we consider to be "ours." (Interestingly, oxytocin may also be why we can so easily distrust or be suspicious of those whom we consider "others," and not "ours.")

So, if oxytocin is such a powerful catalyst for trust and trust is so central to good collaboration, how can we generate more of both?

One of the ways we can stimulate more oxytocin is through our interactions. Especially when those interactions involve generosity, benevolence and sincere caring. As Balboa and Glaser tell us, the aftereffects of our conversations can sometimes remain indefinitely, long after oxytocin levels return to normal: "Conversations have the power to change the brain by boosting the production of hormones and neurotransmitters that stimulate body systems and nerve pathways, changing our body's chemistry, not just for a moment, but perhaps for a lifetime."

So if you want to connect and feel connected with someone else, try being generous by extending curiosity and benevolence, for starters. The Golden Rule may be more than a nice platitude — treating others as we would like to be treated can be a practical strategy for increasing our oxytocin levels and expanding our collaborative performance.

Five Dimensions of Trust

We've seen that trust is a multifaceted thing—it's an action, a feeling and a molecule. Now let's break it down in a different way and look at five ways that we can experience trust in other people and in ourselves.

We often say *I trust her* or *I don't trust him* as if trust is like a light switch, either on or off. When we think about trust in these all-or-nothing terms, we're wielding trust as a blunt instrument. We're limiting our collaborative capacity, our ability to make and sustain contact with others.

By breaking trust out into five distinct dimensions, we can be much more precise about whom and what we are trusting or not trusting, and consequently how we might engage and make commitments with them. These five dimensions are: *Capacity, Reliability, Aligned Commitments, Transparency* and *Shared Context*. We can apply these dimensions to teams and organizations as well as individuals. And of course, each of these are areas of assessment...

Transparency (Candor, Sincerity): Does what she say to me match what she says to herself and/or to others? Are her intentions consistent with her words? Is she sincere? As in, "Will this person actually pay me once I've kept my promise?" Or "Will this person actually follow through diligently on what she says she'll do?"

Most executives you talk to would cite candor and transparency as fundamental factors in good collaboration. While we all know intuitively that they are important, we may not always understand the specific ways in which they matter...

Lack of candor contributes to longer cycle times, slow decision making, and unnecessarily iterative discussions.

In a study of banks during the 2008 global economic crisis, the banks with the poorest returns were those in which their teams scored the lowest on the candor scale. Conversely, those that communicated more candidly about risky securities, lending practices, and other potential problems performed better and preserved shareholder value better.

Research at over 50 large companies concluded that "observable candor" is the behavior that best predicts high-performing teams. This applies not only at the team level, but also at the macro, corporate level, as this example about corporate transparency illustrates...

Our cultures are almost identical

In an acquisition by a West Coast tech company of a smaller mid-west competitor, one of the consulting companies assisting with the integration conducted a survey of employees from both companies. The survey concluded that the cultures of the two companies were very similar.

Executives in the acquiring company jumped on this point and made it a centerpiece of their employee communications, declaring that "the two companies are remarkably similar in their responses and overall cultural alignment, and even in areas where we differ, it's by a small margin..."

When I heard this statement, I cringed. I'd already talked to executives from both companies and the differences to me were glaring. The way major strategic and day-to-day decisions were made by leaders in the two companies were diametrically opposed. The communications practices were different. The mythologies that shaped the companies' cultures were worlds apart, as were the stories people told themselves every day about who their company was and why they were proud to work there. Although there certainly were some similarities, the people in these two companies were living in very different worlds.

As senior leaders from the acquired company began leaving unexpectedly (or being asked to leave) early on in the acquisition, the message of "similar cultures" began to take on a desperate tone. Within a year, there were very few senior leaders from the acquired company remaining, which made the integration of the teams below them much more challenging and stressful.

The "actual" differences between the two companies wasn't ever the issue. Those differences could be (and were eventually) worked through. The issue was that those differences weren't appreciated, explored and acknowledged up front, but were instead glossed over and treated as trivial. So many of the people in the acquired company who were already feeling anxious and uncertain about their future, now also felt crazy, confused or misunderstood—and mistrustful of the leaders in the acquiring company. I knew the executives at the acquiring company quite well and they were—to a person— thoughtful, humane and caring folks, committed to the well-being and success of all their employees. This commitment and goodness may have led them to underplay the cultural differences and over-state the similarities, to shield employees from the anxiety and uncertainty of change. Although it might have been initially uncomfortable for the employees to hear, I think the integration would have gone much more smoothly had the executives in the acquiring company looked more closely at the cultural differences and candidly acknowledged those differences up front.

Capacity (Competence): Can he really do what he says he can do, in the ways he says he can do it? Does he have the knowledge, skills, competence, time, resources to do what I would rely on him to do, to get the job done? Does he know how to listen well to what this customer is really looking for? Or, Does he know how to manage his promises well?

Reliability: Does she have a consistent track record of doing what we need her to do? Has she demonstrated reliability in the past?

Aligned Commitments (Shared Commitments): Does the way he conducts his affairs and manage his commitments align with my own? Does she operate with my best interest in mind, even when it may not be convenient for her? Does she share my operational and ethical standards? Remember that "Care Doesn't Care" example from earlier in the book? It was clear that trust between the two main groups was very weak to start with, and the more they tried to get each other to change, the more they eroded that trust. It wasn't until they started working together to examine the data and to listen to each other's differing perspectives that they were able to recognize the other group as committed, caring people who shared an interest in collaborating well to improve the customer's experience.

Shared Context: Does she have the cultural, social, or professional background and understanding to be effective in this area, or is this her "first rodeo"? Does she have the ability to communicate and address problems effectively when they arise? Can she do what she needs to do, in conformance with conventions of social behavior of the environments in which she'll be operating?

Five Ways We Trust

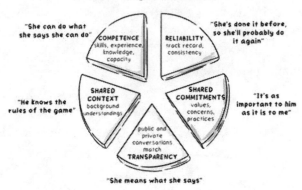

"She can do what she says she can do" — **COMPETENCE** skills, experience, knowledge, capacity

"She's done it before, so she'll probably do it again" — **RELIABILITY** track record, consistency

"He knows the rules of the game" — **SHARED CONTEXT** background understandings

"It's as important to him as it is to me" — **SHARED COMMITMENTS** values, concerns, practices

"She means what she says" — **TRANSPARENCY** public and private conversations match

Trust in Action and the Action in Trust

The issue of trust is often laden with moral significance. It's easy to jump from a negative assessment about someone's trustworthiness in one dimension to their overall moral character as a human being. Sometimes even just raising the issue of trust in conversation can put everyone on edge.

When we treat trust as primarily a moral issue, we limit our opportunities for learning and collaboration. For starters, it's a short step from moralizing about a behavior to characterizing or pathologizing a person in ways that limit both us and them. If they have a track record of not fulfilling their projects on time, for instance, we may pronounce them to be flakes, incompetent, or even liars. From a purely practical perspective, once we've characterized someone in this way, there's not much else to do other than avoid them or try to manipulate them into doing what we want them to do. After all, what can you do about someone who is a flake or liar? Avoidance, coercion, or finding a way to get rid of that person are our primary options.

But if instead we get very specific about trust, examining it from each of the five dimensions—we might move away from this passive moralistic orientation towards a more discerning, curious and active perspective.

Just because we may not trust someone in one or more of these dimensions doesn't mean that we need to write them off as morally inferior or resign ourselves to "who they are." If someone on your team lacks the cultural experience to open up the new office in another country, but otherwise has the skill and commitment to do so (and shares our company's values), then I might find someone else steeped in that culture to help her make the right moves.

By the same token, if I'm considering a new executive hire, even though I assess that he has the perfect skill set, experience and commitment we're looking for, I might not hire him because he wasn't entirely transparent about some aspect of his previous job. Or I might decide to talk with him about that directly (even perhaps going "meta" with him by sharing my concern), to see what else I might learn about him and why he may not have been forthcoming.

Or the person you recently promoted may not yet have the competence to complete the project on his own, but if you trust him in the other dimensions, you might be willing to give him the project anyway, with the understanding that he'll either get training to build his competence, or seek help from someone else who is competent. Of course, this assumes you also trust him to recognize and admit to what he does and doesn't know, and to make the requests needed to get the job done regardless (different types of competence).

I may trust one person on my team to always put the brakes on whenever the conversation turns to something personal. At the same time, I may trust him to always back up his assertions with good data, even while trusting him to never talk about his true feelings. It comes down to discerning which dimensions of trust are most important to me in each situation.

I often ask people which, of the five dimensions, they feel is most critical—which area is a "must have" to be able to trust someone. Many people say it's the dimension of Transparency: If they can't trust a person to be honest and sincere about what they care about, then the other dimensions don't really matter much. Others point to Shared Commitments as the prerequisite. How about you—which of the five dimensions of Trust is a "must have" for *you* to work with them?

Trusting People You Don't Trust

As I just implied, we don't just trust people to do what we want them to do. We can also trust them to do the opposite. And we may still be able to collaborate with them. Self-interest can make strange bedfellows, and sometimes it's the very things we distrust about someone that we can reliably count on them doing in the future.

To trust is to rely upon someone to do things or be certain ways under certain conditions. We can trust people even if their motivation for doing what we're trusting them to do is completely at odds with our own values, self-interest or convenience.

Can I enter into a promise with someone who doesn't seem to care about my own well-being? Who doesn't share my commitment to our mutual success? Possibly. If I assess that, because of their commitment to pursue and satisfy *their own* self-interest, mine will also likely be served, I might be willing to commit to them in certain areas. This describes many geo-political relationships as well as many business relationships. It's why so many businesses which are staunch rivals in the marketplace still enter into partnerships, form coalitions and make alliances.

We may trust some people to consistently make our lives miserable or try to undermine us whenever possible (if that's what their track record suggests). In some ways, this is the definition of an enemy. Yet we still can (and often do) trust our enemies in certain specific ways. We may trust some people to consistently oppose us, while we may trust others to behave erratically or consistently unpredictably towards us.

It's entirely possible to collaborate effectively with someone without trusting them in all five domains. But it's helpful to know in which of the five domains you assess trust and in which you don't, so that you can design your conversations and your commitments accordingly.

Building and Destroying Trust

The cliché goes something like this: *It takes a long time to build trust, but it can be destroyed in an instant.* Here are a few ways to build trust every day with your colleagues (and yourself):

- Create opportunities in your meeting agendas and conversations to talk about Trust itself. Start with yourself—ask your colleagues what you yourself might be doing or not doing that might make it harder to trust you, and in which dimension of trust? Then see if others are willing to follow suit. (The reciprocity principle often helps here.)
- Check-in with each other regularly during a conversation—where are we at, how are we each seeing things? Don't try to rush to conclusions, actions, solutions or "take-aways." This almost always weakens trust and encourages people to distance themselves from the outcome. Instead, take the time to get each person's views on the table and explore them.
- Go through the steps of "grounding" your respective assessments together. Yes, it takes longer up front, but things go much quicker—and better—in the long run.
- Respectfully share sincere assessments with others if they are willing to receive them (I'd ask first). Then be sure

to "own" your assessments for what they are—subjective assessments, not objective reflections of what they're doing or who they are.

- Check your own listening and check others' listening to you throughout your conversations. This helps you remain in contact, which is easier than continually breaking it and then trying to reestablish it.
- Put important points of agreement or commitment in writing for everybody to see and understand.

Respectful physical contact also generates more oxytocin. This is one reason I like to include mindfulness and martial arts-inspired Performance Practices when I work with groups—practices that involve attention, simple movements and light, safe, non-intrusive contact. And I *always* give people the option of just observing if they don't feel comfortable with any of the practices (so that they can trust that I have their well-being in mind).

And here are a few ways to increase your own "trustworthiness" to yourself:

- Make a well-grounded assessment about your current level of competencies in the areas where you want to be trusted. Be sure to get input from others whom you trust.
- Learn and practice new skills to shore up your skill in those areas that matter to you.
- Manage your promises impeccably, including the ones that you may not be able to keep.
- Cultivate your capacity to tolerate strong emotions in others without reacting judgmentally or trying to change them. The more you can stay present with people who share what's truly going on with them—without fear of being judged or fixed by you—the more they'll tend to

trust you. And the more you'll get to learn about them and what makes them tick (valuable for Full Contact!).

Reflection & Practice – Building Trust in Conversations

Let's return to that sheet of paper on which you wrote the names of three people you trust and three you don't trust. For each person, using a scale of 0 to 5 (0 being no trust and 5 being total trust), write down your assessment of trust in each of the five dimensions:

- Transparency
- Capacity
- History
- Aligned Commitments
- Contextual Experience

For each person, what actions might you take to increase the level of trust you assess, and what actions might you take to manage the risk you assess where your level of trust is low?

Part III

Practicing the Internal Art of Full Contact Performance

Throughout this book you've been reading about the action that underlies everything that goes on in our collaborations. You've seen how we each are at the center of that action in very tangible ways, from the way in which we pay attention and interpret things, to the way we express our interpretations and engage with the people and world around us through our words and our bodies.

In Part III, we're going to get even more specific about the role that we, ourselves, play in our collaborative performance. We'll build upon the distinctions of meta-moves and First and Second Order reflection and action and look at the stages of recognition that many managers go through when they're first introduced to these concepts in our workshops and consulting engagements. These are the stages most of us tend to go through as we make deeper contact with ourselves.

We'll then remind ourselves about the importance of practicing whatever it is we want to get better at, including our collaborative performance, and then look at four personal Performance Practices you can do on your own to help you strengthen your contact with your colleagues—especially when collaboration feels challenging.

We'll end with some final thoughts about collaboration...

Chapter 17

Contact with Myself

In this chapter, we'll build upon what we've been calling First and Second Order learning.

If our actions or solutions don't seem to address a problem or are creating new problems, we may make a meta-move to the Second Order, because the options available to us are limited by the First Order we're operating in.

Options Available in the First Order

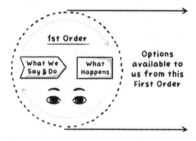

We say and do things, observe and assess what happens, and then say and do more things that make sense from the First Order we're operating in. The options available to us are always limited by the Order we're in.

Like that professional services leadership team that had been trying to solve the "problem" of its leaders, as long as they remained in that First Order thinking, their thinking and conversations remained stuck. This wasn't because they weren't intelligent, experienced or committed; it was because the "givens" that they were operating with limited their thinking and the options available to them. Moving to the Second Order enabled that team to see things they hadn't seen and think things they hadn't thought before.

In the Second Order, our perspective expands, and new possible actions become apparent to us. In essence, our common-sense has changed, which opens the doors to declaring better problems and new solutions.

Options Available in the Second Order

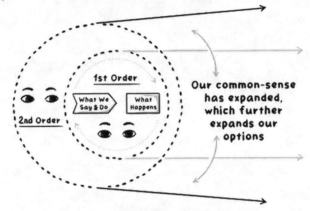

In this new Order, by examining the **givens** (our assumptions, assessments, stories, goals, strategies, etc.), we expand our common-sense and new options become available to us.

Although moving to a new order can vastly expand your options, it still may not always be enough. Perhaps the issues are emotionally super-charged, or maybe you have a history of difficulty with the person or team you're trying to work with. You may have strong critical assessments about them, their attitude, their willingness or even their capacity to collaborate well—and they may have similar assessments about you. Maybe you've tried everything you know—even inviting them into the Second Order with you, but nothing seems to work. You're at an impasse, and the collaboration seems dead in its tracks.

As discouraging as this may feel, it doesn't mean there's nothing more to do, nowhere else to go. This is when you can make another meta-move. But this meta-move is different...

The *Problem* of Me

When you feel you've reached the end of your rope with this person or that group, it may be time for a move to the *Third Order*. This shift requires that you redirect your focus away from the challenging person or the interaction you're stuck in, and shine the light of your attention squarely on yourself. This shift requires no permission or collaboration with anyone else. Nobody even needs to know you're doing it.

Shifting Attention to the Third Order - Ourselves

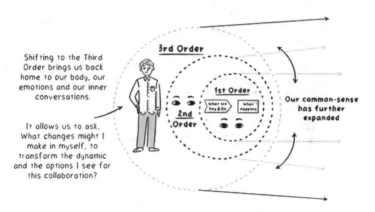

Shifting to the Third Order brings us back home to our body, our emotions and our inner conversations.

It allows us to ask, What changes might I make in myself, to transform the dynamic and the options I see for this collaboration?

3rd Order

1st Order

2nd Order

Our common-sense has further expanded

The shift to the Third Order brings you back home to your body, your emotions and your inner conversations.

The reason this shift is so valuable is that our habitual reactions to what's going on are usually calling the shots. Our habitual assessments and stories, our conditioned emotional triggers, our body's difficulty tolerating discomfort when things aren't going well, all determine the options available to us in these interactions. At these times, we first need to manage ourselves before we can skillfully engage with others. This is why the first "problem" we each need to solve is the problem of *me*. Its why collaboration is fundamentally an internal art.

The value of shifting attention to yourself is that it helps you to loosen the constraints and expand the options available to you for transforming your collaboration.

Focusing inwardly, you can give more attention to what's going on in your body, to the emotions that may be coloring your experience, and to your "inner" conversations.

Along with the public, "outer" conversation we have with others, we're also always running our inner conversations, and although nobody else can hear them, these inner conversations can easily drown out all the other voices in the room.

And it helps to remember that we're not the only ones with our inner conversations. Our colleagues are also each having their own private conversations which aren't accessible to us. This is why Echeverria says that there are at least three conversations going on whenever we're having a conversation with someone else: The spoken conversation that we're both having out loud, and the inner conversations that we are each simultaneously having inside ourselves. Add more people to the mix and it's no wonder collaboration can be so challenging: All of these conversations are taking place in the same room, yet we may have no idea what's actually being said in all those inner conversations.

The challenge is that *our inner conversations drive our outer ones*. They shape the moves we make with that person or group. Even if we try to mask our inner conversations—our true feelings, intentions or strategies—they'll still shape what we do and how we do it.

It's worth repeating here that sometimes the other people out there really *can* impede our collaboration. Other people *can* be really difficult! But those folks out there are never the *sole* problem. They can't be. They're just people doing what they're doing (probably doing their best, like us), until... we tell a story about them: *they don't want to collaborate; they're trying to control things; they don't listen well; they aren't mature enough, they're being assholes, and so forth...*

When we forget that our assessments and stories are just that—*our* assessments and stories, when we treat our beliefs and feelings as true and accurate reflections of what's going on, we lock ourselves into a box of our own thinking, just like the "box" of nine dots. We next drag those other folks right into our box with us and then we're all stuck. Recognizing this imaginary box is the first step into the Third Order, where we can regain some choice about what we are doing and how we're doing it. It's where we find the key that unlocks the box. That key is always stored in our perceptions and thinking.

Stages of Contact with Myself

In workshops and coaching sessions, when I ask managers to reflect carefully on their challenging conversations, they typically go through several stages...

First, there is the initial surprise when they realize that they aren't always doing what they think they're doing in the interaction. They thought they'd been listening well, but realize they weren't. Or they'd assumed that they were being open-minded and inviting dissenting views, when in fact they were subtly shutting them down. With this realization comes the recognition that many of their most ardently held beliefs about their collaborative challenges are not necessarily accurate— they're stories they've invented based on their feelings, biases and frustrations.

And then another realization closely follows: That much of their attention has been focused on those folks *out there*, believing that those folks were the source of the problem. Here, they start to realize that this outward focus is, itself, part of the problem. When they were locked into this mode of outward facing attention, they would naturally strategize and take action that was directed at changing, fixing or controlling those problematic folks (*energy follows attention*). Not only does this outward focus rarely work—it also keeps these managers from examining *their own* role in the situation and prevents them from changing (getting out of that box they are stuck in). It just wouldn't make sense to examine *yourself* if you're certain that the problem lies elsewhere—that's like the drunk person looking for his car keys under the streetlamp, because that's where the light is—not because its where he dropped the keys. *It's as if the "me" in the picture doesn't exist.*

Forgetting the Me in the picture

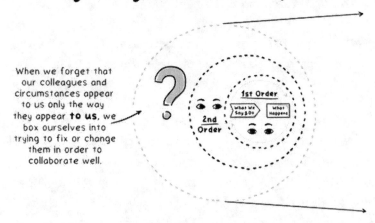

When we forget that our colleagues and circumstances appear to us only the way they appear **to us**, we box ourselves into trying to fix or change them in order to collaborate well.

Around this stage in the process, some managers get frustrated or defensive, occasionally accusing the consultants (me or my colleagues) of "rigging" the exercise—of manipulating the conversation to make them appear to be more responsible for their collaborative challenges than they believe they are. This is when I might remind them that they aren't the only ones with compelling inner conversations and a strong outward focus—all those *other folks* they're having trouble with are probably saying similar things about them. I then ask them whether they would want access to those other folks' inner conversations, if it were hypothetically possible. (Just out of curiosity, if *you* could gain access to your colleagues' inner conversations, would you want to? Many people say *Yes, of course*. But others aren't so sure they'd want to know how other people see them, even if it were somehow possible.)

This is the point in the workshop or coaching session where we begin to explore the principles and practices you've been reading about in this book, helping the managers to gain more awareness of what they're doing with their attention, their words, and their bodies. It's where we give them new practices to expand their collaborative performance and where they begin to recognize that—if making Full Contact with the people with whom they're trying to collaborate is possible—it must start with themselves.

To make full contact with others, we first need to make full contact with ourselves.

From this point forward, things get easier.

As the managers begin to see with new eyes what's going on in their collaborative challenges (by moving to the Second, and then the Third Order), the tension in the room begins to ebb and the mood gets lighter. And something else happens: The managers start to reflect and strategize about how they might learn more about those *other folks'* inner conversations— how they might create the conditions for better conversations by getting more curious and extending legitimacy towards their colleagues. In other words, they start to experience the principles of connectedness and reciprocity, realizing that by changing their own conversations, they can often influence their colleagues' conversations as well.

This three-stage process of learning looks something like this:

1. We start out with our attention fixated on the other person or team being the problem, trying to change them and getting frustrated or discouraged that *they're* not changing.
2. We bring our attention back home to ourselves, so that we can sense, feel and observe ourselves, our attention, and our own active role in the interaction.
3. As we gain more insight into ourselves and what we're doing, we also become more curious and interested in the other person out there and how the world may be showing up for them. As our previously hardened beliefs about the other person soften, the possibility of making full contact with them becomes more tangible, often even effortless.

Put another way, once we've put the *Me* back into the picture, the other folks usually start coming into focus in new ways. Focusing on ourselves enables us to better see them.

Putting the Me Back in the Picture

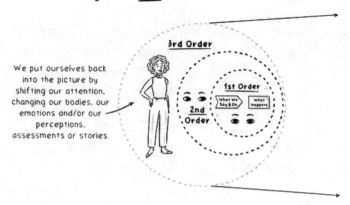

We put ourselves back into the picture by shifting our attention, changing our bodies, our emotions and/or our perceptions, assessments or stories.

To put the missing "me" back into the picture is to make contact with myself, which is where the real leverage lies for

Full Contact Performance. When I change myself, I become an invitation for others to join me. Whether they will always accept my invitation or not is up to them, but regardless of their decision, I've done *my* work and gotten clearer in myself, which is what we might call a "no regrets" scenario.

Changing My Body

When I'm feeling particularly stuck in a painful or uncomfortable emotion, or locked into a negative thought pattern, the best way I've found to shift into the Third Order is to bring my attention to my body. I usually start with a version of the body scanning practice you practiced in Chapter 9, focusing on any clear sensations I experience. Or I may simply begin focusing on my breathing and then expand my attention as other sensations arise. When I let my attention rest on a particular body sensation for a moment or so, I usually notice things start to change, perhaps my breathing slows, some of the heat or tension subsides or sensation may move to another part of the body. This is all quite normal.

The great thing about the body is that it's always present in the here and now — even when our thoughts are far away in the past or the future.

Shifting attention to the body helps us to instantly get more present, to orient ourselves more directly to what's happening right now, and then to move into a more inquisitive, curious frame of mind.

Here are some simple questions you can ask yourself to help shift into the Third Order…

- What are those sensations I'm experiencing in my body — is it a knot in the stomach? Tension in the chest or shoulders? Do I feel tightness or constriction, or perhaps a sense of overall heaviness or fatigue, or some other sensations?

- Am I slumped down in the chair or perhaps holding myself rigidly upright, as if girding for what might happen next?
- Is my breathing shallow, quick, or choppy?
- Where might I feel energy moving through my body, and what's the quality of that energy—is it streaming, vibrating or pulsing in my hands, arms or temples?

These are just a few questions that can help you return to the life of the body and the myriad sensations you might experience. It might also happen that you don't feel much of anything in the body right now, which is also good to notice. There are no "right" sensations you should be experiencing or searching for; the point is simply to notice. Because energy follows attention, just the act of noticing what you're experiencing often begins to change it.

Pulling Myself Together

In any physical endeavor, our power and skill are directly related to how unified and integrated our movement is. On the martial arts mat, tennis court, golf course or softball diamond, if my shoulders are not well coordinated with my hips or my hips are not moving in unison with my legs and feet, my movements will lack power and precision. I'm also much more likely to injure myself. If you've ever tried to push a stalled car or move heavy furniture, you know that you can't just use your hands and arms—you must engage your hips and legs in a coordinated way, or you'll lack power. Although you may not have noticed it at the time, you engaged those stronger muscles in your lower half which helped you unify and coordinate your movements and access your full power.

Same with conversations: If your intention, attention, words and body aren't aligned, you're not going to be very effective and you'll likely cause people to assess you as insincere or "off." You won't be coming from a grounded, centered place and will lack focus and power.

One way you can quickly unify yourself is to do a "grounding and centering" practice. Whether on the martial arts mat, in sports or at the office, when you ground and center yourself, you'll be much better able to deal with challenges from a confident, secure place—without adding to the anxiety or confusion others around you might be feeling. It's a great Third Order practice because just the simple act of grounding and centering yourself can profoundly expand your options while allowing others to relax and feel more comfortable in your presence. I'll provide simple instructions for grounding and centering in the next chapter.

Isn't Focusing on Myself Selfish?

This question sometimes comes up: *Since collaboration is about working with other people, shouldn't I be focused on those other people out there and not on myself? Isn't it selfish to focus on myself when I'm trying to be collaborative with others?*

Absolutely, focusing on the other people matters! To collaborate, we *must* engage with the other folks and give them our deep, curious and benevolent attention. It can't be just about us. But if we're constantly and automatically filtering everything they say and do through our own habitual perceptions and interpretations, then we're not actually being with them in the first place—we're just being with *ourselves*, projecting our beliefs onto them from within our own isolated Universe.

To break that pattern—to become present with *them*, we often need to first return our attention to ourselves. Otherwise, those unexamined habits of perceiving, thinking and feeling will inevitably play themselves out in our interactions, keeping all of us from making contact. It's important enough to restate it: *Our contact with others begins when we make contact with ourselves.*

So, no—focusing on ourselves isn't selfish at all. It's the opposite; it's what allows us to make meaningful contact with the folks around us—even if we don't see eye-to-eye, even if we wish it were someone else sitting across the table from us, even if neither of us has any idea how to proceed. Those situations, in fact, are when shifting to the Third Order and focusing on ourselves can be most helpful.

Chapter 18

Practicing for Full Contact

In working with managers and their teams around the world, my colleagues and I have seen that most people already "know" what works in organizational collaboration. When we ask them to make a list of what works, most of their lists are pretty similar, even across vastly different organizations, industries and cultures. Most of these lists include things like...

- Be candid and transparent
- Respect different viewpoints
- Seek to understand
- Be a good listener
- Make decision based on facts—not just opinions or emotions
- Treat people fairly
- Give everyone in the conversation an opportunity to contribute (and so forth)

These things are important in organizational collaboration and we've addressed many of them in one way or another in this book. But here's the other thing my colleagues and I notice: Even when people *know* what works, they don't always *do* what they know works—especially when they're feeling pressure to "get things done, already." And what's more—even when they do many of these things they know work—those things *still* don't always work as expected.

Knowing what works isn't the same as being able to do what works.

Knowledge and techniques are helpful, but they're not always enough. In the case of organizational collaboration, while concepts like transparency, respect, good listening, fairness, etc., are good, they often remain just concepts. And concepts alone won't help you make Full Contact. They sometimes make collaboration more difficult.

To collaborate effectively, you need to connect your concepts to your actions. And you need to ensure that your intent for the collaboration is clear and supportive of Full Contact, because what matters as much as what you do, is *where you're coming from* as you do it. If you're primarily intent on getting your own needs met and the folks around you are just standing in your way, then your actions will likely convey that intention—regardless of how much you know about good collaboration, active listening or any other techniques you may have learned.

Your intention matters. And so does practice, because to get good at anything, you need to put your nervous system into it.

This is why armies spend so much time drilling their soldiers, why masters in the trades spend years in hands-on apprenticeships, and why good performers in any sport, art or discipline continually practice the basics. People have understood the importance of long-term practice for a long time, but we generally don't apply this knowledge to organizational collaboration.

Today, neuroscientists are quite specific about what happens when we practice: As we practice and gain skill in anything, we literally change our brain—the structure and functioning of our nervous system. The more skilled we become, the more developed and faster become the neurocircuits associated with that skill.

What we call "muscle memory" is actually nervous system memory. Or more specifically, increases in the white matter— the myelination or insulation—around those neural circuits associated with the skill we're practicing—including the thinking or social behaviors we are repeating. Although the physiological processes of neuronal change are complex, the short story is simple: We get better at whatever we repeatedly practice, especially when we're paying attention and getting timely and accurate feedback as we practice. And this applies whether what we're practicing is making us healthier and happier, or more anxious, disconnected and unhappy.

You may be familiar with the "10,000 hour rule," which roughly states that to get really good at something, you need to practice it for at least 10,000 hours. But, as Daniel Goleman says, "The '10,000-hour rule' is only partly true. If you are a duffer at golf, say, and make the same mistakes every time you try a certain swing or putt, 10,000 hours of practicing that error will not improve your game. You'll still be a duffer, albeit an older one." In other words, you'll get pretty good at that lousy swing you keep making.

The key is how you're paying attention while you're practicing, and having a good feedback loop to help you continually self-correct. Mindless, mechanical repetition yields little improvement. So, dancers have mirrors, actors have directors (and often repeat many takes of the same scenes), and world-class athletes have coaches and study videotapes of their performance over and over, to absorb the feedback that lets them recognize and correct errors.

Paying full attention and having reliable and timely feedback also seems to boost the mind's processing speed, strengthen synaptic connections in the brain, and expand the neural networks for whatever it is you're working on.

Pablo Casals was known for practicing scales every day up until the day he died, at age 86. Throughout his later years, he was often asked why—since he was already the greatest living cellist—he continued to practice his scales every day. His common answer: "I'm beginning to see some improvement."

Same for collaboration. The more we "practice" treating our assessments and stories about other people (or ourselves) as true facts, for example, the truer they'll feel, even if they are ruining our relationships and hampering our collaborative performance. We'll get better at whatever we practice.

Full Contact Performance Practices

Since practice is so important, this chapter will introduce you to several "Third Order" practices that can make a big difference in how you respond to difficult collaborations and other types of challenges. These Performance Practices can help you in whatever you're doing. They can often help you to get unstuck when you're stuck and help you get stuck less often.

They are also foundational in that they shape all the other moves you might make. And you can practice them any time and any place—by yourself with nobody else around, or in meetings surrounded by other folks. As a general rule, the more you practice them on your own when you're *not* under pressure, the more available they'll be to you when the pressure is on and you really need them. So don't wait until you are in that tense, conflict-ridden conversation to begin practicing.

Before we look at the specific practices, let's look at some more metaphors we routinely use...

Don't get all spun up about it.
People are getting stirred up.
You seem amped up.
I'm feeling upset.
Calm down.
Don't be so uptight.
He's hot under the collar.
I'm really wound up.

Rooted as they are in our sensate experience, these metaphors point to something fundamental that happens when we get triggered or challenged: *The energy in our body moves up.* Literally. It tends to heat up, rise up and tighten up. As our metaphors also suggest, it's possible to counter these tendencies—to intentionally ground our energy, to lower our temperature and release our tension. Which is why we say things like *calm down, chill out, cool off.* And things like *I need to unwind* and *get grounded.* The following four Performance Practices help with this...

Performance Practice #1 – Grounding & Centering

In the chapter on assessments, we looked at how *grounding* an assessment can help us test and validate the assessment so that we might make better decisions. There, I was using the term *grounding* in a metaphorical sense.

But we know that collaboration—like metaphor—isn't just a head trip. It's a body trip, too. Our relationships and conversations are mutual nervous system encounters in which our bodies are full partners with our words. This Grounding and Centering practice is about the physical source of that "grounding" metaphor—literally, connecting and unifying with the ground under our feet.

Psychologist Russell Lemle reminds us that, in the throes of powerful threat emotions (storylines and bodily states of fear, anxiety or vulnerability), we can rarely simply *think* our way back into a trusting, mutually supportive relationship with our partner or our colleagues. But we can still find ways to interrupt those powerful storylines by switching channels—to the body.

Grounding and Centering is one of the simplest and easiest ways to do this. When we ground our bodies, it's not simply metaphorical—it's experiential, visceral. It involves using attention, sensation and imagination to align ourselves with gravity and connect our body with the ground we are standing on.

Most martial arts and mind-body disciplines include some form of grounding practice.

The following Grounding and Centering practice is simple enough to do anywhere. No special equipment is needed. It helps to quiet and calm the nervous system, increasing your sense of balance and stability, and enhancing your sensitivity to the people and environment around you.

Basic Grounding & Centering Practice

1. Stand with your feet parallel, about shoulder width apart.
2. Gently shift your weight from side to side a few times, sensing how the muscles on each side of your body get activated as you do this. Now let your weight settle in the middle, centered between right and left.
3. Next, gently shift your weight forward and backwards, from the balls of your feet to the heels, sensing the changing pattern of pressure on your feet and how your body organizes itself to keep from falling over in each direction. Now let your weight settle in the middle between front and back—centered in this forward-backward plane.
4. Now bring your attention to your body's height and depth. Gently let your knees bend slightly and then straighten, rising up on your toes slightly. Repeat this movement a few times—literally lowering and raising yourself towards and away from the ground. Now let yourself settle down, knees relaxed. Your body is

upright so that an imaginary plumb line dropped from the crown of the head would pass through the center of the body and between the feet directly towards the center of the earth. This is your center line and it can serve as a reference point for how you are aligned at any given moment. Take a breath and let it out easily, without straining. As you breathe out, imagine that the weight of your head, shoulders, arms, and chest sink straight down through that imaginary center line.

5. Next, place your hand on your lower belly, just a couple of inches below your navel. Your hand will help you to focus your attention here. We'll call this your *center*.

6. Now *ground* yourself by sensing the pressure of your feet on floor. Let the ground support your weight without any effort on your part. Imagine that you have roots reaching down through your feet into the earth. Imagine that your weight continues to settle downward, from your center down through those roots into the ground.

7. Let yourself settle into this centered and grounded position with your knees relaxed, maintaining a slight bounce in your legs. Rest in this easy, relaxed stance for a minute or so, with your attention focused on that imaginary center point in the middle of your body, just below the belly button. Be sure not to strain or work too hard.

That's it—that's all there is to it.

As simple as it is, this Grounding and Centering practice can profoundly impact your sense of stability, calm you down, clear your thinking and shift your mood. By simply shifting focus to the physical sensations of your feet standing on the ground, your body aligning with gravity, your breath moving in and out, you can reset your own internal system. It's like the electrical grounding rod in your house that safely directs the energy of an electrical surge or lightning safely into the ground.

You can Ground and Center yourself in just a few seconds, or you can give it five, ten or more minutes. It's easiest to learn just standing still, but as it becomes more familiar, you can extend the stationary practice to movement, practicing "walking from your center," imagining or sensing your movements emanating or being powered from the center of your body, while also feeling the contact of your feet with the ground. You can do this practice anywhere, from standing in line, to walking, running, riding a bike, playing tennis, or participating in a challenging conversation.

The more you practice, the easier it'll be for you to Ground and Center yourself when you need it—whenever you find yourself getting amped up, when the conversation is driving you and your colleagues further apart, rather than into closer contact together.

Of course, sometimes this is easier to do than at other times. When we notice that the tension or energy in our body, in the room, on the team, in the organization is ramping up, when anxiety is rampant and patience is short, it's hard not to follow suit. Energy, like emotion, is contagious, which is why groups become mobs and chronically impatient and impulsive cultures perpetuate themselves (sometimes until they collapse).

The antidote to getting worked up is to move the energy back down through the body. When you Ground and Center yourself, you are literally shifting your attention and energy down to your own center). If you're not used to doing this, you can start with your imagination—just *imagine* that you are releasing tension, imagine that the energy is descending in the body—down into your center, and then down further through your feet, into the ground beneath you. Just imagining it will start the process, and as you practice more, the actual physical sensations of grounding will become more distinct.

Performance Practice #2 – Slowing Down & Getting Quiet

Moving quickly is important in organizations. Quicker R&D cycles, faster production times, shortening time-to-market, reduced time to resolve customer's issues, accelerating your company's exit strategies... speed matters.

But some of the things we do to speed things up actually slow us down or create other problems (which ultimately slows things down): Rushing to bad decisions; shortening or eliminating conversations in order to be more "efficient"; avoiding contentious topics because they'll take more time to work through; assuming consensus that isn't actually there; setting delivery dates for promises that aren't achievable—they all seem like they should move things along more quickly, but they don't. At least not for very long.

Against the pervasive organizational backdrop of impatience and speed, the maxim "slow down to speed up" has become a cliché. We hear it frequently and we may even preach it to others, but few people heed it. It remains another concept, a good idea—something that other people ought to do, but not *us in this meeting right now*.

Part of the reason is that slowing down seems supremely counter-intuitive when everyone around us is infected with the *speed-it-up* virus.

Slowing down is another one of those meta-moves that defies the common sense of the First Order. But counterintuitive as it may seem, slowing down is often the most efficient path forward.

The point of slowing down isn't to move more slowly—it's to be able to move more quickly later on (although moving more slowly might not always be such a bad thing either).

In my early days as a professional mediator, I had a profound and unnerving experience which has stayed with me: It was the first large multi-party lawsuit that I was mediating on my own. For the previous year or so I had been playing a supporting role in the mediations with my mentor, David Jenkins, taking the lead. But David had a scheduling conflict with another case that day, so I walked alone into the opulent conference room in the Plaintiff's law office in Santa Monica. The lawsuit was a construction defect case in which the Plaintiff (a Homeowner's Association) was claiming damages of more than 40 Million dollars. Seated around the large conference room were 37 people, representing various parties to the lawsuit—the homeowner's association representatives, the many defendants and cross-defendants (the developer, architect, primary contractor, and the various framing, concrete, sheetrock, electrical and plumbing trades), along with their respective attorneys, expert witnesses, and insurance representatives.

The tension I was feeling was oppressive. I had already met most of these players in previous sessions. (These construction cases often involved numerous sessions taking place over six to nine months or longer, and typically included those collaborative fact-finding sessions I described in the Prologue.) But until today, all these folks knew me as David's side-kick—not the lead mediator (*Settlement Referee* is the technical term). As we were approaching the end of this nine-month mediation process, I wasn't the only one feeling anxious. All the other players were also apprehensive about whether we were going to settle this case and how much they'd each have to pay to avoid going to trial (a much more costly consequence for everyone if the case didn't settle). And now in walks Grayson, the "junior" mediator.

I won't keep you in suspense—we settled the case. But not before that "profound and unnerving" experience I mentioned earlier: The morning started out as planned—we went around the room and the attorneys and expert witnesses each took turns sharing their conclusions and proposing their arguments. After lunch, I held a series of private caucuses with several of the larger players, to see how they were assessing their potential liability and to gauge their motivation to settle.

After these caucuses, I reconvened the full group to share, in general terms, the direction I thought the settlement discussions were taking. I wanted to prepare folks for the hard and often painful part of the settlement process—the final negotiations. I wanted the dollar figures that were at stake to feel real to the parties.

At some point in this process, the attorney for the prime contractor (one of the major parties, with significant financial exposure in the case) issued a very clear and provocative verbal challenge to the attorney for the architect (one of the other big players). It was the kind of challenge that threw the whole issue of settling the case into question. I don't actually recall the specifics of the challenge, but I vividly recall how the air suddenly got sucked right out of the room. And in that next instant, all eyes pivoted towards me. Folks were frozen in anticipation and concern, and they were looking to me to figure out a way through this.

The problem was that I suddenly had NO IDEA what to do next. It was as if my years of training and experience as a business leader and mediator just evaporated. For what seemed like an hour (but couldn't have been more than five or ten seconds), I was frozen, along with everyone else. And then I found myself doing the only thing I could apparently manage to do—what I'd been practicing on the Aikido mat for years: I took a slow, deep breath. And then another. This part of the memory is vivid: me sitting there, slowly looking around the room, just breathing, trying to appear calm until I (hopefully) started to feel calm—and praying that some clever words would come to me and rescue us all from this impending disaster.

But no clever words came. Instead, something else happened. As I sat there quietly breathing and willing my body to relax, I noticed that others began to relax their shoulders, release their jaws. Was I just imagining that folks were starting to breathe more slowly? I'll never know. But at that moment, deliverance arrived: One of the attorneys in the room, someone who hadn't been particularly vocal up to this point, made some comment about the progress we seemed to be making in the mediation process... and then everything shifted. Some nodded in agreement, some smiled, and somehow, I regained my center—and my words.

Nobody ever mentioned anything about that moment, and we successfully settled the case. But I continue to reflect on that moment and even now—decades later—the memory speeds up my breathing and brings flutters to my chest.

While it was happening, I had images of the entire case blowing up, the hundreds of thousands of dollars of professional fees wasted, my mediation career coming to an abrupt and humiliating end. Afterwards, I was left with an almost reverent appreciation for the power of slowing down, of quieting down, of breathing, and of the simple act of centering myself (even though while it was happening, my habitual mind and body were screaming, *Do something, quick!*).

A friend of mine, Trathen, is a talented and charismatic leader in both the local and national sustainability movement. He serves on several boards and always seems to have a million projects going on. He once remarked that things were so busy… that he'd better spend more time meditating. He was talking about slowing down inside, in order to keep up with the hectic pace outside.

Getting Quiet

There is an old Zen proverb: "The quieter you become, the more you can hear."

Since that mediation experience, I've seen it play out many times: When the boss, leader, facilitator or consultant slows down and gets quiet, even if only for a moment or two, it creates a potent space. It draws others into that space where they can exercise their autonomy and engage with the conversation or situation on their own terms, which is what you want for Full Contact Performance. The space gives them a sense of shared ownership of what's happening and where it's going, which they might not otherwise feel.

Slowing down and getting quiet is often the only way to actually make contact with people in today's chaotic business climate. To stop being yet another source of input, expectation or demand, and just be still for a few moments can let you— and others— hear and think things you might otherwise miss. Even if it doesn't instantly transform things, slowing down and taking a breath can let the mind disengage for a moment, which often enables you to re-engage with a new perspective. It's a meta-move in its own right.

The Power of Stillness

One form of Tai Chi Chuan practice is called "Push Hands." It's a partner practice that helps you develop sensitivity, timing, groundedness and a unified, harmonious quality of movement. It helps to re-condition your nervous system to meet force with softness, yielding and redirecting it, rather than engaging with force or tension.

It sometimes involves getting very still, so that we can receive and absorb our partner's push, letting their energy circulate down through our body, connect with the ground, and then rebound back out through our partner's body. I know it sounds esoteric and appears on the outside to be fake, but when you experience it, you know it's the real deal. A much bigger and stronger attacker can be toppled or thrown across the room by a skilled practitioner with seemingly no effort or movement. It's a good analogy for what can happen when we slow down, get quiet and really listen to someone speaking to us. They may come to see things they'd never seen before or become open to a different perspective just because they've been listened to so deeply.

So, the next time you find yourself struggling to make contact with someone, take the initiative and get quiet. (I sometimes jokingly tell my clients to "show some leadership and just shut-up for a change.") Instead of trying to push your agenda or wring everything you can out of everyone in the meeting, instead try hitting Pause with yourself and getting very quiet. Let folks know you are still there with them, but don't try to force things in any particular direction. Just let contact happen. If nothing else, it will be a nice break for everyone.

Performance Practice #3 – Relaxing for Performance
Any martial artist will tell you that the easiest people to topple are those who use the most force and carry the most tension in their bodies. My Tai Chi teacher continually shows me where I'm holding tension in my body (even though I'm *certain* that I'm relaxed).

One of the benefits of grounding and centering ourselves is that it helps us to relax our bodies, to let go of any tension, holding or constriction that we don't truly need in order to do whatever it is we're doing.

Watching top athletes, musicians, martial artists or acrobats, you notice that they look relaxed in their bodies. Unless they're injured, they tend to move with ease and a natural rhythm. They simply couldn't perform well otherwise. Because their muscles are generally relaxed, those muscles are available when they're needed to perform the lightning-quick, powerful, or dazzlingly intricate movements that characterize their mastery—seemingly without effort. If their muscles were constantly firing (as in chronically tense), they wouldn't be able to perform their magic. And they'd get tired much too quickly.

Unfortunately, we *do* see many business executives and managers with chronically tense bodies and chronically over-active minds. Ignoring the well-documented health consequences of chronic tension (cardiovascular disease, inflammation, digestive disorders, etc.), what do you think might be the implications for collaborative performance?

When we're relaxed, we tend to feel more stable and secure, less liable to be toppled by daily events. We're less trigger happy and less prone to getting triggered by others. We also tend to be more focused and efficient with our movement because we're using just what we need to get the job done and nothing more.

When I was beginning Aikido, an instructor grabbed my wrist with a very strong grip, tensing his entire arm and shoulder, intending to lock my wrist in place so that I couldn't move it. Although I had to muster some effort, I was able to move my wrist and break his grasp.

He then grabbed my wrist with only his thumb and forefinger, applying light but steady force—just enough pressure to maintain the connection. Using all my force, I couldn't escape his grasp. With a relaxed grip he could sense and track my every move precisely and with minimal effort, adjusting his grasp as needed to maintain contact and keep me from breaking free. As I moved left or right, up or down, he stayed relaxed and was able to continually calibrate to keep my wrist in his grasp.

This applies to many other things as well. Keeping a light, easy grasp on the situation allows for sensing and adjusting to the changes that we encounter. When we relax, we are calmer, more present, better able to connect and muster our power as needed, rather than being in a state of continual "on" which is what happens when we are tense or hypervigilant. We're also more pleasant to be around.

Whenever we feel that somebody or some challenging situation is bearing down on us, it's easy to be thrown off balance, both physically and mentally. Our first impulse is often to tighten up, to gird against the onslaught, as if that will protect us. But it has the opposite effect—we just become less stable and less grounded. This is why practicing relaxing ourselves mentally and physically when we're *not* under pressure is so important. It's how we build "the muscle" of relaxing under pressure when we do need it.

Less Effort Isn't Slacking

One dimension of *Relaxing for Performance* involves not working so hard at everything. The instruction to "work harder" starts early and only escalates through school and careers. When was the last time you were told by your teacher or boss to *not* work so hard? (Or if you were told this, when was the last time you actually heeded this advice?)

Contrary to our conditioning, more effort doesn't always equal better performance. It also doesn't always equate to greater commitment. Working harder at the "wrong" solution (or the wrong problem) won't solve the problem. It doesn't make us smarter or more efficient; just more tired.

We can see this clearly in our own body: Tight, held muscles are not strong or efficient muscles—they're dysfunctional muscles, literally. As with those elite athletes, when our muscles are already activated, they're no longer available to do their work because the muscle fibers are already engaged.

A tense muscle is also a buffer to sensation. When our muscles are tense, we're unable to feel our subtle movement and energy, and to perceive the movements, energy and balance of another person. When we're tense and "up-tight," we're not going to be able to sense or make good contact with the people around us—like our muscles, we become less sensitive and attuned to our surroundings.

It's easy to see when people are working too hard on the Aikido mat: Beginners tend to move around too much, and usually too quickly. They use too much force and involve unnecessary muscles in the effort. Instead of displacing their partner's balance and making them light and easy to move, they make their training partner heavier and more difficult to displace. In other words, by trying too hard, they've made their work even harder. This is one of the things that distinguishes beginners from more advanced practitioners.

When we work too hard, we also aren't learning much about ourselves or our partner. We don't learn about how our opponent is approaching the situation; we don't pick up the signals they may be giving us about what they're going to do next.

Many business meetings are exhausting for the same reasons. People have spent the last hour, day or year of meetings running circles around each other or pushing hard against their colleagues' views or challenges, avoiding meaningful talk about difficult issues. Or trying to force their agenda onto each other while trying hard to not appear controlling or anxious about failing.

Some Tai Chi teachers tell their students to never use more than about 75% effort—because any more than that and you're just introducing more tension into the body. I think of this often when I'm in meetings and people are working especially hard to make things happen.

Performance Practice #4 – Extending Legitimacy

This fourth Performance Practice may also be the most challenging. Earlier in the book I introduced the concept of *extending legitimacy* as a fundamental practice for good listening and for genuine collaborative inquiry. Now, we'll look at how to get better at doing it, especially when our assessments or stories about the person sitting across from us may be strongly critical.

I recognize that this may seem like a strange thing to contemplate: *How do I change my assessments about someone if those are my "true and genuine" assessments?* To answer the question, we'll build on what we already know about *attention* and *words*.

First, a review: Extending legitimacy to another person doesn't mean that you agree, support, or must go along with their views, values or intentions. It just means that you recognize their humanity, their basic okay-ness, underneath those differences.

In terms of how to do it, we'll start where this book started—with the basic premise that to do almost anything—and especially to change what we're doing—we need to gain more awareness of what we're already doing.

So, the first step is to shift to the Third Order—to bring your attention to yourself: what you are feeling, thinking and doing in relation to the person or people you may be struggling with. Become familiar with the assessments you're making, the stories you're telling yourself, the characterizations you may be using to describe them, the sensations you feel in your body when you interact with them. As you already know, just noticing and acknowledging what's going on in our mind and/or body can often in itself bring about a change. Also, ask yourself what your honest intention is in this interaction or relationship. Just get your internal bearings.

Next, you can try out any of the following practices to see what might work for you. Going through one or more of them, you may notice that the power and hold of your assessments, stories or characterizations starts to soften. They lose some of their charge. You may experience a warming in your attitude towards this person. Just continue to be attentive to what's going on in you, regardless of what happens. And remember, you can do all of this alone—you need nobody's permission or participation to do any of these practices.

Examine those critical assessments you are making about this person. This means reminding yourself that these are, in fact, assessments that are never true or false. Go through the five questions for Grounding Assessments (from Chapter 6) and do it sincerely. Here are the five questions again...

1. *Towards what end are we making this assessment?* (and, if applicable, *What's the arena of action?*)

2. *What are the relevant facts (assertions) we're relying on to make this assessment?*
3. *What are the standards we're using to make this assessment?*
4. *How might our emotions be influencing this assessment?*
5. *How might other people whose opinions we value assess this?*

Find or invent a new focus for your attention. You already know that your attention is like a magnet for your energy (and often for others' energy as well). When you find yourself dwelling on someone or something, just intentionally shifting your attention can help to weaken its hold on you. And there are many ways you can shift your attention. Here are just a few:

Clarify your intention. Focus on the larger objective, goal or mission that you and the other person share. This is a focal point often touted by team building, conflict resolution and leadership experts, and for good reason. Keeping this focus in mind and returning to it frequently can help you remember why you are trying to collaborate in the first place and may help you get through some tough points in the process together.

Bring focus to your bodily sensations. As you've already seen, a shift to your bodily experience can ground, stabilize and relax you, often bringing about a change in your mood and mental outlook. Just relaxing your eyes and taking a few full, conscious breaths can bring about big changes.

Bring to mind some person or setting in your life that has been a source of unconditional support or love. It could be a child, sibling or spouse; a parent, beloved aunt, uncle or grandparent; a teacher or mentor — even a favorite pet. It could be any person or creature who evokes positive feelings when you think of them. Next, imagine that the person you are struggling with is also probably loved and appreciated by her or his family and friends (and if not, that's also a good reason to feel compassion for them).

Invent and practice a new story. Imagine that you own the company in which you and the other person are working. Rather than criticizing, competing or opposing them, you can instead think about how best to understand and support them. You care about their success just as you care about your business. (Yes, of course it's pretend, but as you'll recall, the point of a good story isn't necessarily to be accurate, but to connect you to what's important.) Another Aikido teacher of mine, Wendy Palmer, is masterful at using her attention to radically change the trajectory and impact of attacks by much larger training partners. Sometimes she might imagine her own energy bubbling up in her body, which instantly lightens the attacker's force as well. Or she may focus her attention on all of the empty space surrounding her and the attacker (using soft eyes), which—because attention can be so magnetic— also diffuses the attacker's focus on her as a target. I know it sounds weird, but when you watch her do it (or try attacking her yourself, as I have done countless times), you realize that it really works. The focus could even be on some place in nature, or anywhere else where you feel comfortable, inspired or expansive. Holding that image will change your body and your attitude, if only temporarily.

Invent a compassionate narrative. I have a little story I sometimes tell myself when I find myself delegitimizing someone else. It goes something like this: If I were living his life—in his role, with his challenges, his body, his life experiences, would I be showing up very different from how he's showing up to me right now? Probably not. Just as he might be showing up a lot like me if our lives and roles were reversed. This gives me a little more compassion and curiosity about what his experience might be like.

<u>Change the setting</u>. If you always meet with this person or team at the same time, same office space (which usually also means same seating routines), mix it up. Try meeting later in the day or earlier, outside or in a room with only chairs. Or have a walking conversation. Just changing the physical environment can sometimes be enough to change the habitual dynamic. At the very least, ask if folks are willing to change seats.

<u>Check out their assessments about you</u>. Consider the possibility that your colleagues may be relating to you similarly to how you are relating to them. Wonder aloud (without putting words in their mouth) how you imagine *you* might be showing up for *them* right now, even naming all the worst things you can imagine them thinking about you (their assessments and characterizations of you). Be sure you do this respectfully and with curiosity—not with an accusatory or defensive intent. Once you've shared your curiosity about how they might see you, don't try to change or fix it—just stay curious about it. You might even speculate about how difficult it might be for them to be trying to collaborate with you, if they see you this way. Doing this sincerely and without adding your own judgments to it, can dissolve some of the tension you both may be feeling, and open things up for a different conversation.

<u>Change the conversation</u>. Consider inviting this person out to lunch, tea, or a drink. Suggest that you not focus on business at all, but instead just take some time to learn more about each other's backgrounds and interests—to connect a little on a personal level. They might appreciate the invitation and take it up or not, but the consideration itself sometimes can dissolve some of the charge between you. It reminds you both that you

are human beings underneath everything else that may be going on in the relationship.

This is not an exhaustive list, but I've seen and used all these suggestions at various times with good results. As usual, my intent is not to give you formulas or techniques to apply mechanically, but to stimulate your thinking about how you might expand your capacity to extend legitimacy and make contact when you find yourself struggling to do so with someone else.

The Performance Practices you've just learned about can absolutely help you improve your collaborative performance, as well as your personal performance. But they only work if you practice them—first on your own and with fairly easy challenges, and then taking them into your more challenging collaborative encounters.

Chapter 19

Final Thoughts

The saying "Wherever you go, there you are" has long been a popular meme. (Some attribute it to Confucius, others to Buckaroo Bonzai in the movie *The Adventures of Buckaroo Banzai Across the 8th Dimension*. I think they both might have said it, although in different contexts.) As cliché as the saying is, it still reminds me of what this book is about. It also reminds me about what frequently happens to me when I travel abroad...

Over the years, my work has involved a lot of international travel. When I'm in unfamiliar cities and especially in different cultures, I've developed an evening routine—call it a practice. At the end of the day of meetings, or an even longer day of meetings plus dinner with clients, I'll take a long walk.

I head out alone and just start wandering the streets, following my curiosity and my gut. Sometimes I'll check out the action on the busier streets where people are hanging out; other times I'll let the lights, sounds, smells or emptiness of the streets pull me along. Not having a destination on these walks helps me to relax. Sometimes my mind wanders home to family and friends, or to work, but most of the time I'll just give myself to the place I find myself in—walking this street, noticing these lights and shadows in the park, wondering about that family in the lit window, or imagining what it's like to be living the lives of the people passing me on the street. And then returning to the simplicity of my body walking down the street.

After a few minutes of this and once I'm away from the familiar neighborhood of my hotel, I settle into a rhythm of being alone with myself. There's a mood that usually comes on during these walks. It's hard to describe, but it has elements of sweetness, longing, surrender, and a relaxed yet vigilant sense of aliveness. The more I walk, the more I feel my connection with the ground under my feet. The more I feel the swing of my arms with each step and the sense of the uneven sidewalk under my feet. The more vivid become the lights, sounds and smells. And as I settle further into myself, I feel more connected with the place I'm in and the people around me. I remember—no, I fully experience—that *I am here*, wherever here happens to be.

These walks usually last a couple of hours, and by the time I make it back to the hotel, I feel as if I've been on a long journey in a distant land (which sometimes is literally true). I also feel that the journey has brought me home to myself in a very visceral way. In a way that is easy to lose touch with when I'm caught up in my normal everyday activities.

Somebody else—again, I'm not sure who—said that the best journey is the one that brings you back to yourself.

For most of us, collaboration starts out being about other people. We can spend hours, days, years trying to solve the problem of *them*—trying to figure out how to get the people we work with to come around, to be more collaborative.

My intent with this book is that—by examining the ways in which you use your attention, your words, your body and your intention—you are starting to see collaborative performance in a new light. My hope is that this journey we've been on called Full Contact Performance, has helped you to come back to yourself as the primary focus of your attention and the primary source of your actions as you engage with the people in your life to get important stuff done.

Our collaborative challenges are *never* simply the result of the poor collaboration skills, lack of interest or ill will of those folks out there. We are *never* just passive recipients or victims of our collaborative challenges. We are always active participants, because what's happening with them is in some ways also about us. And vice versa.

To make Full Contact with someone else, we must first make Full Contact with ourselves. It's not that we are responsible for everything that happens or for everything that others do in our collaborations – those other folks are, of course, also active participants doing whatever it is they are doing, and we usually have little control over that. But we do have influence over how we relate to it. And over the intention we're holding as we interact with them.

Not Every Collaboration Works

Nothing in this book is a magic pill. No amount of awareness, understanding or practice will always work in every situation. And not every collaborative challenge or roadblock you face may be "fixable." There are projects that simply may not succeed, and people who may not have the interest, motivation, or even capacity to engage constructively in every collaboration, no matter how skillful you are.

Although we play much more of a role in our collaborations than we may have previously thought, we can't control everything. Even when we're doing everything "right," things can still fizzle. We won't make the deal, complete the project on time or hit our numbers. We probably can't make Full Contact with everyone.

There are times when it's time to cut our losses and end the conversation or even the relationship. There are times when decisive, unilateral action may be needed. Or when shutting up and accommodating may be the best answer. In some cases, hard-nosed transactional negotiating to maximize your own gains may be exactly what you'll want to do. That's up to you to determine. But even in those situations, the principles, practices and moves we've covered here can still be helpful.

Morihei Ueshiba, the Japanese founder of Aikido said that "True victory is victory over oneself." Regardless of what ultimately happens, if you've been clear in your intention to make Full Contact with your colleagues; if you've been unified in your attention, words, body and intention, then you'll probably be more at peace with the outcome, whatever it is—even if the collaboration doesn't succeed. Because you'll have made Full Contact with yourself, you'll have achieved full victory.

Acknowledgements

This book reflects a collaborative journey with many folks. I offer a deep bow of gratitude to you all for being such generous and committed "training partners." You've each helped me see things I hadn't clearly seen before, make new connections I hadn't recognized before, and just keep going when I lost my way. Specifically...

For their incisive editorial insight, support and honesty: Taylor Ray, Stephen Powers, Dan Waldman, Paul Bowman, Russel Lemle, Victoria Beckner and Tom Bowman. A very special call-out to my sister, Jan Bowman, who devoted countless hours reading through the many iterations of this book, challenging my thinking every step of the way with her laser-sharp comments and questions.

To my Aikido teachers George Leonard, Richard Strozzi-Heckler, Wendy Palmer, Frank Doran, Hiroshi Ikeda and Mitsugi Saotome, for their inspiration and guidance on the mat and off, with a special callout to Richard Strozzi-Heckler for his deep support, guidance and friendship spanning so many years and so many life changes.

To Alan Vann Gardner, my Aiki-brother and fellow explorer, and my many other training partners at Two Rock Aikido, Tamalpais Aikido and the many other dojos, seminars and retreats where I've had the good fortune to practice. To Tai Chi Sifu Hal Mosher for his inspiring embodiment of the art.

To Julio Olalla and Rafael Echeverria for introducing me to the world of Ontological Coaching, and to Bob Dunham for helping me learn how to integrate Ontological thinking and practice in my client engagements. I am especially grateful to Rafael Echeverria for his pioneering development of the approach to human behavior and performance known as the Ontology of Language and for the opportunity to learn and work with him. So much of my work, and this book, is inspired by his teaching, coaching and his personal embodiment of the Ontological principles he articulates through his many books and programs.

To my many clients for their trust and the opportunities they've given me over the years to cultivate and practice my craft with their teams and organizations. Special gratitude and appreciation goes to Lucy Norris, Paul Segre, Tom Eggemeier, Mark Friedman, Keith Pearce and John Baxter.

To my colleagues from whom I've learned so much: Dorene Mahoney, Barry Smith, Merle McKinley, Jay Stewart, John Kinsella and Roger Dillan. Another special shout-out to Roger Dillan for our long and deep friendship and for regularly blowing my cognitive circuits and expanding my thinking.

For their friendship and support in keeping me on this path: Charles Kremer, Naomie Kremer, Allen Noren, Peter Kindfield and Bruce Ecker.

To KT and her great staff (and great food) at the Tea Room Cafe in Petaluma, CA, where much of this book was written.

And special gratitude to...

My sister, Jan Bowman, and brother-in-law, Paul Bowman. I can't imagine a more generous, thoughtful and dedicated sibling and sibling-in-law.

My son, Laiken, for being the bright, funny and boundary-pushing young man he is. He might not know it, but he has been inspiring and teaching me about Full Contact since his first breath.

And finally, to my wife, Kathy, for her loving, caring presence and support. I don't know how to express my love and gratitude for our 30+ years together. It's always been a mystery how she puts up with me in general, but how she put up with me-working-on-this-book—unfathomable! Regardless, may the mystery continue.

About the Author

Grayson has been helping executives and their teams around the world transform their collaborative leadership performance for over 30 years. He is recognized for his unique and potent application of mind-body practices to results-oriented business performance. In addition to coaching senior executives and teams, he facilitates organizational change initiatives and is designer of the highly acclaimed Full Contact collaborative leadership workshops.

Former CEO of a nationally recognized private school system in the San Francisco Bay Area cited as a model school for the future in *Esquire* Magazine, Grayson has also started and led nonprofits focused on homelessness and sustainable local food systems. He holds a 6th Degree Black Belt in Aikido and is a senior instructor at Two Rock Aikido in Petaluma, California.

For more information or to contact Grayson directly, go to: www.fullcontactinstitute.com or email him at grayson@fullcontactinstitute.com.

BUSINESS
BOOKS

Business Books

Business Books publishes practical guides
and insightful non-fiction for beginners and professionals.
Covering aspects from management skills, leadership and
organizational change to positive work environments, career
coaching and self-care for managers, our books are a valuable
addition to those working in the world of business.

Modern Day Selling
Unlocking Your Hidden Potential
Brian Barfield
Learn how to reconnect sales associates with customers and unlock hidden sales potential.
Paperback: 978-1-78099-457-4 ebook: 978-1-78099-458-1

The Most Creative, Escape the Ordinary, Excel at Public Speaking Book Ever
All the Help You Will Ever Need in Giving a Speech
Philip Theibert
The 'everything you need to give an outstanding speech' book, complete with original material written by a professional speech-writer.
Paperback: 978-1-78099-672-1 ebook: 978-1-78099-673-8

On Business And For Pleasure
A Self-Study Workbook for Advanced Business English
Michael Berman
This workbook includes enjoyable challenges and has been designed to help students with the English they need for work.
Paperback: 978-1-84694-304-1

Small Change, Big Deal
Money as if People Mattered
Jennifer Kavanagh
Money is about relationships: between individuals and between communities. Small is still beautiful, as peer lending model, micro-credit, shows.
Paperback: 978-1-78099-313-3 ebook: 978-1-78099-314-0

Readers of ebooks can buy or view any of these bestsellers
by clicking on the live link in the title. Most titles are published
in paperback and as an ebook. Paperbacks are available in
traditional bookshops. Both print and ebook formats
are available online.
Find more titles and sign up to our readers' newsletter at
http://www.jhpbusiness-books.com/
Facebook: https://www.facebook.com/JHPNonFiction/
Twitter: @JHPNonFiction